C-1287   CAREER EXAMINATION SERIES

*This is your
PASSBOOK for...*

Fire Fighter (FDNY)

*Test Preparation Study Guide
Questions & Answers*

COPYRIGHT NOTICE

This book is SOLELY intended for, is sold ONLY to, and its use is RESTRICTED to individual, bona fide applicants or candidates who qualify by virtue of having seriously filed applications for appropriate license, certificate, professional and/or promotional advancement, higher school matriculation, scholarship, or other legitimate requirements of education and/or governmental authorities.

This book is NOT intended for use, class instruction, tutoring, training, duplication, copying, reprinting, excerption, or adaptation, etc., by:

1) Other publishers
2) Proprietors and/or Instructors of "Coaching" and/or Preparatory Courses
3) Personnel and/or Training Divisions of commercial, industrial, and governmental organizations
4) Schools, colleges, or universities and/or their departments and staffs, including teachers and other personnel
5) Testing Agencies or Bureaus
6) Study groups which seek by the purchase of a single volume to copy and/or duplicate and/or adapt this material for use by the group as a whole without having purchased individual volumes for each of the members of the group
7) Et al.

Such persons would be in violation of appropriate Federal and State statutes.

PROVISION OF LICENSING AGREEMENTS – Recognized educational, commercial, industrial, and governmental institutions and organizations, and others legitimately engaged in educational pursuits, including training, testing, and measurement activities, may address request for a licensing agreement to the copyright owners, who will determine whether, and under what conditions, including fees and charges, the materials in this book may be used them. In other words, a licensing facility exists for the legitimate use of the material in this book on other than an individual basis. However, it is asseverated and affirmed here that the material in this book CANNOT be used without the receipt of the express permission of such a licensing agreement from the Publishers. Inquiries re licensing should be addressed to the company, attention rights and permissions department.

All rights reserved, including the right of reproduction in whole or in part, in any form or by any means, electronic or mechanical, including photocopying, recording, or by any information storage and retrieval system, without permission in writing from the Publisher.

Copyright © 2024 by
National Learning Corporation

212 Michael Drive, Syosset, NY 11791
(516) 921-8888 • www.passbooks.com
E-mail: info@passbooks.com

PUBLISHED IN THE UNITED STATES OF AMERICA

PASSBOOK® SERIES

THE *PASSBOOK® SERIES* has been created to prepare applicants and candidates for the ultimate academic battlefield – the examination room.

At some time in our lives, each and every one of us may be required to take an examination – for validation, matriculation, admission, qualification, registration, certification, or licensure.

Based on the assumption that every applicant or candidate has met the basic formal educational standards, has taken the required number of courses, and read the necessary texts, the *PASSBOOK® SERIES* furnishes the one special preparation which may assure passing with confidence, instead of failing with insecurity. Examination questions – together with answers – are furnished as the basic vehicle for study so that the mysteries of the examination and its compounding difficulties may be eliminated or diminished by a sure method.

This book is meant to help you pass your examination provided that you qualify and are serious in your objective.

The entire field is reviewed through the huge store of content information which is succinctly presented through a provocative and challenging approach – the question-and-answer method.

A climate of success is established by furnishing the correct answers at the end of each test.

You soon learn to recognize types of questions, forms of questions, and patterns of questioning. You may even begin to anticipate expected outcomes.

You perceive that many questions are repeated or adapted so that you can gain acute insights, which may enable you to score many sure points.

You learn how to confront new questions, or types of questions, and to attack them confidently and work out the correct answers.

You note objectives and emphases, and recognize pitfalls and dangers, so that you may make positive educational adjustments.

Moreover, you are kept fully informed in relation to new concepts, methods, practices, and directions in the field.

You discover that you are actually taking the examination all the time: you are preparing for the examination by "taking" an examination, not by reading extraneous and/or supererogatory textbooks.

In short, this PASSBOOK®, used directedly, should be an important factor in helping you to pass your test.

FIREFIGHTER

DUTIES:
Under supervision, Firefighters assist in the control and extinguishment of fires, in providing pre-hospital emergency medical care, and in the enforcement of laws, ordinances, rules and regulations regarding the prevention, control and extinguishment of fires, as well as perform fire safety education activities; perform inspections and related enforcement duties, such as issuing criminal court summonses and vacate orders, to assure compliance with provisions of the fire prevention code and applicable sections of the building code, multiple dwelling code, housing maintenance code, labor law and other laws, rules and regulations, within enforcement purviews of the Fire Department; perform inspections of equipment and schedule as necessary the maintenance of various tools and equipment, including but not limited to power tools, company apparatus, self-contained breathing apparatus (S.C.B.A) and other personal safety equipment; and perform related work.

THE EXAMINATION:
The examination is designed to assess important abilities and aptitudes that are required to successfully learn and perform the-work of a Firefighter. The test will evaluate basic abilities, such as reading, listening, problem solving, basic arithmetic and related areas. It also will assess the way candidates approach work, interact with others, and concentrate on details.

HOW TO TAKE A TEST

I. YOU MUST PASS AN EXAMINATION

A. *WHAT EVERY CANDIDATE SHOULD KNOW*

Examination applicants often ask us for help in preparing for the written test. What can I study in advance? What kinds of questions will be asked? How will the test be given? How will the papers be graded?

As an applicant for a civil service examination, you may be wondering about some of these things. Our purpose here is to suggest effective methods of advance study and to describe civil service examinations.

Your chances for success on this examination can be increased if you know how to prepare. Those "pre-examination jitters" can be reduced if you know what to expect. You can even experience an adventure in good citizenship if you know why civil service exams are given.

B. *WHY ARE CIVIL SERVICE EXAMINATIONS GIVEN?*

Civil service examinations are important to you in two ways. As a citizen, you want public jobs filled by employees who know how to do their work. As a job seeker, you want a fair chance to compete for that job on an equal footing with other candidates. The best-known means of accomplishing this two-fold goal is the competitive examination.

Exams are widely publicized throughout the nation. They may be administered for jobs in federal, state, city, municipal, town or village governments or agencies.

Any citizen may apply, with some limitations, such as the age or residence of applicants. Your experience and education may be reviewed to see whether you meet the requirements for the particular examination. When these requirements exist, they are reasonable and applied consistently to all applicants. Thus, a competitive examination may cause you some uneasiness now, but it is your privilege and safeguard.

C. *HOW ARE CIVIL SERVICE EXAMS DEVELOPED?*

Examinations are carefully written by trained technicians who are specialists in the field known as "psychological measurement," in consultation with recognized authorities in the field of work that the test will cover. These experts recommend the subject matter areas or skills to be tested; only those knowledges or skills important to your success on the job are included. The most reliable books and source materials available are used as references. Together, the experts and technicians judge the difficulty level of the questions.

Test technicians know how to phrase questions so that the problem is clearly stated. Their ethics do not permit "trick" or "catch" questions. Questions may have been tried out on sample groups, or subjected to statistical analysis, to determine their usefulness.

Written tests are often used in combination with performance tests, ratings of training and experience, and oral interviews. All of these measures combine to form the best-known means of finding the right person for the right job.

II. HOW TO PASS THE WRITTEN TEST

A. NATURE OF THE EXAMINATION

To prepare intelligently for civil service examinations, you should know how they differ from school examinations you have taken. In school you were assigned certain definite pages to read or subjects to cover. The examination questions were quite detailed and usually emphasized memory. Civil service exams, on the other hand, try to discover your present ability to perform the duties of a position, plus your potentiality to learn these duties. In other words, a civil service exam attempts to predict how successful you will be. Questions cover such a broad area that they cannot be as minute and detailed as school exam questions.

In the public service similar kinds of work, or positions, are grouped together in one "class." This process is known as *position-classification*. All the positions in a class are paid according to the salary range for that class. One class title covers all of these positions, and they are all tested by the same examination.

B. FOUR BASIC STEPS

1) Study the announcement

How, then, can you know what subjects to study? Our best answer is: "Learn as much as possible about the class of positions for which you've applied." The exam will test the knowledge, skills and abilities needed to do the work.

Your most valuable source of information about the position you want is the official exam announcement. This announcement lists the training and experience qualifications. Check these standards and apply only if you come reasonably close to meeting them.

The brief description of the position in the examination announcement offers some clues to the subjects which will be tested. Think about the job itself. Review the duties in your mind. Can you perform them, or are there some in which you are rusty? Fill in the blank spots in your preparation.

Many jurisdictions preview the written test in the exam announcement by including a section called "Knowledge and Abilities Required," "Scope of the Examination," or some similar heading. Here you will find out specifically what fields will be tested.

2) Review your own background

Once you learn in general what the position is all about, and what you need to know to do the work, ask yourself which subjects you already know fairly well and which need improvement. You may wonder whether to concentrate on improving your strong areas or on building some background in your fields of weakness. When the announcement has specified "some knowledge" or "considerable knowledge," or has used adjectives like "beginning principles of…" or "advanced … methods," you can get a clue as to the number and difficulty of questions to be asked in any given field. More questions, and hence broader coverage, would be included for those subjects which are more important in the work. Now weigh your strengths and weaknesses against the job requirements and prepare accordingly.

3) Determine the level of the position

Another way to tell how intensively you should prepare is to understand the level of the job for which you are applying. Is it the entering level? In other words, is this the position in which beginners in a field of work are hired? Or is it an intermediate or advanced level? Sometimes this is indicated by such words as "Junior" or "Senior" in the class title. Other jurisdictions use Roman numerals to designate the level – Clerk I, Clerk II, for example. The word "Supervisor" sometimes appears in the title. If the level is not indicated by the title, check the description of duties. Will you be working under very close supervision, or will you have responsibility for independent decisions in this work?

4) Choose appropriate study materials

Now that you know the subjects to be examined and the relative amount of each subject to be covered, you can choose suitable study materials. For beginning level jobs, or even advanced ones, if you have a pronounced weakness in some aspect of your training, read a modern, standard textbook in that field. Be sure it is up to date and has general coverage. Such books are normally available at your library, and the librarian will be glad to help you locate one. For entry-level positions, questions of appropriate difficulty are chosen – neither highly advanced questions, nor those too simple. Such questions require careful thought but not advanced training.

If the position for which you are applying is technical or advanced, you will read more advanced, specialized material. If you are already familiar with the basic principles of your field, elementary textbooks would waste your time. Concentrate on advanced textbooks and technical periodicals. Think through the concepts and review difficult problems in your field.

These are all general sources. You can get more ideas on your own initiative, following these leads. For example, training manuals and publications of the government agency which employs workers in your field can be useful, particularly for technical and professional positions. A letter or visit to the government department involved may result in more specific study suggestions, and certainly will provide you with a more definite idea of the exact nature of the position you are seeking.

III. KINDS OF TESTS

Tests are used for purposes other than measuring knowledge and ability to perform specified duties. For some positions, it is equally important to test ability to make adjustments to new situations or to profit from training. In others, basic mental abilities not dependent on information are essential. Questions which test these things may not appear as pertinent to the duties of the position as those which test for knowledge and information. Yet they are often highly important parts of a fair examination. For very general questions, it is almost impossible to help you direct your study efforts. What we can do is to point out some of the more common of these general abilities needed in public service positions and describe some typical questions.

1) General information

Broad, general information has been found useful for predicting job success in some kinds of work. This is tested in a variety of ways, from vocabulary lists to questions about current events. Basic background in some field of work, such as sociology or economics, may be sampled in a group of questions. Often these are principles which have become familiar to most persons through exposure rather than through formal training. It is difficult to advise you how to study for these questions; being alert to the world around you is our best suggestion.

2) Verbal ability

An example of an ability needed in many positions is verbal or language ability. Verbal ability is, in brief, the ability to use and understand words. Vocabulary and grammar tests are typical measures of this ability. Reading comprehension or paragraph interpretation questions are common in many kinds of civil service tests. You are given a paragraph of written material and asked to find its central meaning.

3) Numerical ability

Number skills can be tested by the familiar arithmetic problem, by checking paired lists of numbers to see which are alike and which are different, or by interpreting charts and graphs. In the latter test, a graph may be printed in the test booklet which you are asked to use as the basis for answering questions.

4) Observation

A popular test for law-enforcement positions is the observation test. A picture is shown to you for several minutes, then taken away. Questions about the picture test your ability to observe both details and larger elements.

5) Following directions

In many positions in the public service, the employee must be able to carry out written instructions dependably and accurately. You may be given a chart with several columns, each column listing a variety of information. The questions require you to carry out directions involving the information given in the chart.

6) Skills and aptitudes

Performance tests effectively measure some manual skills and aptitudes. When the skill is one in which you are trained, such as typing or shorthand, you can practice. These tests are often very much like those given in business school or high school courses. For many of the other skills and aptitudes, however, no short-time preparation can be made. Skills and abilities natural to you or that you have developed throughout your lifetime are being tested.

Many of the general questions just described provide all the data needed to answer the questions and ask you to use your reasoning ability to find the answers. Your best preparation for these tests, as well as for tests of facts and ideas, is to be at your physical and mental best. You, no doubt, have your own methods of getting into an exam-taking mood and keeping "in shape." The next section lists some ideas on this subject.

IV. KINDS OF QUESTIONS

Only rarely is the "essay" question, which you answer in narrative form, used in civil service tests. Civil service tests are usually of the short-answer type. Full instructions for answering these questions will be given to you at the examination. But in case this is your first experience with short-answer questions and separate answer sheets, here is what you need to know:

1) Multiple-choice Questions

Most popular of the short-answer questions is the "multiple choice" or "best answer" question. It can be used, for example, to test for factual knowledge, ability to solve problems or judgment in meeting situations found at work.

A multiple-choice question is normally one of three types—
- It can begin with an incomplete statement followed by several possible endings. You are to find the one ending which *best* completes the statement, although some of the others may not be entirely wrong.
- It can also be a complete statement in the form of a question which is answered by choosing one of the statements listed.

- It can be in the form of a problem – again you select the best answer.

Here is an example of a multiple-choice question with a discussion which should give you some clues as to the method for choosing the right answer:

When an employee has a complaint about his assignment, the action which will *best* help him overcome his difficulty is to
- A. discuss his difficulty with his coworkers
- B. take the problem to the head of the organization
- C. take the problem to the person who gave him the assignment
- D. say nothing to anyone about his complaint

In answering this question, you should study each of the choices to find which is best. Consider choice "A" – Certainly an employee may discuss his complaint with fellow employees, but no change or improvement can result, and the complaint remains unresolved. Choice "B" is a poor choice since the head of the organization probably does not know what assignment you have been given, and taking your problem to him is known as "going over the head" of the supervisor. The supervisor, or person who made the assignment, is the person who can clarify it or correct any injustice. Choice "C" is, therefore, correct. To say nothing, as in choice "D," is unwise. Supervisors have and interest in knowing the problems employees are facing, and the employee is seeking a solution to his problem.

2) True/False Questions

The "true/false" or "right/wrong" form of question is sometimes used. Here a complete statement is given. Your job is to decide whether the statement is right or wrong.

SAMPLE: A roaming cell-phone call to a nearby city costs less than a non-roaming call to a distant city.

This statement is wrong, or false, since roaming calls are more expensive.

This is not a complete list of all possible question forms, although most of the others are variations of these common types. You will always get complete directions for answering questions. Be sure you understand *how* to mark your answers – ask questions until you do.

V. RECORDING YOUR ANSWERS

Computer terminals are used more and more today for many different kinds of exams.

For an examination with very few applicants, you may be told to record your answers in the test booklet itself. Separate answer sheets are much more common. If this separate answer sheet is to be scored by machine – and this is often the case – it is highly important that you mark your answers correctly in order to get credit.

An electronic scoring machine is often used in civil service offices because of the speed with which papers can be scored. Machine-scored answer sheets must be marked with a pencil, which will be given to you. This pencil has a high graphite content which responds to the electronic scoring machine. As a matter of fact, stray dots may register as answers, so do not let your pencil rest on the answer sheet while you are pondering the correct answer. Also, if your pencil lead breaks or is otherwise defective, ask for another.

Since the answer sheet will be dropped in a slot in the scoring machine, be careful not to bend the corners or get the paper crumpled.

The answer sheet normally has five vertical columns of numbers, with 30 numbers to a column. These numbers correspond to the question numbers in your test booklet. After each number, going across the page are four or five pairs of dotted lines. These short dotted lines have small letters or numbers above them. The first two pairs may also have a "T" or "F" above the letters. This indicates that the first two pairs only are to be used if the questions are of the true-false type. If the questions are multiple choice, disregard the "T" and "F" and pay attention only to the small letters or numbers.

Answer your questions in the manner of the sample that follows:

32. The largest city in the United States is
    A. Washington, D.C.
    B. New York City
    C. Chicago
    D. Detroit
    E. San Francisco

1) Choose the answer you think is best. (New York City is the largest, so "B" is correct.)
2) Find the row of dotted lines numbered the same as the question you are answering. (Find row number 32)
3) Find the pair of dotted lines corresponding to the answer. (Find the pair of lines under the mark "B.")
4) Make a solid black mark between the dotted lines.

VI. BEFORE THE TEST

Common sense will help you find procedures to follow to get ready for an examination. Too many of us, however, overlook these sensible measures. Indeed, nervousness and fatigue have been found to be the most serious reasons why applicants fail to do their best on civil service tests. Here is a list of reminders:

- Begin your preparation early – Don't wait until the last minute to go scurrying around for books and materials or to find out what the position is all about.
- Prepare continuously – An hour a night for a week is better than an all-night cram session. This has been definitely established. What is more, a night a week for a month will return better dividends than crowding your study into a shorter period of time.
- Locate the place of the exam – You have been sent a notice telling you when and where to report for the examination. If the location is in a different town or otherwise unfamiliar to you, it would be well to inquire the best route and learn something about the building.
- Relax the night before the test – Allow your mind to rest. Do not study at all that night. Plan some mild recreation or diversion; then go to bed early and get a good night's sleep.
- Get up early enough to make a leisurely trip to the place for the test – This way unforeseen events, traffic snarls, unfamiliar buildings, etc. will not upset you.
- Dress comfortably – A written test is not a fashion show. You will be known by number and not by name, so wear something comfortable.

- Leave excess paraphernalia at home – Shopping bags and odd bundles will get in your way. You need bring only the items mentioned in the official notice you received; usually everything you need is provided. Do not bring reference books to the exam. They will only confuse those last minutes and be taken away from you when in the test room.
- Arrive somewhat ahead of time – If because of transportation schedules you must get there very early, bring a newspaper or magazine to take your mind off yourself while waiting.
- Locate the examination room – When you have found the proper room, you will be directed to the seat or part of the room where you will sit. Sometimes you are given a sheet of instructions to read while you are waiting. Do not fill out any forms until you are told to do so; just read them and be prepared.
- Relax and prepare to listen to the instructions
- If you have any physical problem that may keep you from doing your best, be sure to tell the test administrator. If you are sick or in poor health, you really cannot do your best on the exam. You can come back and take the test some other time.

VII. AT THE TEST

The day of the test is here and you have the test booklet in your hand. The temptation to get going is very strong. Caution! There is more to success than knowing the right answers. You must know how to identify your papers and understand variations in the type of short-answer question used in this particular examination. Follow these suggestions for maximum results from your efforts:

1) Cooperate with the monitor

The test administrator has a duty to create a situation in which you can be as much at ease as possible. He will give instructions, tell you when to begin, check to see that you are marking your answer sheet correctly, and so on. He is not there to guard you, although he will see that your competitors do not take unfair advantage. He wants to help you do your best.

2) Listen to all instructions

Don't jump the gun! Wait until you understand all directions. In most civil service tests you get more time than you need to answer the questions. So don't be in a hurry. Read each word of instructions until you clearly understand the meaning. Study the examples, listen to all announcements and follow directions. Ask questions if you do not understand what to do.

3) Identify your papers

Civil service exams are usually identified by number only. You will be assigned a number; you must not put your name on your test papers. Be sure to copy your number correctly. Since more than one exam may be given, copy your exact examination title.

4) Plan your time

Unless you are told that a test is a "speed" or "rate of work" test, speed itself is usually not important. Time enough to answer all the questions will be provided, but this does not mean that you have all day. An overall time limit has been set. Divide the total time (in minutes) by the number of questions to determine the approximate time you have for each question.

5) Do not linger over difficult questions

If you come across a difficult question, mark it with a paper clip (useful to have along) and come back to it when you have been through the booklet. One caution if you do this – be sure to skip a number on your answer sheet as well. Check often to be sure that you have not lost your place and that you are marking in the row numbered the same as the question you are answering.

6) Read the questions

Be sure you know what the question asks! Many capable people are unsuccessful because they failed to *read* the questions correctly.

7) Answer all questions

Unless you have been instructed that a penalty will be deducted for incorrect answers, it is better to guess than to omit a question.

8) Speed tests

It is often better NOT to guess on speed tests. It has been found that on timed tests people are tempted to spend the last few seconds before time is called in marking answers at random – without even reading them – in the hope of picking up a few extra points. To discourage this practice, the instructions may warn you that your score will be "corrected" for guessing. That is, a penalty will be applied. The incorrect answers will be deducted from the correct ones, or some other penalty formula will be used.

9) Review your answers

If you finish before time is called, go back to the questions you guessed or omitted to give them further thought. Review other answers if you have time.

10) Return your test materials

If you are ready to leave before others have finished or time is called, take ALL your materials to the monitor and leave quietly. Never take any test material with you. The monitor can discover whose papers are not complete, and taking a test booklet may be grounds for disqualification.

VIII. EXAMINATION TECHNIQUES

1) Read the general instructions carefully. These are usually printed on the first page of the exam booklet. As a rule, these instructions refer to the timing of the examination; the fact that you should not start work until the signal and must stop work at a signal, etc. If there are any *special* instructions, such as a choice of questions to be answered, make sure that you note this instruction carefully.

2) When you are ready to start work on the examination, that is as soon as the signal has been given, read the instructions to each question booklet, underline any key words or phrases, such as *least, best, outline, describe* and the like. In this way you will tend to answer as requested rather than discover on reviewing your paper that you *listed without describing*, that you selected the *worst* choice rather than the *best* choice, etc.

3) If the examination is of the objective or multiple-choice type – that is, each question will also give a series of possible answers: A, B, C or D, and you are called upon to select the best answer and write the letter next to that answer on your answer paper – it is advisable to start answering each question in turn. There may be anywhere from 50 to 100 such questions in the three or four hours allotted and you can see how much time would be taken if you read through all the questions before beginning to answer any. Furthermore, if you come across a question or group of questions which you know would be difficult to answer, it would undoubtedly affect your handling of all the other questions.

4) If the examination is of the essay type and contains but a few questions, it is a moot point as to whether you should read all the questions before starting to answer any one. Of course, if you are given a choice – say five out of seven and the like – then it is essential to read all the questions so you can eliminate the two that are most difficult. If, however, you are asked to answer all the questions, there may be danger in trying to answer the easiest one first because you may find that you will spend too much time on it. The best technique is to answer the first question, then proceed to the second, etc.

5) Time your answers. Before the exam begins, write down the time it started, then add the time allowed for the examination and write down the time it must be completed, then divide the time available somewhat as follows:
   - If 3-1/2 hours are allowed, that would be 210 minutes. If you have 80 objective-type questions, that would be an average of 2-1/2 minutes per question. Allow yourself no more than 2 minutes per question, or a total of 160 minutes, which will permit about 50 minutes to review.
   - If for the time allotment of 210 minutes there are 7 essay questions to answer, that would average about 30 minutes a question. Give yourself only 25 minutes per question so that you have about 35 minutes to review.

6) The most important instruction is to *read each question* and make sure you know what is wanted. The second most important instruction is to *time yourself properly* so that you answer every question. The third most important instruction is to *answer every question*. Guess if you have to but include something for each question. Remember that you will receive no credit for a blank and will probably receive some credit if you write something in answer to an essay question. If you guess a letter – say "B" for a multiple-choice question – you may have guessed right. If you leave a blank as an answer to a multiple-choice question, the examiners may respect your feelings but it will not add a point to your score. Some exams may penalize you for wrong answers, so in such cases *only*, you may not want to guess unless you have some basis for your answer.

7) Suggestions
   a. Objective-type questions
      1. Examine the question booklet for proper sequence of pages and questions
      2. Read all instructions carefully
      3. Skip any question which seems too difficult; return to it after all other questions have been answered
      4. Apportion your time properly; do not spend too much time on any single question or group of questions

5. Note and underline key words – *all, most, fewest, least, best, worst, same, opposite*, etc.
6. Pay particular attention to negatives
7. Note unusual option, e.g., unduly long, short, complex, different or similar in content to the body of the question
8. Observe the use of "hedging" words – *probably, may, most likely*, etc.
9. Make sure that your answer is put next to the same number as the question
10. Do not second-guess unless you have good reason to believe the second answer is definitely more correct
11. Cross out original answer if you decide another answer is more accurate; do not erase until you are ready to hand your paper in
12. Answer all questions; guess unless instructed otherwise
13. Leave time for review

  b. Essay questions
1. Read each question carefully
2. Determine exactly what is wanted. Underline key words or phrases.
3. Decide on outline or paragraph answer
4. Include many different points and elements unless asked to develop any one or two points or elements
5. Show impartiality by giving pros and cons unless directed to select one side only
6. Make and write down any assumptions you find necessary to answer the questions
7. Watch your English, grammar, punctuation and choice of words
8. Time your answers; don't crowd material

8) Answering the essay question

Most essay questions can be answered by framing the specific response around several key words or ideas. Here are a few such key words or ideas:

M's: manpower, materials, methods, money, management
P's: purpose, program, policy, plan, procedure, practice, problems, pitfalls, personnel, public relations

  a. Six basic steps in handling problems:
1. Preliminary plan and background development
2. Collect information, data and facts
3. Analyze and interpret information, data and facts
4. Analyze and develop solutions as well as make recommendations
5. Prepare report and sell recommendations
6. Install recommendations and follow up effectiveness

  b. Pitfalls to avoid
1. *Taking things for granted* – A statement of the situation does not necessarily imply that each of the elements is necessarily true; for example, a complaint may be invalid and biased so that all that can be taken for granted is that a complaint has been registered

2. *Considering only one side of a situation* – Wherever possible, indicate several alternatives and then point out the reasons you selected the best one
3. *Failing to indicate follow up* – Whenever your answer indicates action on your part, make certain that you will take proper follow-up action to see how successful your recommendations, procedures or actions turn out to be
4. *Taking too long in answering any single question* – Remember to time your answers properly

IX. AFTER THE TEST

Scoring procedures differ in detail among civil service jurisdictions although the general principles are the same. Whether the papers are hand-scored or graded by machine we have described, they are nearly always graded by number. That is, the person who marks the paper knows only the number – never the name – of the applicant. Not until all the papers have been graded will they be matched with names. If other tests, such as training and experience or oral interview ratings have been given, scores will be combined. Different parts of the examination usually have different weights. For example, the written test might count 60 percent of the final grade, and a rating of training and experience 40 percent. In many jurisdictions, veterans will have a certain number of points added to their grades.

After the final grade has been determined, the names are placed in grade order and an eligible list is established. There are various methods for resolving ties between those who get the same final grade – probably the most common is to place first the name of the person whose application was received first. Job offers are made from the eligible list in the order the names appear on it. You will be notified of your grade and your rank as soon as all these computations have been made. This will be done as rapidly as possible.

People who are found to meet the requirements in the announcement are called "eligibles." Their names are put on a list of eligible candidates. An eligible's chances of getting a job depend on how high he stands on this list and how fast agencies are filling jobs from the list.

When a job is to be filled from a list of eligibles, the agency asks for the names of people on the list of eligibles for that job. When the civil service commission receives this request, it sends to the agency the names of the three people highest on this list. Or, if the job to be filled has specialized requirements, the office sends the agency the names of the top three persons who meet these requirements from the general list.

The appointing officer makes a choice from among the three people whose names were sent to him. If the selected person accepts the appointment, the names of the others are put back on the list to be considered for future openings.

That is the rule in hiring from all kinds of eligible lists, whether they are for typist, carpenter, chemist, or something else. For every vacancy, the appointing officer has his choice of any one of the top three eligibles on the list. This explains why the person whose name is on top of the list sometimes does not get an appointment when some of the persons lower on the list do. If the appointing officer chooses the second or third eligible, the No. 1 eligible does not get a job at once, but stays on the list until he is appointed or the list is terminated.

X. HOW TO PASS THE INTERVIEW TEST

The examination for which you applied requires an oral interview test. You have already taken the written test and you are now being called for the interview test – the final part of the formal examination.

You may think that it is not possible to prepare for an interview test and that there are no procedures to follow during an interview. Our purpose is to point out some things you can do in advance that will help you and some good rules to follow and pitfalls to avoid while you are being interviewed.

What is an interview supposed to test?

The written examination is designed to test the technical knowledge and competence of the candidate; the oral is designed to evaluate intangible qualities, not readily measured otherwise, and to establish a list showing the relative fitness of each candidate – as measured against his competitors – for the position sought. Scoring is not on the basis of "right" and "wrong," but on a sliding scale of values ranging from "not passable" to "outstanding." As a matter of fact, it is possible to achieve a relatively low score without a single "incorrect" answer because of evident weakness in the qualities being measured.

Occasionally, an examination may consist entirely of an oral test – either an individual or a group oral. In such cases, information is sought concerning the technical knowledges and abilities of the candidate, since there has been no written examination for this purpose. More commonly, however, an oral test is used to supplement a written examination.

Who conducts interviews?

The composition of oral boards varies among different jurisdictions. In nearly all, a representative of the personnel department serves as chairman. One of the members of the board may be a representative of the department in which the candidate would work. In some cases, "outside experts" are used, and, frequently, a businessman or some other representative of the general public is asked to serve. Labor and management or other special groups may be represented. The aim is to secure the services of experts in the appropriate field.

However the board is composed, it is a good idea (and not at all improper or unethical) to ascertain in advance of the interview who the members are and what groups they represent. When you are introduced to them, you will have some idea of their backgrounds and interests, and at least you will not stutter and stammer over their names.

What should be done before the interview?

While knowledge about the board members is useful and takes some of the surprise element out of the interview, there is other preparation which is more substantive. It *is* possible to prepare for an oral interview – in several ways:

1) Keep a copy of your application and review it carefully before the interview

This may be the only document before the oral board, and the starting point of the interview. Know what education and experience you have listed there, and the sequence and dates of all of it. Sometimes the board will ask you to review the highlights of your experience for them; you should not have to hem and haw doing it.

2) Study the class specification and the examination announcement

Usually, the oral board has one or both of these to guide them. The qualities, characteristics or knowledges required by the position sought are stated in these documents. They offer valuable clues as to the nature of the oral interview. For example, if the job involves supervisory responsibilities, the announcement will usually indicate that knowledge of modern supervisory methods and the qualifications of the candidate as a supervisor will be tested. If so, you can expect such questions, frequently in the form of a hypothetical situation which you are expected to solve. NEVER go into an oral without knowledge of the duties and responsibilities of the job you seek.

3) Think through each qualification required

Try to visualize the kind of questions you would ask if you were a board member. How well could you answer them? Try especially to appraise your own knowledge and background in each area, *measured against the job sought*, and identify any areas in which you are weak. Be critical and realistic – do not flatter yourself.

4) Do some general reading in areas in which you feel you may be weak

For example, if the job involves supervision and your past experience has NOT, some general reading in supervisory methods and practices, particularly in the field of human relations, might be useful. Do NOT study agency procedures or detailed manuals. The oral board will be testing your understanding and capacity, not your memory.

5) Get a good night's sleep and watch your general health and mental attitude

You will want a clear head at the interview. Take care of a cold or any other minor ailment, and of course, no hangovers.

What should be done on the day of the interview?

Now comes the day of the interview itself. Give yourself plenty of time to get there. Plan to arrive somewhat ahead of the scheduled time, particularly if your appointment is in the fore part of the day. If a previous candidate fails to appear, the board might be ready for you a bit early. By early afternoon an oral board is almost invariably behind schedule if there are many candidates, and you may have to wait. Take along a book or magazine to read, or your application to review, but leave any extraneous material in the waiting room when you go in for your interview. In any event, relax and compose yourself.

The matter of dress is important. The board is forming impressions about you – from your experience, your manners, your attitude, and your appearance. Give your personal appearance careful attention. Dress your best, but not your flashiest. Choose conservative, appropriate clothing, and be sure it is immaculate. This is a business interview, and your appearance should indicate that you regard it as such. Besides, being well groomed and properly dressed will help boost your confidence.

Sooner or later, someone will call your name and escort you into the interview room. *This is it.* From here on you are on your own. It is too late for any more preparation. But remember, you asked for this opportunity to prove your fitness, and you are here because your request was granted.

What happens when you go in?

The usual sequence of events will be as follows: The clerk (who is often the board stenographer) will introduce you to the chairman of the oral board, who will introduce you to the other members of the board. Acknowledge the introductions before you sit down. Do not be surprised if you find a microphone facing you or a stenotypist sitting by. Oral interviews are usually recorded in the event of an appeal or other review.

Usually the chairman of the board will open the interview by reviewing the highlights of your education and work experience from your application – primarily for the benefit of the other members of the board, as well as to get the material into the record. Do not interrupt or comment unless there is an error or significant misinterpretation; if that is the case, do not hesitate. But do not quibble about insignificant matters. Also, he will usually ask you some question about your education, experience or your present job – partly to get you to start talking and to establish the interviewing "rapport." He may start the actual questioning, or turn it over to one of the other members. Frequently, each member undertakes the questioning on a particular area, one in which he is perhaps most competent, so you can expect each member to participate in the examination. Because time is limited, you may also expect some rather abrupt switches in the direction the questioning takes, so do not be upset by it. Normally, a board member will not pursue a single line of questioning unless he discovers a particular strength or weakness.

After each member has participated, the chairman will usually ask whether any member has any further questions, then will ask you if you have anything you wish to add. Unless you are expecting this question, it may floor you. Worse, it may start you off on an extended, extemporaneous speech. The board is not usually seeking more information. The question is principally to offer you a last opportunity to present further qualifications or to indicate that you have nothing to add. So, if you feel that a significant qualification or characteristic has been overlooked, it is proper to point it out in a sentence or so. Do not compliment the board on the thoroughness of their examination – they have been sketchy, and you know it. If you wish, merely say, "No thank you, I have nothing further to add." This is a point where you can "talk yourself out" of a good impression or fail to present an important bit of information. Remember, *you close the interview yourself.*

The chairman will then say, "That is all, Mr. _____, thank you." Do not be startled; the interview is over, and quicker than you think. Thank him, gather your belongings and take your leave. Save your sigh of relief for the other side of the door.

How to put your best foot forward

Throughout this entire process, you may feel that the board individually and collectively is trying to pierce your defenses, seek out your hidden weaknesses and embarrass and confuse you. Actually, this is not true. They are obliged to make an appraisal of your qualifications for the job you are seeking, and they want to see you in your best light. Remember, they must interview all candidates and a non-cooperative candidate may become a failure in spite of their best efforts to bring out his qualifications. Here are 15 suggestions that will help you:

1) Be natural – Keep your attitude confident, not cocky

If you are not confident that you can do the job, do not expect the board to be. Do not apologize for your weaknesses, try to bring out your strong points. The board is interested in a positive, not negative, presentation. Cockiness will antagonize any board member and make him wonder if you are covering up a weakness by a false show of strength.

2) Get comfortable, but don't lounge or sprawl

Sit erectly but not stiffly. A careless posture may lead the board to conclude that you are careless in other things, or at least that you are not impressed by the importance of the occasion. Either conclusion is natural, even if incorrect. Do not fuss with your clothing, a pencil or an ashtray. Your hands may occasionally be useful to emphasize a point; do not let them become a point of distraction.

3) Do not wisecrack or make small talk

This is a serious situation, and your attitude should show that you consider it as such. Further, the time of the board is limited – they do not want to waste it, and neither should you.

4) Do not exaggerate your experience or abilities

In the first place, from information in the application or other interviews and sources, the board may know more about you than you think. Secondly, you probably will not get away with it. An experienced board is rather adept at spotting such a situation, so do not take the chance.

5) If you know a board member, do not make a point of it, yet do not hide it

Certainly you are not fooling him, and probably not the other members of the board. Do not try to take advantage of your acquaintanceship – it will probably do you little good.

6) Do not dominate the interview

Let the board do that. They will give you the clues – do not assume that you have to do all the talking. Realize that the board has a number of questions to ask you, and do not try to take up all the interview time by showing off your extensive knowledge of the answer to the first one.

7) Be attentive

You only have 20 minutes or so, and you should keep your attention at its sharpest throughout. When a member is addressing a problem or question to you, give him your undivided attention. Address your reply principally to him, but do not exclude the other board members.

8) Do not interrupt

A board member may be stating a problem for you to analyze. He will ask you a question when the time comes. Let him state the problem, and wait for the question.

9) Make sure you understand the question

Do not try to answer until you are sure what the question is. If it is not clear, restate it in your own words or ask the board member to clarify it for you. However, do not haggle about minor elements.

10) Reply promptly but not hastily

A common entry on oral board rating sheets is "candidate responded readily," or "candidate hesitated in replies." Respond as promptly and quickly as you can, but do not jump to a hasty, ill-considered answer.

11) Do not be peremptory in your answers

A brief answer is proper – but do not fire your answer back. That is a losing game from your point of view. The board member can probably ask questions much faster than you can answer them.

12) Do not try to create the answer you think the board member wants

He is interested in what kind of mind you have and how it works – not in playing games. Furthermore, he can usually spot this practice and will actually grade you down on it.

13) Do not switch sides in your reply merely to agree with a board member

Frequently, a member will take a contrary position merely to draw you out and to see if you are willing and able to defend your point of view. Do not start a debate, yet do not surrender a good position. If a position is worth taking, it is worth defending.

14) Do not be afraid to admit an error in judgment if you are shown to be wrong

The board knows that you are forced to reply without any opportunity for careful consideration. Your answer may be demonstrably wrong. If so, admit it and get on with the interview.

15) Do not dwell at length on your present job

The opening question may relate to your present assignment. Answer the question but do not go into an extended discussion. You are being examined for a *new* job, not your present one. As a matter of fact, try to phrase ALL your answers in terms of the job for which you are being examined.

Basis of Rating

Probably you will forget most of these "do's" and "don'ts" when you walk into the oral interview room. Even remembering them all will not ensure you a passing grade. Perhaps you did not have the qualifications in the first place. But remembering them will help you to put your best foot forward, without treading on the toes of the board members.

Rumor and popular opinion to the contrary notwithstanding, an oral board wants you to make the best appearance possible. They know you are under pressure – but they also want to see how you respond to it as a guide to what your reaction would be under the pressures of the job you seek. They will be influenced by the degree of poise you display, the personal traits you show and the manner in which you respond.

ABOUT THIS BOOK

This book contains tests divided into Examination Sections. Go through each test, answering every question in the margin. We have also attached a sample answer sheet at the back of the book that can be removed and used. At the end of each test look at the answer key and check your answers. On the ones you got wrong, look at the right answer choice and learn. Do not fill in the answers first. Do not memorize the questions and answers, but understand the answer and principles involved. On your test, the questions will likely be different from the samples. Questions are changed and new ones added. If you understand these past questions you should have success with any changes that arise. Tests may consist of several types of questions. We have additional books on each subject should more study be advisable or necessary for you. Finally, the more you study, the better prepared you will be. This book is intended to be the last thing you study before you walk into the examination room. Prior study of relevant texts is also recommended. NLC publishes some of these in our Fundamental Series. Knowledge and good sense are important factors in passing your exam. Good luck also helps. So now study this Passbook, absorb the material contained within and take that knowledge into the examination. Then do your best to pass that exam.

EXAMINATION SECTION

EXAMINATION SECTION
TEST 1

DIRECTIONS: Each question or incomplete statement is followed by several suggested answers or completions. Select the one that BEST answers the question or completes the statement. *PRINT THE LETTER OF THE CORRECT ANSWER IN THE SPACE AT THE RIGHT.*

1. Of the following, the BASIC purpose of Fire Department inspection of private property is to
    A. make sure that Fire Department equipment is properly maintained
    B. secure proper maintenance of all entrance and exit facilities
    C. obtain correction of conditions creating undue fire hazards
    D. make sure that walls are properly plastered and painted in order to prevent the spread of fire
    E. impress upon owners and occupants the importance of fire prevention

    1.____

2. Fire drills should be held frequently in school buildings CHIEFLY in order to
    A. impress upon pupils the necessity for discipline
    B. conform to the rules of the Fire Department and the Board of Education
    C. acquaint pupils with Fire Department regulations
    D. train pupils to leave the building quickly and in an orderly manner
    E. lead pupils to respect law and order

    2.____

3. "Sometimes at a fire, an officer endures great punishment in order to reach a desired position which could have been reached more quickly and with less hardship."
    Of the following, the CHIEF implication of the above statement is that
    A. one should take time off during a fire to think completely through problems presented
    B. courage is an important asset in a firefighter
    C. training is an important factor in firefighting
    D. modern firefighting requires alert firefighters
    E. no two fires are every exactly the same

    3.____

4. "Fire records indicate that in many fires caused by heating equipment, insufficient clearance from combustible materials is an important factor."
    From this observation it follows that the MAJOR reason, of those listed, that fires increase in cold weather is that
    A. cold weather makes combustible materials more inflammable
    B. combustible materials tend to expand when heated
    C. heating equipment is in operation
    D. hot air from heating equipment is more inflammable
    E. heating equipment tends to become defective

    4.____

5. A survey of dip tank fires in large cleaning establishments shows that the majority of these fires started with such an obvious hazard as cutting and welding torches.
This experience indicates MOST strongly a need for
   A. a law prohibiting the use of welding torches
   B. fire-safety programs in this industry
   C. a law requiring welders to be licensed
   D. eliminating the use of dip tanks
   E. the location of additional fire companies in the neighborhood of dip tank users

5.____

6. In order to reduce the number of collisions between fire apparatus and private automobiles, a number of suggestions have been made regarding the training and selection of drivers.
Of the following courses of action, the one which is LEAST likely to lead to the reduction of accidents is to
   A. select drivers who have the longest driving experience
   B. require all members of a company to drive fire apparatus
   C. select drivers who have experience in driving trucks
   D. select an alternate driver for every piece of fire apparatus
   E. require drivers to practice driving and maneuvering fire apparatus

6.____

7. "Automobile parking on city streets is becoming daily a greater menace to effective firefighting."
Of the following effects of automobile parking, the LEAST serious is that
   A. access to the fire building may be obstructed
   B. ladder and rescue work may be retarded
   C. traffic congestion may make it difficult for fire apparatus to get through
   D. greater lengths of hose may be needed in fighting a fire
   E. street width is reduced so that fire apparatus has difficulty in maneuvering

7.____

8. Suppose that you are driving the first due engine to a fire. At an intersection, a civilian points to another fire in a direction different from the way you are going.
In general, the BEST action for you to take is to
   A. halt your engine at the intersection and wait until you receive further orders from the Battalion Chief
   B. continue to the fire for which your company was summoned
   C. halt your engine at the intersection to permit your Lieutenant to telephone to the Chief Telegraph Dispatcher for further instructions
   D. proceed to the fire to which the man is pointing
   E. go to the fire to which the man is pointing, leave half of the men and transport the rest to the other fire

8.____

9. Assume that you are a firefighter fighting a fire on the third story of a six-story building.
   Generally, it can be expected that the heat from this fire will spread
   A. upwards
   B. downwards
   C. sideways along the joists
   D. sideways along the walls
   E. evenly in all directions

10. If during a fire it is observed that the water draining away from the fire is cold, it may be concluded that
    A. the water has played a negligible part in putting out the fire
    B. the hoses are placed to the windward
    C. the heat waves are forcing the water streams away from the fire
    D. more hose lines are needed to fight the fire
    E. the water pressure is too low

11. "In fighting a fire, a firefighter should use fresh water wherever possible in preference to salt water."
    The PRIMARY reason for this recommendation is that fresh water
    A. has a higher specific gravity
    B. evaporates more quickly
    C. puts out fires more quickly
    D. is less injurious to a firefighter's hands
    E. produces less water damage

12. After a fire of considerable size has been extinguished, your company has been ordered back to the third floor of a building.
    Of the following acts, the one which should be taken FIRST is to
    A. determine whether or not it is safe to go on that floor
    B. collect in one or more piles all personal articles found on the fire floor
    C. search for any spark or fire that may remain on the floor
    D. place something over holes which have been cut in the floor
    E. remove any broken timbers or glass found on that floor

13. "You are descending a flight of wooden stairs which have become charred during a fire and which may be weakened. The safest way for you to descend is backwards, keeping close to the wall and feeling each step with your foot."
    Of the following, the CHIEF reason for this procedure is that
    A. stairs are less worn near the wall
    B. it is not necessary to depend upon the handrail for support while descending
    C. it is easier to call for help when facing the head of the stairs
    D. should the entire stairway fall, it is easier to get to safety
    E. the stairs are probably more firmly supported next to the wall

14. "A fire will occur when a flammable material is sufficiently heated in the presence of oxygen."
It follows from this statement that a fire will occur whenever there is sufficient
   A. heat, hydrogen, and fuel
   B. oxygen, hydrogen, and fuel
   C. heat, air, and fuel
   D. gasoline, heat, and fuel
   E. oxygen, air, and heat

15. Of the following, the CHIEF reason why firefighters avoid wearing gas masks, whenever possible, is that masks tend to
   A. become defective quickly
   B. irritate the face
   C. be costly
   D. be unsanitary
   E. hamper working ability

16. A wet cloth or handkerchief is frequently placed over a person's mouth and nose to give protection at a fire.
Of the following, this gives protection against
   A. smoke particles only
   B. harmful gases only
   C. smoke particles and carbon dioxide
   D. smoke particles and carbon monoxide
   E. harmful gases and lack of oxygen

17. "It is customary to indicate the top or tip of ground ladders with white paint and the base or butt with black paint."
The MAJOR reason for these markings is to facilitate
   A. identifying the company to which the ladder belongs
   B. determining the length of the ladder
   C. identifying the end to which rope should be tied when hoisting the ladder to a roof
   D. placing and raising the ladder
   E. placing the ladder on the fire truck

18. "At a fire at which visibility is poor, it is advisable to get down on your hands and knees and crawl, keeping your free hand in front of you with fist clenched."
Of the following, the CHIEF reason for holding your free hand in this manner is that
   A. your reach will be increased
   B. your sense of touch will be better
   C. you will be more stable while crawling
   D. you will be less likely to hurt your hand
   E. you will be able to advance more

19. Suppose that you are in a burning building on the floor above the fire floor and that you wish to get to a window.
    Of the following, you should
    A. cross the center of the floor if this is the shortest path to the window
    B. follow a wall around to the window
    C. crawl on your hands and knees
    D. tie a handkerchief over your mouth and nose
    E. run to the window

20. "The firefighter must not only know how to make the proper knots, but he must know how to make them quickly."
    Of the following, the CHIEF justification for this statement is that
    A. a firefighter uses many kinds of knots
    B. a slowly tied knot slips more easily than one tied quickly
    C. haste makes waste
    D. it is more important for a knot to be tied correctly than quickly
    E. in most fire operations, speed is important

21. "The fire of rags and paper was quenched in a short time."
    As used in this sentence, the word *quenched* means MOST NEARLY
    A. burned out   B. kindled   C. extinguished
    D. started   E. diverted

22. "A driver should make periodic inspections of his vehicle."
    As used in this sentence, the word *periodic* means MOST NEARLY
    A. regular   B. personal   C. careful

23. "The official noted the effect of each detonation."
    As used in this sentence, the word *detonation* means MOST NEARLY
    A. attachment   B. explosion   C. acid
    D. injury   E. audible sound

24. "The structure had a large number of windows exposed to radiant heat across a narrow alley."
    As used in this sentence, the word *radiant* means MOST NEARLY
    A. emitted   B. absorbed   C. dense
    D. dangerous   E. visible

25. "Oil fires can propagate in many ways."
    As used in this sentence, the word *propagate* means MOST NEARLY to
    A. destroy   B. spread   C. burn
    D. be extinguished E. be controlled

26. "A study was made of the efficiency of personnel and equipment under simulated air raid conditions."
    As used in this sentence, the word *simulated* means MOST NEARLY
    A. activated   B. difficult   C. reduced
    D. differentiated E. pretended

27. "The pump faults were rectified."
    As used in this sentence, the word *rectified* means MOST NEARLY
    A. worsened B. overlooked C. corrected
    D. discovered E. recorded

28. "Obstacles which might interfere with quick egress during a fire should be removed."
    As used in this sentence, the word *egress* means MOST NEARLY
    A. movement B. progress C. assistance
    D. communication E. departure

29. "Carbon tetrachloride is a volatile liquid."
    As used in this sentence, the word *volatile* means MOST NEARLY
    A. having a high boiling point B. having a low freezing point
    C. evaporating quickly D. poisonous
    E. odorous

30. "The order was rescinded."
    As used in this sentence, the word *rescinded* means MOST NEARLY
    A. repeated B. cancelled C. verified
    D. relayed E. executed

KEY (CORRECT ANSWERS)

1.	C	11.	E	21.	C
2.	D	12.	A	22.	A
3.	C	13.	E	23.	B
4.	C	14.	C	24.	A
5.	B	15.	E	25.	B
6.	B	16.	A	26.	E
7.	D	17.	D	27.	C
8.	B	18.	D	28.	E
9.	A	19.	B	29.	C
10.	A	20.	E	30.	B

TEST 2

DIRECTIONS: Each question or incomplete statement is followed by several suggested answers or completions. Select the one that BEST answers the question or completes the statement. *PRINT THE LETTER OF THE CORRECT ANSWER IN THE SPACE AT THE RIGHT.*

1. "Some of the training exercises are very intricate."
   As used in this sentence, the word *intricate* means MOST NEARLY
   A. intense   B. educational   C. effective
   D. useless   E. complicated

   1.____

2. "Few states attempt to compile vital statistics on fires and fire losses."
   As used in this sentence, the word *compile* means MOST NEARLY
   A. collect   B. distribute   C. conceal
   D. interpret   E. simplify

   2.____

3. "The heat waves and explosions compelled the firefighters to operate on the periphery of the fire."
   As used in this sentence, the word *periphery* means MOST NEARLY
   A. outer boundary   B. center   C. coolest part
   D. hottest part   E. most dangerous

   3.____

4. "The equipment was dismantled."
   As used in this sentence, the word *dismantled* means MOST NEARLY
   A. partly salvaged   B. cleaned thoroughly   C. taken apart
   D. repaired   E. replaced

   4.____

5. "Under stringent regulations, persons cannot shirk their responsibilities."
   As used in this sentence, the word *stringent* means MOST NEARLY
   A. explicit   B. severe   C. adjustable
   D. legal   E. equitable

   5.____

6. "A lack of buoyancy in the smoke made fighting the cellar fire more difficult."
   As used in this sentence, the word *buoyancy* means MOST NEARLY having the ability to
   A. reflect light   B. rise   C. absorb moisture
   D. cool   E. reflect heat

   6.____

7. "These were the alleged causes for the fire."
   As used in this sentence, the word *alleged* means MOST NEARLY
   A. known   B. proved   C. secret
   D. declared   E. real

   7.____

8. "The result of the action was that the smoke nuisance was eradicated."
   As used in this sentence, the word *eradicated* means MOST NEARLY
   A. changed   B. discovered   C. increased
   D. abolished   E. blamed

   8.____

9. "The problem was aggravated by these new actions."
   As used in this sentence, the word *aggravated* means MOST NEARLY
   A. solved
   B. publicized
   C. revealed
   D. increased
   E. lightened

10. "The members of the company extricated the firefighter."
    As used in this sentence, the word *extricated* means MOST NEARLY
    A. revived
    B. complimented
    C. freed
    D. supported
    E. criticized

Questions 11-20.

DIRECTIONS: Questions 11 through 20 are to be answered on the basis of the following paragraphs.

Air conditioning systems are complex and are made up of several processes. The circulation of the air is produced by fans and ducts; the heating is produced by steam, hot water coils, coal, gas or oil-fired furnaces; the cooling is done by ice or mechanical refrigeration and the cleaning is done by air washers or filters.

Air conditioning systems in large buildings generally should be divided into several parts with wholly separate ducts for each part or floor. The ducts are then extended through fire partitions. As a safeguard, whenever ducts pass through fire partitions, automatic fire dampers should be installed in the ducts. Furthermore, the ducts should be lined on the inside with fire-resistant materials. In addition, a manually operated fan shut-off should be installed at a location which will be readily accessible under fire conditions.

Most air conditioning systems recirculate a considerable portion of the air and when this is done an additional safeguard has to be taken to have the fan arrange to shut down automatically in case of fire. A thermostatic device in the return air duct will operate the shut-off device whenever the temperature of the air coming to the fan becomes excessive. The air filters are frequently coated with oil to help catch dust. Such oil should be of a type that does not ignite readily. Whenever a flammable or toxic refrigerant is employed for air cooling, coils containing such refrigerant should not be inserted in any air passage.

11. According to the preceding paragraphs, fan shut-offs in the air conditioning system should be installed
    A. near the air ducts
    B. next to the fire partitions
    C. near the fire dampers
    D. where fires may start
    E. where they can be reached quickly

12. On the basis of the preceding paragraphs, whenever a fire breaks out in a building containing an air conditioning system which recirculates a portion of the air,
    A. the fan will shut down automatically
    B. the air ducts will be opened
    C. the thermostat will cease to operate
    D. the fire partitions will open
    E. it will be extinguished

13. The preceding paragraphs state that on every floor of a large building where air conditioning systems are used, there should be a(n)
    A. automatic fire damper
    B. thermostatic device
    C. air filter
    D. manually operated fan shut-off
    E. separate duct

14. From the preceding paragraphs, the conclusion can be drawn that in an air conditioning system flammable refrigerants
    A. may be used if certain precautions are observed
    B. should be used sparingly and only in air passages
    C. should not be used under any circumstances
    D. may be more effective than other refrigerants
    E. may be less effective than other refrigerants

15. According to the preceding paragraphs, the spreading of dust by means of the fans in the air conditioning system is reduced by
    A. shutting down the fan automatically
    B. lining the inside of the air ducts
    C. cleaning the circulated air with filters
    D. coating the air filters with oil
    E. cooling the circulated air with refrigerants

16. According to the preceding paragraphs, the purpose of a thermostatic device is to
    A. regulate the temperature of the air conditioning system
    B. shut off the fan when the temperature of the air rises
    C. operate the fan when the temperature of the air falls
    D. assist the recirculation of the air
    E. operate the air duct automatically in case of fire

17. According to the preceding paragraphs, hot water coils in the air conditioning system are limited to
    A. cooling
    B. heating
    C. heating and cooling
    D. heating and cleaning
    E. cooling and cleaning

18. The parts of an air conditioning system which the preceding paragraphs state should be made of fire-resistant materials are the
    A. hot water coils
    B. automatic fire dampers
    C. air duct linings
    D. thermostatic devices
    E. air filters

19. According to the preceding paragraphs, automatic fire dampers should be installed
    A. on oil-fired furnaces
    B. on every floor of a large building
    C. in ducts passing through fire partitions
    D. next to the hot water coils
    E. near the thermostatic device

4 (#2)

20. On the basis of the preceding paragraphs, the MOST accurate statement is 20._____
that coils containing toxic refrigerants should be
   A. used only when necessary
   B. lined with fire-resistant materials
   C. coated with non-flammable oil
   D. kept out of any air passage
   E. kept from overheating

Questions 21-30.

DIRECTIONS: Questions 21 through 30 are to be answered on the basis of the following paragraphs.

    Fire regulations require that every liquefied petroleum gas installation should be provided with the means for shutting off the supply to a building in case of an emergency. The installation of a shut-off valve immediately inside a building, which is sometimes done for the convenience of the user, does not comply with this regulation. An outside shut-off valve just outside the building seems to be the logical solution. However, the possibility of tampering illustrates the danger of such an arrangement. A shut-off valve so located might be placed in a locked box. However, this has no advantage over a valve provided within the locked cabinet containing the cylinder or an enclosure provided over the top of the cylinders. Keys may be carried by firefighters or in an emergency the lock may be broken. Where no valve is visible, the firefighters should not hesitate to break the lock to the cylinder enclosure. The means for shutting off the gas varies considerably in the numerous types of equipment in use. When the cover to the enclosure has been opened, the gas may be shut off as follows:
    Close the tank or cylinder valves to which the supply line is connected. Such valves always turn to the right. If the valve is not provided with a handwheel, an adjustable wrench can be used. If conditions are such that shutting off the supply at once is imperative and this cannot be accomplished as above, the tubing which is commonly employed as the supply line can be flattened to the extent of closure by a hammer. If the emergency is such as to require the removal of the cylinder, the supply line should be disconnected and the cylinder removed to a safe location. A tank buried in the ground is safe against fire. When conditions indicate the need of removing a cylinder or tank, and this cannot be done due to the severity of exposure, pressures within the container can be kept within control of the safety valve by means of a hose stream played on the surface of the container. The melting of the fuse plug may also be prevented in this way.

21. According to the preceding paragraphs, in an emergency a firefighter should 21._____
break the lock of a cylinder enclosure whenever the shut-off valve
   A. fails to operate
   B. has no handwheel
   C. has been tampered with
   D. cannot be seen
   E. is installed inside the building

22. According to the preceding paragraphs, shut-off valves for liquefied petroleum 22._____
gas installations
   A. always turn to the right
   B. always turn to the left
   C. sometimes turn to the right and sometimes turn to the left
   D. are generally pulled up
   E. are generally pushed down

23. According to the preceding paragraphs, if a cylinder should be moved but cannot because of the severity of exposure, the pressure can be kept under control by
    A. opening the shut-off valve
    B. playing a hose stream on the cylinder
    C. disconnecting the supply line into the cylinder
    D. removing the fuse plug
    E. closing the cabinet containing the cylinder

24. The preceding paragraphs state that the supply line should be disconnected when the
    A. fuse plug melts
    B. cylinder is removed to another location
    C. supply line becomes defective
    D. cylinder is damaged
    E. shut-off valve fails to operate

25. The preceding paragraphs state that shut-off valves for liquefied petroleum gas installations are sometimes placed inside buildings
    A. so that firefighters will be able to find the valves more easily
    B. because it is more convenient for the occupants
    C. in order to hide the valves from public view
    D. as this makes it easier to keep the valves in good working condition
    E. to insure that the valves cannot be tampered with

26. It is suggested in the preceding paragraphs that during an emergency the supply line tubing should be flattened to the extent of closure when the
    A. supply line becomes defective
    B. shut-off valve cannot be opened
    C. shut-off valve cannot be closed
    D. supply line is very near a fire
    E. shut-off valve is located inside the building

27. According to the preceding paragraphs, fire regulations require that liquefied petroleum gas installations should
    A. be made in safe places
    B. be tamper-proof
    C. have shut-off valves
    D. not exceed a certain size
    E. contain cylinders

28. The preceding paragraphs state that an adjustable wrench may be used in turning the shut-off valve when the valve
    A. turns to the right
    B. turns to the left
    C. is open
    D. is closed
    E. is without a handwheel

29. The preceding paragraphs state the means for shutting off liquefied petroleum gas flowing from a cylinder
    A. varies in the many types of equipment
    B. is the same for nearly all types of equipment
    C. varies with the size of the equipment
    D. varies with the age of the equipment
    E. is the same in some installations using portable equipment

30. As suggested in the preceding paragraphs, the fuse plug may be prevented from melting by
    A. using an adjustable wrench
    B. disconnecting the supply line
    C. putting water on the surface of the tank
    D. removing the heated contents of the tank
    E. locking the valve

31. When administering first aid for the accidental swallowing of poison, water is given CHIEFLY to
    A. increase energy
    B. quiet the nerves
    C. weaken the poison
    D. prevent choking
    E. prevent vomiting

32. The CHIEF purpose of administering artificial respiration in first aid is to
    A. exert regular pressure on the heart
    B. force the blood into circulation by pressure
    C. force air into the lungs
    D. keep the person warm by keeping his body in motion
    E. keep the person awake

33. When severe shock occurs, it is important for the person being treated to have
    A. sedatives and cold drinks
    B. warmth and low head position
    C. hot drinks and much activity
    D. sedatives and sitting position
    E. cold drinks and high head position

34. When administering first aid, a tourniquet is used to
    A. sterilize the injured area
    B. hold the splints in place
    C. hold the dressing in place
    D. stop the loss of blood
    E. close an open wound

35. Heat exhaustion and sunstroke are alike in that in both cases the person affected
    A. has hot dry skin and a red face
    B. should lie with head high
    C. should be given stimulants
    D. has a very high temperature
    E. has been exposed to heat

KEY (CORRECT ANSWERS)

1.	E	11.	E	21.	D	31.	C
2.	A	12.	A	22.	A	32.	C
3.	A	13.	E	23.	B	33.	B
4.	C	14.	A	24.	B	34.	D
5.	B	15.	D	25.	B	35.	E
6.	B	16.	B	26.	C		
7.	D	17.	B	27.	C		
8.	D	18.	C	28.	E		
9.	D	19.	C	29.	A		
10.	C	20.	D	30.	C		

EXAMINATION SECTION

TEST 1

DIRECTIONS: Each question or incomplete statement is followed by several suggested answers or completions. Select the one that BEST answers the question or completes the statement. *PRINT THE LETTER OF THE CORRECT ANSWER IN THE SPACE AT THE RIGHT.*

1. Suppose that, as a firefighter, you are holding the nozzle of an operating hose line in the center of a large, smoke-filled basement. The water supply suddenly fails, causing the hose line to go limp. The smoke has become so dense that no exit from the basement is immediately apparent.
   Of the following, the BEST action for you to take in order to escape from the basement is to
   A. follow the nearest wall to your left until a door is reached
   B. follow the nearest wall to your right until a door is reached
   C. proceed rapidly to the nearest stairway
   D. attempt to locate a large window
   E. follow the hose line back to its source

1._____

2. Suppose that, while fighting a fire, you are on the fire escape of a building. You are ordered to break a pane of glass in a window so that you can insert your hand to unfasten the window catch.
   Of the following, the LEAST appropriate procedure to follow in carrying out this order is to
   A. give warning to men working below so that they can get out of the way of falling glass
   B. use an axe or other long-handled tool so that you can break the glass without cutting your hands
   C. stand directly in front of the window so that the broken pieces of glass can follow down the handle of the tool used
   D. make the hole close to the catch so that you can easily reach the catch through the broken window
   E. make the hole large enough so that you will not cut your arm on jagged edges of glass

2._____

3. "Just as it takes more than red paint and polished brass to make a fire engine, so also does it require more than muscle and a strong back to make a firefighter."
   Of the following, the CHIEF implication of the above quotation is that
   A. strong men make good firefighters
   B. firefighting is a technical job
   C. equipment should be kept polished
   D. polishing fire apparatus is difficult work
   E. few fire engines are painted red

3._____

4. Suppose that, as a firefighter, you wish to force a locked window open so that you can enter a burning building. It is the usual double-hung type of window which slides up and down.
Of the following, the BEST action for you to take is to insert the blade of an axe
   A. between the upper and lower halves of the window and twist sharply
   B. beneath the base of the lower sash and pry upward
   C. between the window and the window frame on the right side and pry inward
   D. between the upper window pane and sash and twist gently
   E. between the window and the window frame on the left side and pry outward

4.____

5. Suppose that you have stretched a line of hose up a fire ladder. You are holding the nozzle and are about to signal the pump operator to start the water.
Of the following, the BEST reason for first strapping yourself to the ladder is that
   A. water leaving a nozzle exerts a backward force
   B. the hose line containing the water may be very short
   C. there may be several sharp kinks in the hose line
   D. the ladder may be damaged or weakened
   E. the nozzle is considerably above the level of the pump

5.____

6. Assume that you are a firefighter. During the course of your training, you are instructed not to open the nozzle of a hose line until you have actually located the fire.
Of the following, the BEST justification for these instructions is that starting the flow of water from a hose line in a burning building before the fire is located may
   A. force smoke out of the roof and windows
   B. produce large quantities of fumes
   C. cut off possible retreat
   D. cause excessive water damage
   E. smother the fire

6.____

7. Assume that it is your function, when your company responds to a fire alarm, to sound the siren which warns other vehicles of the approach of fire apparatus. You are warned by your superior officer to interrupt sounding the siren for a few seconds when the apparatus approaches an intersection.
Of the following, the BEST reason for this warning is that
   A. it may be necessary for the driver of fire apparatus to concentrate on his driving when he approaches an especially dangerous intersection
   B. most accidents involving fire apparatus and civilian automobiles occur at intersections
   C. in an emergency, speed is more important than safety
   D. other emergency vehicles may be sounding their own sirens as they approach the intersection from other directions
   E. it is at intersections that a fire engine is driven most rapidly

7.____

8. Assume that a fire has occurred in a tenement house. It is necessary to determine whether the fire is spreading inside the wall of a room, some distance away from the origin of the fire.
Of the following, the circumstances which indicate LEAST strongly that the fire is spreading inside the wall is that
   A. the door leading into the room is warped
   B. parts of the wall feel hot
   C. smoke is issuing through cracks in the wall
   D. the wallpaper is rapidly becoming discolored
   E. the paint on the wall is blistering

8.____

9. "After a fire has been extinguished, every effort should be made to determine how the fire started."
Of the following, the CHIEF reason for determining the origin of the fire is to
   A. reduce the amount of damage caused by the fire
   B. determine how the fire should have been fought
   C. eliminate causes of fire in the future
   D. explain delays in fighting the fire
   E. improve salvage operations

9.____

10. "A partially filled gasoline drum is a more dangerous fire hazard than a full one." Of the following, the BEST justification for this statement is that
    A. a partially filled gasoline drum contains relatively little air
    B. gasoline is difficult to ignite
    C. when a gasoline drum is full, the gasoline is more explosive
    D. gasoline vapors are more explosive than gasoline itself
    E. air is not combustible

10.____

11. The first engine company to arrive at a fire in a tenement building is usually required to stretch a hose line to the interior stairway of the building.
Of the following, the BEST justification for this practice is that
    A. the stairway is a relatively safe and rapid means of evacuating tenants
    B. it may be possible to extinguish the fire in a few minutes
    C. using a stairway for storage is a violation of the fire rules
    D. stairways are required by law to be fireproof
    E. even old law tenements are required to have fire escapes

11.____

12. Suppose that you are a member of an engine company. Your company is notified to respond to a fire near Box 3234. En route, your company encounters another fire in a warehouse. For your company to stop to extinguish the warehouse fire would be unwise CHIEFLY because
    A. warehouses are usually well protected with sprinkler systems
    B. your company may be the only engine company notified to respond to the fire near Box 3234
    C. warehouse fires, if neglected, may develop into serious proportions
    D. other engine companies may also be responding to the fire near Box 3234
    E. time would be wasted in summoning another engine company to the warehouse fire

12.____

13. "The fire alarm box is an important element of the city's fire protection system."
The one of the following factors which is of LEAST value in helping a citizen to send a fire alarm quickly by means of a fire alarm box is that
    A. the mechanism of a fire alarm box is simple to operate
    B. fire alarm boxes are placed at very frequent intervals throughout the city
    C. there are several different types of fire alarm boxes in use
    D. specific directions for sending an alarm appear on each fire alarm box
    E. fire alarm boxes are painted a distinctive color

14. "Chief officers shall instruct their aides that when transmitting particulars of a fire, they shall include the fact that foods are involved if the fire involves premises where foodstuffs are sold or stored."
Of the following, the BEST justification for this regulation is that, when foodstuffs are involved in a fire,
    A. the fire may reach serious proportions
    B. police protection may be desirable in preventing looting
    C. relatively little firefighting equipment may be needed
    D. there is a strong likelihood of arson
    E. inspection to detect contamination may be desirable

15. "One or more public ambulances may be called to a street box by sending on the Morse key therein the following signals in the order given: the preliminary signal 777, the number of the street box, and the number to indicate how many ambulances are wanted."
In accordance with these instruction, the PROPER signal for calling four public ambulances to Box 423 is
    A. 4-777-423   B. 7777-423   C. 423-777-4
    D. 777-423-4   E. 7-423-4

16. It has been found that, during winter months, the percentage of drivers of civilian vehicles involved in accidents with fire apparatus who claim that they did not hear the fire sirens is larger than the percentage during summer months.
Of the following, the MOST probable explanation for this situation is that
    A. the sound of fire sirens travels faster in cold air than in warm air
    B. there is less traffic on the streets during winter months than during summer months
    C. drivers tend to be more alert during the winter than during the summer
    D. more drivers tend to keep car windows closed during winter months than during summer months
    E. snow and ice make driving conditions more hazardous during winter months than during summer months

17. "No firefighter is expected to use a measuring stick to determine the exact amount of hose needed to stretch a line from the entrance of the burning building to the seat of the fire. He should be guided generally by the following rule—one length of hose for every story."
This rule assumes MOST directly some degree of uniformity in
   A. fire hazards
   B. building construction
   C. causes of fires
   D. window areas
   E. street widths

18. It has been suggested that all fire companies now quartered in individual firehouses in Manhattan be combined and quartered in a few large fire stations located at strategic points.
The one of the following LEAST accurately considered a possible advantage of the proposed scheme is that
   A. duplication of work in individual firehouses would be reduced
   B. fewer officers would be required to supervise maintenance of buildings and equipment
   C. fire apparatus would be able to respond more quickly to the scene of a fire
   D. flow of correspondence and reports between fire headquarters and individual fire companies would be simplified
   E. valuable land and property now in the hands of the city could be leased or sold

19. "The taxpayer type of building is usually located in the busiest sections of a city."
Of the following, the LEAST valid implication of the above statement is that, when a fire in a taxpayer occurs during working hours,
   A. heavy traffic may be a handicap to firefighting operations
   B. precautions may be necessary to avoid panic among employees or shoppers
   C. police lines may be needed to keep back pedestrians
   D. failure to get the fire under control quickly may result in high property damage
   E. the fire may burn for a long period of time before it is detected

20. "Installation of a modern fire alarm system will mean smaller fires."
Of the following, the BEST justification for this statement is that
   A. if summoned quickly, firefighters can control a fire before it has a chance to spread
   B. if the alarm system is modern, firefighters can be given a complete picture of a fire even before they respond
   C. some fires, such as fires resulting from explosions, assume large proportions in a few seconds
   D. most industrial establishments depend on more than one method of transmitting fire alarms
   E. an efficient fire alarm system would discourage arsonists from setting fires intentionally

21. The one of the following circumstances concerning a fire which indicates MOST strongly the possibility of arson is that
    A. there was heavy charring of wood around the point of origin of the fire
    B. three fires apparently broke out simultaneously in different parts of the building
    C. the heat was so intense that glass in the building became molten and fused
    D. when the firefighters arrived the smoke was very heavy
    E. the fire apparently started in an oil-soaked mop

22. Of the following, the BEST justification for a firefighter to practice important routine duties until they become definite habits is that
    A. habits are rarely formed consciously
    B. conscious habits are ineffective
    C. habits are not often forgotten
    D. routine duties are usually unimportant
    E. bad habits are difficult to practice

23. Of the following, the CHIEF advantage likely to be derived from installing a short wave radio receiving set in every piece of fire apparatus is that
    A. fire companies could be communicated with while they are in the field
    B. fire department headquarters could be notified as soon as a fire company has returned to its quarters from a fire
    C. traffic accidents involving fire department apparatus would be reduced
    D. fewer men would require technical fire training
    E. a definite wave band could be set aside for exclusive use by the fire department

24. Suppose that your company is operating at a fire in a three-story factory. Your commanding officer orders you to open the skylight on the roof to ventilate the building.
    Openings for ventilation are usually made in the roof of a burning building CHIEFLY because
    A. hot air tends to flow towards the point of greatest pressure
    B. air is much lighter than smoke
    C. a rush of fresh air might cause the fire to spread
    D. smoke tends to remain close to the seat of the fire
    E. hot gases and smoke tend to rise

25. As a firefighter, you may be assigned to inspect buildings for fire hazards. The one of the following MOST appropriately used for fire-retardant coating of wood is
    A. varnish   B. shellac   C. wood stain
    D. lacquer   E. white wash

26. The competent firefighter should know that, of the following, the BEST conductor of heat is
    A. concrete   B. porcelain   C. pine wood
    D. steel   E. bricks

27. "Even a single 2½ inch hose line with a 1 inch nozzle will load a fire floor with more than a ton of water per minute."
Of the following, the CHIEF implication of the above statement is that
   A. a hose line should not be placed too close to the fire
   B. building collapse is a serious possibility in firefighting
   C. a 2½ inch hose line is generally too small for fighting fires
   D. more than one hose line is usually needed to extinguish a fire
   E. a single firefighter can usually handle a hose line satisfactorily

28. A large, heavy stream of water should be used in preference to a small stream in fighting a fire when the
   A. area involved in the fire is small, such as a closet
   B. fire is confined, with little danger of extension
   C. fire must be fought at a great distance
   D. fire is almost extinguished
   E. fire is in its initial stages

29. "In a fog stream, the water is divided into a large number of tiny droplets."
The proficient firefighter, therefore, should realize that a fog stream is better able to absorb heat than a solid stream of water because a fog stream
   A. has a greater surface area
   B. has a greater density
   C. is more continuous
   D. dissolves less air
   E. delivers a greater weight of water

30. Suppose that a firefighter has burned his hand while working at a fire.
Of the following, the POOREST first aid remedy for burns is
   A. baking soda solution
   B. Epsom salts
   C. picric acid
   D. iodine
   E. tannic acid

31. "Before entering a room filled with carbon monoxide, tie a wet cloth over your mouth and nose."
The competent firefighter should realize that the procedure described in the above quotation
   A. is useless
   B. is effective only for preventing asphyxiation
   C. is valuable for no longer than 5 minutes, by which time the water will have evaporated from the handkerchief
   D. will furnish protection against carbon monoxide but not against carbon dioxide
   E. will be effective as long as the handkerchief remains moist

32. By a compound fracture is generally meant a fracture in which
   A. the broken bone has penetrated the skin
   B. the bone is broken at more than one point
   C. the bone has not been broken but has been dislocated as well
   D. more than one bone has been broken
   E. the fracture is complicated by internal bleeding

33. "Never forget to loosen a tourniquet every once in a while and let the blood flow."
Of the following, the BEST justification for this statement is that
    A. a tourniquet is merely an emergency measure
    B. a tourniquet tends to lose its effectiveness unless it is tightened frequently
    C. continued flow of blood may lead to infection of the wound
    D. heavy loss of blood may weaken the victim seriously
    E. prolonged interruption of blood circulation may cause gangrene

34. In his first aid training, the newly appointed firefighter is cautioned: "Do not disturb blood clots."
Of the following, the BEST justification for this recommendation is that
    A. blood clots are a source of germs and serious infection
    B. the blood of most persons clots very easily
    C. a blood clot has already accomplished the first aider's purpose in stopping bleeding
    D. it is possible to apply pressure to a blood vessel even when the blood has clotted
    E. the fact that the victim's blood has clotted does not indicate whether a vein or artery is involved

35. Suppose that ½ of the firefighters in the fire department have served for more than 5 years and $1/3$ for more than 10 years.
Then the fraction of firefighters having served between 5 and 10 years is MOST NEARLY
    A. $2/3$ B. $1/3$ C. $1/5$ D. $1/6$ E. $1/12$

36. Suppose that it is necessary to compute the number of gallons of water contained in a length of hose 50 feet long and 2½ inches in diameter.
Of the following, the CHIEF additional item of information required is the
    A. radius of the hose
    B. circumference of the hose
    C. pressure of a gallon of water
    D. velocity of the water passing through the hose
    E. number of cubic inches in a gallon

37. Suppose that a piece of fire apparatus averages 20 runs a month during each of 3 summer months and 30 runs a month during each of 2 winter months.
Then the average number of runs made by this apparatus over the 5 month period is MOST NEARLY
    A. 22   B. 24   C. 25   D. 26   E. 28

38. A basement is being flooded by means of fire hose. At the end of 6 minutes, the basement is one-third flooded. At the same rate of flooding, a basement with a capacity for holding twice as much water could be completely flooded in _____ minutes.
    A. 12   B. 18   C. 24   D. 36   E. 64

39. Assume that, during a certain period, there were in New York 300 fires and 200 false alarms of fire.
If the number of fires were doubled and the number of false alarms were also doubled, the ratio of fires to false alarms would be
   A. four times as large
   B. twice as large
   C. unchanged
   D. one-half as large
   E. one-quarter as large

40. Assume that, during a given period of time, the number of third alarms was 80 percent of the number of second alarms.
Then, of the following, the MOST accurate statement is that
   A. the number of second and third alarms combined was at least 80 percent of all first alarms
   B. at least 80 percent of all alarms higher than first alarms higher than first alarms were second alarms
   C. the number of second alarms was 20 percent of the number of third alarms
   D. there were one-quarter as many third as second alarms
   E. there were 1¼ times as many second as third alarms

KEY (CORRECT ANSWERS)

1.	E	11.	A	21.	B	31.	A
2.	C	12.	B	22.	C	32.	A
3.	B	13.	C	23.	A	33.	E
4.	B	14.	E	24.	E	34.	C
5.	A	15.	D	25.	E	35.	D
6.	D	16.	D	26.	D	36.	E
7.	D	17.	B	27.	B	37.	B
8.	A	18.	C	28.	C	38.	D
9.	C	19.	E	29.	A	39.	C
10.	D	20.	A	30.	D	40.	E

TEST 2

DIRECTIONS: Each question or incomplete statement is followed by several suggested answers or completions. Select the one that BEST answers the question or completes the statement. *PRINT THE LETTER OF THE CORRECT ANSWER IN THE SPACE AT THE RIGHT.*

1. Assume that, of the 130 runs made by fire department apparatus during a certain period of time, 50 percent were made by engine companies, 40 percent by truck companies, and the remainder by miscellaneous companies.
   Then, of the following, the MOST accurate statement is that
   A. truck companies made fewer than 50 runs
   B. engine companies made more than 75 runs
   C. truck companies made 10 runs more than engine companies
   D. miscellaneous companies made more than 10 runs
   E. engine companies and truck companies together made fewer than 100 runs

   1.____

2. "Reports should include all pertinent material."
   The word *pertinent* means MOST NEARLY
   A. directly observed by the writer
   B. required by rules, procedure, or law
   C. having to do with the subject being considered
   D. tending to fix responsibility
   E. requested by one's superior

   2.____

3. A firefighter who is *nimble* is BEST described as
   A. able to perform tasks of great importance
   B. quick and light in motion
   C. fatigued by heavy work
   D. capable of learning efficiently
   E. injured seriously

   3.____

4. "A firefighter's work may sometimes be tedious."
   The word *tedious* means MOST NEARLY
   A. boring   B. dangerous   C. unproductive
   D. difficult   E. solitary

   4.____

5. "The firefighter was reproved for his action."
   The word *reproved* means MOST NEARLY
   A. praised highly   B. censured mildly   C. rewarded
   D. cited publicly   E. exonerated

   5.____

6. "When at a fire, the firefighter must avoid any action that is superfluous."
   The word *superfluous* means MOST NEARLY
   A. irresponsible   B. uncertain   C. uncoordinated
   D. risky   E. unnecessary

   6.____

2 (#2)

7. Fumes which are *toxic* are BEST described as
   A. dense
   B. concentrated
   C. poisonous
   D. offensive
   E. odorous

8. "Officers will submit a report of all obsolete equipment."
   The word *obsolete* means MOST NEARLY
   A. failing to operate
   B. difficult to replace
   C. out of date
   D. unusually effective
   E. highly expensive

9. "Firefighters performing inspection duty should note any conditions that are hazardous."
   The word *hazardous* means MOST NEARLY
   A. negligent
   B. congested
   C. illegal
   D. dangerous
   E. unusual

10. "The principle of operation of a fire pump is complex.
    The word *complex* means MOST NEARLY
    A. important
    B. uniform
    C. universal
    D. intricate
    E. fundamental

11. A firefighter who is *intrepid* is MOST NEARLY
    A. prudent
    B. competent
    C. fearless
    D. responsible
    E. intelligent

12. Instructions which are *tentative* in nature are BEST described as
    A. precisely stated
    B. subject to change
    C. detailed in form
    D. very clear
    E. especially meaningful

13. "Possibility of the collapse of the building was remote.
    The word *remote* means MOST NEARLY
    A. slight
    B. imminent
    C. real
    D. serious
    E. obvious

14. To say that evidence of arson is *inconclusive* means MOST NEARLY that the evidence
    A. is entirely reasonable
    B. has been gathered irregularly
    C. is irrelevant and immaterial
    D. fails to establish definite proof
    E. has not been subjected to tests

15. A firefighter who is *meticulous* in his work is MOST NEARLY
    A. alert and cooperative
    B. unusually susceptible to errors
    C. courageous in emergencies
    D. a rapid but careless worker
    E. excessively careful in small details

16. "The report on the accident involving the fire apparatus was written tersely." 16.____
    The word *tersely* means MOST NEARLY
    A. concisely
    B. competently
    C. immediately afterwards
    D. poorly
    E. in accordance with instructions

Questions 17-23.

DIRECTIONS: Questions 17 through 23 are to be answered on the basis of the following paragraph.

An out-of-service disk is a metallic disk with either a 3" or 2½" hole at its center, so that it may be placed on the 3" or 2½" nozzle of a fire hydrant. All disks are colored white. Some 3" disks, in addition, have a 1" black stripe painted across the center of both sides. Whenever a low pressure or high pressure fire hydrant or any independent outlet of a high pressure fire hydrant is found unserviceable from any cause, including all fire hydrants which are frozen or which are not supplied with water or which are connected to water mains that have been temporarily shut off, an out-of-service disk shall be placed thereon in accordance with the following procedure. If a low pressure fire hydrant is unserviceable, a white painted out-of-service disk shall be placed on the nozzle of the 2½" outlet to indicate that the fire hydrant cannot be used. If only one or two independent outlets of a high pressure fire hydrant are unserviceable, a 3" white painted out-of-service disk shall be placed on the nozzle of each unserviceable outlet to indicate that such outlet or outlets cannot be used. If three or all four independent outlets of a high pressure hydrant are unserviceable, a white painted out-of-service disk having a 1" black stripe painted across the center of both sides thereof shall be placed on the nozzle of the outlet nearest the roadway to indicate that the fire hydrant cannot be used.

17. On the basis of the above paragraph, it is evident that the CHIEF purpose of 17.____
    the out-of-service disk is to
    A. prevent damage to fire hydrants by careless operation
    B. prevent loss of pressure in fire lines due to friction
    C. indicate quickly to the firefighters exactly how much pressure can be obtained from a hydrant
    D. avoid loss of valuable time when connections are made to defective hydrants
    E. prevent two or more pumpers from connecting to the same hydrant

18. If two independent outlets of a high pressure hydrant are unserviceable, 18.____
    the PROPER action to take is to place a white colored disk
    A. on the nozzle nearest the roadway
    B. on each of the unserviceable nozzles
    C. having a black stripe on the nozzle nearest the roadway
    D. on each of the unserviceable nozzles and a white colored disk on each of the unserviceable nozzles
    E. on each of the unserviceable nozzles and a white colored disk having a black stripe on the nozzle nearest the roadway

19. Of the following, the MOST accurate statement on the basis of the above paragraph is that a
    A. 3" white colored disk having a black stripe should be placed on a high pressure hydrant only
    B. 3" white colored disk should be placed on a low pressure hydrant only
    C. 2½" white colored disk should be placed on a high pressure hydrant only
    D. 2½" white colored disk having a black stripe should be placed on a low pressure hydrant only
    E. 2½" white colored disk having a black stripe should be placed on a high pressure hydrant only

19.____

20. Of the following, the BEST justification for placing an out-of-service disk on the nozzle nearest the roadway, as suggested in the above paragraph, is that a disk attached to the nozzle nearest the roadway is
    A. not likely to be removed by unauthorized persons
    B. not likely to interfere with normal firefighting operations
    C. easily removed in case of an emergency
    D. likely to be close to the scene of the fire
    E. not likely to be overlooked by firefighters arriving at the scene

20.____

21. Of the following, the MOST accurate statement on the basis of the above paragraph is that a _____ pressure hydrant has at least _____ nozzle(s).
    A. low; one 3"   B. high; one 2½"   C. low; one 2½"
    D. high; five 3"   E. low; one 3½"

21.____

22. If one independent outlet of a high pressure hydrant is defective, the PROPER action is to place a
    A. 2½" white colored disk on the defective nozzle
    B. 3" white colored disk on the defective nozzle
    C. 2½" white colored disk having a black stripe on the nozzle nearest the roadway
    D. 3" white colored disk having a black stripe on the defective nozzle
    E. 3" white colored disk on the nozzle nearest the roadway

22.____

23. The instructions in the above paragraph are LEAST complete with respect to the specific action to be taken if
    A. neither of the two outlets of a low pressure hydrant is serviceable
    B. all four outlets of a high pressure hydrant are unserviceable
    C. a low pressure hydrant cannot be used at all for fire department purposes
    D. only one of the 3" outlets of a high pressure hydrant is unserviceable
    E. the 4½" nozzle of a high pressure hydrant is the only unserviceable outlet

23.____

Questions 24-30.

DIRECTIONS: Questions 24 through 30 are to be answered on the basis of the following paragraph which is adapted from a typical firefighting manual.

In the foam type of fire extinguisher, the three principal chemicals used are aluminum sulphate, bicarbonate of soda, and a stabilizer. Generally about 50 percent water solution of aluminum sulphate is used in the small inner chamber. The large outer chamber contains about 8 percent bicarbonate of soda, 3 percent stabilizer, and 89 percent water. The purpose of the stabilizer is to make the bubbles smaller in size and more tenacious. The method of operating the extinguisher is by inverting it, whereupon the chemicals in the two chambers are mixed to produce not only the foam but pressure to expel the foam. The principal extinguishing agent consists of minute bubbles of carbon dioxide gas entrapped in walls of insoluble aluminum hydrate, to form a strong, tough, elastic and adhesive foam that will stand considerable abuse. In volume, more than 90 percent of the foam is carbon dioxide gas, but foam contains more than 85 percent water by weight. The foam forms a blanket of bubbles over the burning material, excluding the air and at the same time cooling the surface. The aluminum hydrate gives strength to the bubble wall and renders cloth and other cellulose products fire resistant. The foam coats both horizontal and vertical surfaces with a heat insulating layer which clings wherever applied and floats on even light liquids. It is harmless to the operator and has a lesser wetting effect than water. The force, length, and duration of the stream are not dependent on the operator. The extinguisher is not effective on alcohol fires and must be protected from low temperatures.

24. According to the above paragraph, a foam extinguisher is NOT effective on
    A. fires involving liquids B. fires involving chemicals
    C. burning wood   D. burning alcohol
    E. burning cloth

25. With respect to the total contents of the fire extinguisher described in the above paragraph, the MOST accurate statement is that there is, by volume,
    A. less water than aluminum sulphate
    B. more stabilizer than aluminum sulphate
    C. less stabilizer than bicarbonate of soda
    D. more bicarbonate of soda than water
    E. less water in the outer chamber than in the inner chamber

26. Of the following, the BEST explanation for the fact that foam is 90 percent carbon dioxide by volume and 85 percent water by weight is that
    A. water has a greater density than carbon dioxide
    B. water occupies a greater volume than carbon dioxide
    C. carbon dioxide is heavier than air
    D. carbon dioxide is not a pure gas
    E. the water in the extinguisher is in solution

27. The CHIEF purpose of the stabilizer in the foam extinguisher is to prevent
    A. premature chemical reaction of the contents
    B. rapid breaking up of the carbon dioxide bubbles
    C. evaporation of the aluminum sulphate
    D. adhesion of the foam to the extinguisher
    E. excessive gas pressure in the extinguisher

27._____

28. The CHIEF reason for excluding air from burning material by means of a coating of foam is that
    A. the nitrogen in air is essential for combustion
    B. a coating of foam allows radiated heat to escape
    C. foam lowers the ignition temperature of burning material
    D. carbon dioxide is decomposed by the heat of the fire
    E. a fire needs oxygen to continue burning

28._____

29. The foam is expelled from a foam extinguisher by
    A. the force of gravity
    B. contraction of the water in the inner cylinder
    C. a hand pump operated by the firefighter
    D. the force of the stabilizer acting in solution
    E. the pressure of gas created by chemical reaction

29._____

30. The one of the following which describes MOST accurately a limitation of the foam extinguisher is that
    A. it may decompose cellulose products
    B. it may give off dangerous gases
    C. it may freeze in low temperatures
    D. foam is a poor conductor of electricity
    E. foam bubbles are rather small in size

30._____

KEY (CORRECT ANSWERS)

1.	D	11.	C	21.	C
2.	C	12.	B	22.	B
3.	B	13.	A	23.	E
4.	A	14.	D	24.	D
5.	B	15.	E	25.	C
6.	E	16.	A	26.	A
7.	C	17.	D	27.	B
8.	C	18.	B	28.	E
9.	D	19.	A	29.	E
10.	D	20.	E	30.	C

EXAMINATION SECTION
TEST 1

DIRECTIONS: Each question or incomplete statement is followed by several suggested answers or completions. Select the one that BEST answers the question or completes the statement. *PRINT THE LETTER OF THE CORRECT ANSWER IN THE SPACE AT THE RIGHT.*

1. Suppose that you are a firefighter and that your company has responded to a fire at a large apartment house. You are on a ladder, about to enter a smoke-filled room through the window in order to search for a woman reported to be still in the burning building.
   Of the following, the BEST action for you to take first before you enter the room is to
   A. make certain that there is at least one other means of exit from the room in the event of an emergency
   B. lash the ladder securely to a heavy piece of furniture in the room
   C. note the layout of the room in relation to all stairways in the building
   D. test the flooring around the window cautiously with one foot to determine whether the flooring will hold your weight
   E. determine quickly whether the fire is spreading through the walls of the building

   1.____

2. Suppose that a fire has occurred in a drugstore basement where a large stock of chemicals is stored on open shelves and in wooden boxes. As a member of an engine company, you take a line of hose down into the basement. The smoke is very thick, but flames can be seen behind a row of boxes.
   Of the following, the CHIEF precaution for you to take is to avoid
   A. upsetting and mixing the chemicals, lest there be an explosion
   B. wetting any wooden boxes near the flames, lest a chemical reaction results from the effect of water on wood
   C. wetting the walls, lest a short circuit be caused in the electric wiring
   D. opening any windows in the basement, lest the smoke be allowed to escape
   E. throwing water directly on the fire, lest excessive smoke be produced

   2.____

3. Suppose that, in a fire in an unfinished warehouse, several iron and steel structural supports are heated to a point where they are red hot.
   Of the following, the BEST reason for not directing water against the heated supports is that
   A. the action of water on heated metal may produce a sudden burst of flame
   B. iron and steel are very poor conductors of heat
   C. hot sparks may be produced, causing the fire to spread to other parts of the warehouse
   D. smoke may be given off in excessively large quantities
   E. iron and steel supports may buckle when cooled quickly, causing the roof to collapse

   3.____

4. "The firefighter assigned to Housewatch Duty is responsible for giving and receiving alarms, not all of which come by way of telegraph signals." Suppose that, while you are on duty, a woman runs up to you. Breathless and almost hysterical, she shouts "Fire!"
Of the following, the MOST important question for you, as House Watchman, to ask is
   A. What is your name and address?
   B. Where is the fire?
   C. How serious is the fire?
   D. Did you actually see the fire yourself?
   E. How far is the fire from here?

5. As a firefighter, you may be assigned to drive a piece of fire apparatus. Suppose that you are responding to a fire alarm. As you approach a street intersection, it would be MOST wise for you to
   A. increase your rate of speed in order to avoid collisions with cross-traffic at the intersection
   B. increase your rate of speed in order to avoid delaying cross-traffic, which may have halted to allow you to pass
   C. maintain your normal rate of speed, lest a rear-end collision occur should you stop suddenly
   D. decrease your rate of speed so that you may have time to decide which turn to make, if necessary
   E. decrease your rate of speed so that you may be able to stop more quickly, if necessary

6. "Adequate firefighting equipment is necessary and should be provided, but even the best equipment may be ineffectual unless used intelligently."
This statement emphasizes CHIEFLY the importance of
   A. inspecting fire equipment frequently to make certain that it is adequate
   B. purchasing fire equipment intelligently
   C. designing fire equipment properly
   D. training personnel in methods of firefighting
   E. eliminating inadequate fire equipment

7. Suppose that you are a firefighter assigned to a hook and ladder company. An alarm is received at your fire station to which your company responds.
Of the following, the BEST reason for not riding the side of the hook and ladder truck until it reaches the street is that
   A. oncoming traffic is usually warned by means of the fire bell that the truck is leaving the fire station
   B. the truck may be delayed a minute or two in leaving for the fire
   C. The driver may not be able to follow the usual route to the fire because of street obstructions
   D. hook and ladder trucks are difficult even for skilled drivers to handle in narrow spaces
   E. the driver of the hook and ladder truck is naturally expected to be the first to mount the vehicle

8. Suppose that you are holding the nozzle of a hose line and directing a stream of water on a fire. Your officer directs you to close the controlling valve in the nozzle that shuts off the flow of water from the nozzle.
Of the following, the BEST reason for you to close the valve slowly is to avoid
   A. formation of a vacuum in the nozzle
   B. having the stream of water issuing from the nozzle break into a spray
   C. a sudden increase in pressure in the hose
   D. a gradual seepage of air into the nozzle
   E. escape of air from the hose

8.____

9. "Delays in getting started in response to a fire alarm often result in accidents on the road."
Of the following, the BEST justification for this statement is that
   A. most delays in getting to the scene of a fire occur on the road rather than in getting started
   B. most accidents involving fire vehicles occur within a few minutes of getting started
   C. time lost in responding to a fire alarm can never be regained at the fire
   D. most drivers who start quickly tend to drive quickly
   E. some drivers attempt to make up on the road for lost time

9.____

10. "Hose lines should not be charged with water until brought to the point from which they will operate."
Of the following, the CHIEF justification for this rule is that
   A. in many cases water will spread a fire rather than extinguish it
   B. pump operators should usually be told the precise location of the fire in the building
   C. fire hose usually varies in length and diameter
   D. running water weighs less than standing water
   E. a charged hose line weighs more than an uncharged hose line

10.____

11. "In extremely cold weather, it is wise to leave the nozzle of a charged hose line partly open at all times when the line is not in use."
Of the following, the CHIEF reason for following this recommendation is to
   A. prevent a falling off of water pressure due to the normal contraction of water in cold weather
   B. maintain a constant pressure at the nozzle despite fluctuations in temperature
   C. prevent interruption of the water supply due to freezing of the water in the hose
   D. prevent bursting of the hose due to a gradual increase in water pressure
   E. maintain the water in the hose at a fairly constant temperature

11.____

12. Suppose that, while you are driving a piece of fire apparatus to a fire, your officer cautions you to avoid driving over any fire hose being used to throw water on the fire.
Of the following, the CHIEF reason for this order is that
   A. damage to its tires may leave a piece of fire apparatus stranded
   B. burst hose may leave an operating company in a precarious position
   C. interference with the maneuverability of fire apparatus may lead to a fire getting out of hand
   D. the area in front of a fire must be kept clear of encumbrances
   E. the area in front of a burning building is the point in greatest danger of collapsing walls

13. Suppose that a firefighter has been injured. He has received a deep puncture in his right arm. The one of the following steps which should NOT be taken in administering first aid to this firefighter is to
   A. wash the wound
   B. remove all soiled clothing around the wound
   C. apply an antiseptic
   D. apply a sterile dressing
   E. treat for shock

14. "The Fire Department should receive full information on all extensive street repairs." Such information is valuable to the Fire Department CHIEFLY because it indicates
   A. areas requiring very careful inspection for fire hazards involving construction materials stored in the streets
   B. necessary changes in planned routes to be followed by Fire Department equipment in response to fire alarms
   C. possible damage to water mains affecting neighborhoods far removed from the points of street damage
   D. that the experience of Fire Department vehicles in responding to fire alarms is an important consideration determining the need for street repairs
   E. a logical explanation for some of the traffic accidents involving Fire Department vehicles which may have occurred previously in the areas under repair

15. "Keep in mind that floor boards are, as a rule, laid lengthwise in a room." This advice can be MOST helpful to a firefighter in
   A. keeping the amount of hose necessary to fight a fire at a minimum
   B. locating the path of a fire spreading within the walls of a room
   C. escaping from a room filled with dense smoke
   D. avoiding unnecessary damage to property while extinguishing a fire
   E. determining the exact location of a fire hidden by thick smoke

16. Suppose that the duty of the fire company to which you are attached is to remove hose from the hose wagon, connect the hose to the pumper, and advance into the burning building with the hose line so that water may be thrown upon the fire. You are cautioned by your officer not to tangle the hose during this maneuver.
    Of the following, the result LEAST likely to be achieved by observing your officer's warning is to
    A. allow the firefighter with the nozzle to advance readily into the burning building
    B. maintain the hose line close to the pumper where it can be constantly observed
    C. reduce friction loss in the hose line
    D. prevent total blocking of the water by creases in the hose line
    E. allow gathering up the hose line rapidly after the fire has been extinguished

16.____

17. The one of the following which is NOT a recommended procedure for treating shock is
    A. administering stimulants
    B. placing in a horizontal position
    C. applying heat
    D. covering
    E. applying direct pressure

17.____

18. Suppose that you are throwing water on a fire by means of a fire hose line. Your lieutenant orders you to direct the stream from the nozzle so as to hit the ceiling midway between the fire and the point at which you are standing.
    As an alert firefighter, you should realize that the CHIEF reason for this order is probably that
    A. the fire covers a large area
    B. the fire is dying out gradually but perceptibly
    C. pressure in the hose is so great that it is difficult for one firefighter to direct the stream of water accurately
    D. there is insufficient smoke to locate the exact position of the fire accurately
    E. the fire is smoldering heavily

18.____

19. "Firefighter holding a life net should keep their eyes on the person jumping from a burning building."
    Of the following, the BEST justification for this recommendation is that
    A. a person attempting to jump into a life net may overestimate the distance of the net from the building
    B. some persons will not jump into a life net unless given confidence
    C. a person jumping into a life net may be seriously injured if the net is not allowed to "give" slightly at the moment of impact
    D. firefighters holding a life net should be evenly spaced around the net at the moment of impact in order to distribute the shock
    E. an open net is suggestive and leads some people to jump unnecessarily

19.____

20. Suppose that a gasoline stove explodes in the kitchen of your apartment. For you to close all the kitchen doors immediately would be _____ because such action would _____.
    A. *unwise*; allow more heat to generate
    B. *unwise*; limit the amount of air available for combustion
    C. *wise*; limit the area exposed to the flames
    D. *wise*; prevent the formation of carbon dioxide
    E. *unwise*; allow heated gases to accumulate

20.____

21. "A program of inspections and re-inspections may be prosecuted vigorously but cannot be expected to eliminate all risk of fire."
    On the basis of the above statement, it follows MOST accurately that
    A. some fire hazards, even when recognized, cannot be removed completely
    B. a program of inspections and re-inspections must be prosecuted vigorously if all risk of fire is to be eliminated
    C. the more carefully re-inspections are made, the less significant the original inspection in detecting the risk of fire
    D. inspections are evidently of little value in reducing the risk of fire
    E. at least some inspections are indirect fire hazards

21.____

22. "Firefighting reduces the financial loss suffered by property owners because of fires. The difference between organized and makeshift methods of fighting fires in this respect to the property owner is not measured simply by the money value of property saved from destruction."
    Of the following, the BEST additional measure of the difference between organized and makeshift methods of fighting fires, in accordance with the above statement, is the
    A. location and origin of the fire
    B. bulk and weight of the property saved
    C. continued usefulness of the property saved to its owner
    D. number of firefighters required to save the property
    E. amount of fire equipment necessary to save the property

22.____

23. Suppose that you are the driver of a Fire Department hose wagon. Your officer cautions you, as you drive the hose wagon onto a pier where your company is fighting a fire at the river end, to turn the vehicle around so that it faces the pier entrance.
    As an alert firefighter, you should realize that the CHIEF reason for this warning is that
    A. additional hose may be unnecessary if the fire should be extinguished quickly
    B. other hose wagons may be called to the scene of the fire on the second alarm
    C. manpower is more important than apparatus in fighting pier fires
    D. there may not be sufficient time to turn the hose wagon around at a later time if the fire should spread rapidly
    E. water may have to be drafted from the river if no other hose wagon should appear at the scene of the fire

23.____

24. "Most modern buildings are equipped with locks and other devices designed to bar the entrance of those not possessing the necessary keys."
On the basis of the above statement, it follows MOST accurately that
    A. locks and other devices for barring entrance to buildings are unnecessary fire hazards
    B. skill in the use of forcible entry tools is essential for firefighters
    C. fires in modern buildings are the most difficult to handle
    D. firefighters should be equipped with a sufficient number of master keys to open all ordinary types of locks
    E. firefighters should strive to extinguish fires without breaking doors or windows

25. "Every firefighter, regardless of his immediate assignment, should be able to handle all types of apparatus and to act in any desired capacity."
Of the following, the BEST justification for this statement is that
    A. firefighters rarely receive immediate assignments
    B. few firefighters can act in more than one capacity
    C. very much the same apparatus is handled by all firefighters, regardless of immediate assignment
    D. routine assignments must be changed in emergency situations
    E. immediate assignments tend to become routine assignments

26. "When cutting a hole through a floor with an axe, always cut near the supporting timber. This will make the work easier, as the floor boards will not spring. Never cut the timber itself."
Of the following, the BEST reason for not cutting the timber is that
    A. supporting timbers prevent collapse of whole floor sections
    B. fire spreads easily from floor boards to seasoned timber
    C. supporting timbers counteract the spring of floor boards
    D. supporting timbers are difficult to cut because they are thicker than floor boards
    E. supporting timbers are usually inaccessible because they are completely covered by floor boards

27. As a firefighter, you will be taught the use of knots in lashing hose lines and in numerous other tasks incident to the fighting of fires. "Methods of tying knots are standardized so that every firefighter will tie knots in the same way, and not in some peculiar way of his own, no matter how good his own way may be. It is important that every firefighter be able to untie a knot tied by another firefighter."
The importance of instructing all firefighters to tie knots in the same way is BEST illustrated by the situation in which it is necessary for a firefighter to
    A. lash himself to an aerial ladder for security while holding a line of hose
    B. tie a "cradle" by which he may be lowered into a subcellar
    C. fasten a portable ladder to a rope so that the ladder may be hoisted to the roof of a three-story building

D. lash himself to an icy fire escape in order to avoid slipping or falling on the ice
E. lash a nozzle to a roof parapet so that he can better direct the stream of water

28. "Comparative tests show that, at a speed of 20 miles per hour, the average piece of fire apparatus will continue to travel approximately 60 feet before it can be brought to a complete stop."
Of the following, the CHIEF implication of the above statement for a firefighter assigned to drive fire apparatus is that
    A. fire trucks should rarely be driven at such a speed that they cannot be halted in less than 60 feet
    B. a driver who cannot see the road more than 60 feet ahead of him should be driving at less than 20 miles per hour
    C. the optimum rate of speed for a fire truck is 20 miles per hour
    D. most fire trucks can be brought to a complete stop in less than 60 feet
    E. the average distance in which any fire truck can be brought to a complete stop, on the basis of comparative tests, is about 60 feet

29. "Water possesses certain advantages as an extinguishing agent."
Of the following, the CHIEF advantage of water as an extinguishing agent is that water
    A. enters into chemical union with certain substances, producing heat
    B. has a high freezing point
    C. is lighter than oil and will not mix with it
    D. has a great capacity for absorbing heat
    E. is decomposed, producing combustible gases, when in contact with hot metals

30. The one of the following which is NOT a recommended procedure when administering artificial respiration to another firefighter is to
    A. continue the process without interruption
    B. keep a regular and definite rhythm
    C. keep the patient's nose and mouth free for breathing
    D. loosen tight clothing about the patient's neck and chest
    E. administer liquid stimulants at frequent intervals

31. Suppose that the number of fires in New York City during May increased 5 percent over the number of fires during April, but that the number of fires during June decreased 5 percent as compared with the number of fires during May.
Then the one of the following statements which is MOST accurate is that there were
    A. exactly as man fires during April as there were during June
    B. more fires during June than during May
    C. more fires during April than during May
    D. fewer fires during June than during April
    E. fewer fires during May than during June

9 (#1)

32. Suppose that a fire truck is undergoing tests. If the distance traversed by the truck, where the distance is expressed in yards, is divided by the time required by the truck to cover that distance, where the time is expressed in minutes, then the quotient is equal to the
    A. maximum rate of speed at which the truck travelled during any one minute
    B. average rate of speed of the truck, measured in yards per minute
    C. average distance travelled by the truck, measured in yards
    D. number of miles per hour at which the truck travelled
    E. total distance travelled by the truck, measured in miles

32.____

33. In an engine pumps G gallons of water per minute, then the number of gallons pumped in half an hour may be found by
    A. taking one-half of G
    B. multiplying G by 60 and then dividing the product by two
    C. dividing 60 by twice G
    D. dividing G by 30 and then multiplying the quotient by two
    E. dividing 30 by G

33.____

34. Suppose that two 60-foot ladders have been placed against the side of a building. The base of the first ladder is 10 feet from the building, and the base of the second ladder is 20 feet from the building.
    Then, of the following, the MOST accurate statement is that
    A. the first ladder will make a larger angle with the ground than the second ladder will make
    B. the top of the second ladder is higher above the ground than the top of the first ladder
    C. both ladders will reach to the same height above the ground
    D. the first ladder will make a larger angle with the building than the second ladder will make
    E. both ladders will make the same angle with the building

34.____

35. Suppose that the total number of fires reported in New York City during the year is equal to F and that the number of fires reported by telephone during that time is P. The ratio of the number of fires reported by telephone to the total number of fires reported is R. Then, the product of R and F is equal to the
    A. ratio of fires not reported by telephone
    B. number of fires not reported by telephone
    C. number of fires reported by telephone
    D. ratio of fires reported by telephone
    E. total number of fires reported

35.____

36. Suppose that water is being pumped from an engine into a hose at a pressure of R pounds and that the friction loss in the hose is P pounds per foot of hose. The pressure loss in the hose due to friction will equal the pump pressure when the length of the hose is equal to
    A. P divided by R feet   B. R minus P feet
    C. 12 times P feet   D. R feet
    E. R divided by P feet

36.____

37. Suppose that for a certain period of time studied, the percentage of telephone alarms which were false alarms was less than the percentage of fire box alarms which were false alarms.
Then, the one of the following which is MOST accurate, solely on the basis of the above statement, is that during the period studied
    A. more alarms were transmitted by telephone than by fire box
    B. more alarms were transmitted by fire box than by telephone
    C. relatively fewer false alarms were transmitted by telephone than by fire box
    D. relatively fewer false alarms were transmitted by fire box than by telephone
    E. the number of false telephone alarms was less than the number of false fire box alarms

38. "There are more engine companies than hook and ladder companies. However, to conclude that the number of firefighters assigned to engine companies exceeds the number of firefighters assigned to hook and ladder companies is to make a basic assumption."
Of the following, the MOST accurate statement of the basic assumption referred to in this quotation is that
    A. the number of hook and ladder companies does not differ greatly from the number of engine companies
    B. about the same number of firefighters, on the average, are assigned to each type of company
    C. an engine company, on the average, has fewer firefighters than a hook and ladder company
    D. the largest engine company is no larger than the largest hook and ladder company
    E. there is no fixed relationship between the size of engine companies and hook and ladder companies

39. "During the year, 25 percent of all the fires in New York City were in buildings of Type A, 40 percent were in buildings of Type B, and 15 percent were in buildings of Type C."
Of the following, the MOST accurate statement is that the total number of fires in New York City during the year was
    A. equal to the sum of the percentages of fires in the three types of buildings, divided by 100
    B. less than 100 percent
    C. one-fourth the number of fires in buildings of Type B
    D. equal to the sum of the number of fires in buildings of Types A, B, and C
    E. four times the number of fires in buildings of Type A

40. If the fire company due to arrive first at a fire arrived one minute before the company second due, and the company third due arrived four minutes after the alarm was sent, then the one of the following statements which is MOST accurate is that the
    A. second due company arrived three minutes before the third due company
    B. third due company arrived three minutes after the first due company

C. second due company arrived two minutes after the alarm was sent
D. second due company arrived one minute after the first due company
E. first due company arrived five minutes before the third due company

KEY (CORRECT ANSWERS)

1.	D	11.	C	21.	A	31.	D
2.	A	12.	B	22.	C	32.	B
3.	E	13.	A	23.	D	33.	B
4.	B	14.	B	24.	B	34.	A
5.	E	15.	C	25.	D	35.	C
6.	D	16.	B	26.	A	36.	E
7.	D	17.	E	27.	C	37.	C
8.	C	18.	A	28.	B	38.	B
9.	E	19.	A	29.	D	39.	E
10.	E	20.	C	30.	E	40.	D

TEST 2

DIRECTIONS: Each question or incomplete statement is followed by several suggested answers or completions. Select the one that BEST answers the question or completes the statement. *PRINT THE LETTER OF THE CORRECT ANSWER IN THE SPACE AT THE RIGHT.*

1. "Firefighting, like many other specialized activities, makes use of certain words and phrases that should carry clear and definite meaning to every firefighter. For example, every competent firefighter should know what is meant by a centrifugal pump."
   The word *centrifugal* means MOST NEARLY
   A. economical
   B. single purpose
   C. proceeding from the center outward
   D. designed to produce fluid motion
   E. maximally efficient

   1._____

2. "The important point for a firefighter to remember is that gases have a tendency to diffuse."
   The word *diffuse* means MOST NEARLY
   A. explode suddenly   B. contract under pressure
   C. absorb air   D. spread widely
   E. interact chemically

   2._____

3. "Water is the solvent in some fire extinguishers."
   The word *solvent* means MOST NEARLY the liquid
   A. by means of which the fire is extinguished
   B. in which a chemical is dissolved
   C. which is not soluble
   D. which constitutes the active element
   E. which evolves from the extinguisher

   3._____

4. "There will be a spattering of molten metal whenever water is present."
   The word *molten* means MOST NEARLY
   A. pulverized   B. exploded   C. burning
   D. heated   E. melted

   4._____

5. "A stream of water has kinetic energy."
   The word *kinetic* means MOST NEARLY
   A. capable of being measured   B. highly variable
   C. capable of being used   D. due to motion
   E. concrete

   5._____

6. "The firefighter will find at many fires that heat is spread by convection."
   The word *convection* refers MOST NEARLY to transfer of heat by
   A. direct contact with the blazing object
   B. radiation
   C. currents of air
   D. molecular attraction
   E. close proximity

7. "Firefighters must be acquainted with the viscosity of various fluids."
   The word *viscosity* means MOST NEARLY
   A. boils at low temperatures
   B. forms inflammable mixtures
   C. does not react to heat
   D. does not flow easily
   E. extinguishes fires effectively

8. "An alert firefighter will soon realize that many formulas are empirical."
   The word *empirical* means MOST NEARLY
   A. based upon experience
   B. theoretical
   C. highly valuable
   D. easy to memorize
   E. fallacious

9. "Acoustic material presents a fire hazard sufficiently serious to warrant a special fire prevention bulletin."
   The word *acoustic* means MOST NEARLY
   A. stored in confined places
   B. relating to paints and varnishes
   C. stored in containers
   D. relating to sound
   E. relating to business machines

10. "To find the pressure at the orifice, a simple formula may be employed."
    The word *orifice* means MOST NEARLY
    A. point under discussion
    B. lowest point
    C. relatively small opening
    D. highest point
    E. lateral depression

11. To say that a substance has been *oxidized* means MOST NEARLY that the substance has
    A. replaced oxygen
    B. produced oxygen
    C. combined with oxygen
    D. become heat resistant because of exclusion of oxygen
    E. become a form of free oxygen

12. "Evaporation is accompanied by the absorption of a definite amount of heat, which is called the latent heat of vaporization."
    The word *latent* means MOST NEARLY
    A. not visible or apparent
    B. tangible
    C. maximum
    D. not sufficient or complete
    E. not constant

13. "Pressure applied to a confined body of water from without is transmitted without diminution."
    The word *diminution* means MOST NEARLY
    A. change in form
    B. reduction in magnitude
    C. noticeable expansion
    D. need for control
    E. change of direction

14. A weight is said to be in *equilibrium* when
    A. it is in a state of balance
    B. a force is being applied
    C. its velocity is constant
    D. friction is non-existent
    E. it is accelerating regularly

15. "Some gases are inert."
    The word *inert* means MOST NEARLY
    A. not compressible
    B. ineffective
    C. inactive
    D. insoluble
    E. unstable

Questions 16-25.

DIRECTIONS: "Knowledge of the principal properties of everyday chemicals is a part of the stock in trade of every scientific firefighter." Column I below lists ten chemicals. Column II lists four descriptive statements. For each of the chemicals in Column I, write the letter of the statement in Column II which BEST describes that chemical.

COLUMN I
16. Carbon dioxide
17. Hydrogen
18. Nitric acid
19. Carbon tetrachloride
20. Methane
21. Sulphur
22. Carbon monoxide
23. Ethyl chloride
24. Hydrogen sulphide
25. Sodium chloride

COLUMN II
A. A gas at ordinary temperatures which has a characteristic color or odor
B. A gas at ordinary temperatures which is lighter than air
C. A gas at ordinary temperatures which is non-inflammable
D. A chemical which is not a gas at ordinary temperatures

Questions 26-32.

DIRECTIONS: Questions 26 through 32 are to be answered on the basis of the following paragraph, which relates to the work of firefighters.

Everyone knows that "water seeks its own level"; that it will always flow to the lowest accessible point. If restrained, it exerts pressure against the restraining object, whether this be the walls of a drinking glass, a giant dam, or a pipe to conduct it from one place to another. The degree of pressure exerted upon the walls of a container at any point depends, not on the quantity of water stored, but on the vertical height to which it is backed up; in other words, the difference in elevation between the point where the pressure is measured and the surface of the continuous body of water that is restrained. The technical term for this difference of elevation is "head", and in this country it is usually measured in feet. Firefighters are more accustomed to thinking of water pressure in terms of pounds per square inch, usually abbreviated to "pounds." It is very easy to convert pressure in terms of "head" to "pounds"; simply multiply the head in feet by 0.433, and the result is pressure in terms of pounds per square inch.

26. According to the above paragraph, the "head" at a point 4 feet above the bottom of a tank which is 12 feet deep and is filled with water to within 2 feet of the top of the tank is _____ feet.
    A. 4   B. 6   C. 8   D. 10   E. 12

27. The above paragraph explains what is meant by the principle "water seeks its own level".
    Of the following, the practice which is based MOST directly upon this principle is
    A. using chemicals rather than water in fire extinguishers
    B. placing sprinkler systems in basements rather than in the upper stories of a building
    C. using 2½ inch hose for fighting fires rather than 3 inch hose
    D. placing fire hydrants at frequent intervals along the street
    E. placing a water tank on the roof of a building

28. The number 0.433 mentioned in the above paragraph is BEST defined as the
    A. temperature of water at a specific atmospheric pressure
    B. area of the base of a specific restraining container
    C. "head" at a point one foot below the surface of the water
    D. weight of a specific quantity of water
    E. quantity of water stored in a specific container

29. According to the above paragraph, water pressure is zero
    A. unless "head" is measured in pounds per square inch
    B. where the quantity of water stored is excessively large
    C. when water is flowing through a fire hose
    D. if the pipe conducting the water from one place to another is less than one square inch in diameter
    E. at the surface of a large body of water restrained by a dam

30. Suppose that water is confined in a tank. According to the above paragraph, pressure is exerted by the water
    A. against the walls of the tank
    B. in a direction level with the tank
    C. only if the water seeks its own level
    D. equivalent to atmospheric pressure
    E. inversely with depth

31. According to the above paragraph, to say that the water pressure at a given point is 200 pounds means MOST NEARLY that
    A. the weight of all the water above the restraining point is 200 pounds
    B. the force exerted by the water at that point is 200 pounds per square inch
    C. the "head" is 200 pounds
    D. a cubic foot of water at that point weighs 200 pounds
    E. the vertical height of the water exceeds the equivalent of 200 pounds

32. On the basis of the above paragraph, "head" may also be accurately expressed in
    A. cubic feet
    B. square inches
    C. foot pounds
    D. degrees
    E. yards

Questions 33-40.

DIRECTIONS: Questions 33 through 40 are to be answered on the basis of the following paragraph, which relates to the work of firefighters.

When a pumper engine is drafting water, the pump exhausts air from the suction hose and creates a partial vacuum, and air pressure on the body of water surrounding the suction hose forces water through it to the pump. The pressure of the atmosphere is approximately 14.7 pounds per square inch, so that if a perfect vacuum could be secured in the suction hose, water could be raised a maximum vertical distance of 34 feet. This theoretical maximum cap can never be obtained in practice because no pump is efficient enough to create a perfect vacuum. Furthermore, friction losses in the suction line must be met, so that the maximum height through which a small quantity of water can be drafted is about 28 feet, while a lift of 24½ feet could be considered the practical maximum. The lift is measured from the surface of the water to the center of the pump suction. The atmospheric pressure of 14.7 pounds per square inch (less than this at altitudes above sea level) cannot be increased; it is the maximum pressure available. The more of it that is used up in balancing the water column in the suction hose, the less that remains available for friction losses, and the smaller the quantities of water that can be pumped. Also, the friction loss increases with the length of the suction hose.

33. According to the above paragraph, the theoretical maximum vertical distance of 34 feet that water can be drafted by suction is measured MOST accurately from
    A. one end of the suction hose to the other
    B. the surface of the water to the center of the pump suction
    C. the open end of the suction hose to the surface of the water
    D. the surface of the water to the center of the hose
    E. the open end of the suction hose to a point 24½ feet below the surface of the water

33.____

34. According to the above paragraph, in order to draw a maximum amount of water through the suction hose
    A. the vertical lift should be kept as short as possible
    B. the suction hose should be as long as possible
    C. the suction hose should be as narrow as possible
    D. the engine should be operated as slowly as possible
    E. friction should be increased as much as possible

34.____

35. The maximum vertical distance that water can be raised depends LEAST on the
    A. amount of air left in the suction hose by the pump
    B. distance of the pump above sea level
    C. amount of friction in the hose
    D. efficiency of the pump in creating a vacuum
    E. quantity of water surrounding the hose

35.____

36. According to the above paragraph, water is forced through the suction hose by
    A. pump pressure
    B. engine pressure
    C. vacuum resistance
    D. atmospheric pressure
    E. friction loss

36.____

37. The information in the above paragraph is MOST directly applicable to
    A. drawing water from a low pressure hydrant
    B. drawing water from a high pressure hydrant
    C. pumping water to fires in the upper stories of buildings
    D. pumping water to fires located in a distance from the hydrant
    E. drawing sea water for use at a fire

37.____

38. To say that atmospheric pressure is 14.7 pounds per square inch at sea level means MOST NEARLY that
    A. there is a pressure of 14.7 pounds on each square inch of the surface of the water
    B. a body with a density of more than 14.7 pounds per square inch will float on water
    C. water pressure is at least 14.7 pounds per square inch at the surface
    D. suction pumps exert a minimum pressure of 14.7 pounds per square inch
    E. water issues from suction pumps at a pressure of 14.7 pounds per square inch

38.____

39. "Friction losses," as used in the above paragraph, refers MOST PROBABLY to friction between
    A. air bubbles and pump blades
    B. water and pump blades
    C. air and hose walls
    D. atmospheric pressure and water pressure
    E. water and hose walls

40. According to the above paragraph, if the pump were operating considerably above sea level,
    A. a larger quantity of water could be pumped in the same period of time
    B. a less perfect vacuum would be required for the same degree of pumping efficiency
    C. the theoretical maximum would approach the practical maximum
    D. the maximum vertical lift would be decreased
    E. atmospheric pressure would be increased

KEY (CORRECT ANSWERS)

1.	C	11.	C	21.	D	31.	B
2.	D	12.	A	22.	B	32.	E
3.	B	13.	B	23.	A	33.	B
4.	E	14.	A	24.	A	34.	A
5.	D	15.	C	25.	D	35.	E
6.	C	16.	C	26.	B	36.	D
7.	D	17.	B	27.	E	37.	E
8.	A	18.	D	28.	D	38.	A
9.	D	19.	D	29.	E	39.	E
10.	C	20.	B	30.	A	40.	D

EXAMINATION SECTION
TEST 1

DIRECTIONS: Each question or incomplete statement is followed by several suggested answers or completions. Select the one that BEST answers the question or completes the statement. *PRINT THE LETTER OF THE CORRECT ANSWER IN THE SPACE AT THE RIGHT.*

1. A large fire occurs which you, as a firefighter, are helping to extinguish. An emergency arises and you believe that a certain action should be taken. Your superior officer directs you to do something else which you consider to be undesirable.
   You should
   A. take the initiative and follow what you originally thought to be the superior line of action
   B. think the matter over for a few minutes and weigh the virtues of the two lines of action
   C. waste no time but refer the problem immediately to another superior officer
   D. attempt to convince the superior officer that your plan has greater merit than his
   E. obey orders despite the fact that you disagree

   1.____

2. A fire breaks out simultaneously in six different parts of a large building. It is MOST reasonable to believe that the fire is the result of
   A. arson   B. carelessness
   C. spontaneous combustion   D. explosives
   E. enzymic action

   2.____

3. Fire losses in a certain city have been reduced from $300.00 per capital in 2012 to $51.00 in 2014, $27.40 in 2015, and $3.80 in 2016. The BEST inference from these data is that the city
   A. managed to rid itself of incendiaries in 2014
   B. increased its water supply in 2012
   C. erected a large number of fireproof buildings in 2011
   D. underwent a decided population shift in 2013
   E. instituted a program of fire prevention in 2013

   3.____

4. "At two o'clock in the morning, Mrs. Smart wakened her husband and said the house was on fire. Mr. Smart dressed hurriedly, ran seventeen blocks past five fire alarm boxes to the fire station, and told the firefighters that his house was on fire. When Mr. Smart and the firefighters had returned, the house had burned down." This is an illustration of the
   A. need for a plentiful supply of fire alarm boxes
   B. fact that fire is no respecter of persons
   C. necessity of preventing fires
   D. desirability of educating the public
   E. need for more fire stations

   4.____

5. Suppose hydrants with a flowing capacity of less than 500 gallons per minute to be painted red, hydrants with a flowing capacity between 500 and 1000 gallons to be painted yellow, and hydrants with a flowing capacity of 1000 gallons or greater per minute to be painted green.
   The PRINCIPAL advantage of such a scheme is that
   A. fewer fires would occur
   B. more water would become available at a fire
   C. citizens would become more acutely aware of the importance of hydrants
   D. parking in front of hydrants would be reduced
   E. firefighters would save time

6. Assume that you are a firefighter, off duty and in uniform in the basement of a department store. A large crowd is present. There are two stairways, 50 feet apart. A woman whom you cannot see screams "Fire!"
   You should FIRST
   A. rush outside and sound the alarm at a fire alarm box
   B. find the woman who shouted "Fire!", ascertain where the fire has occurred, and proceed to extinguish the fire
   C. jump on top of a nearby counter, order everyone to be quiet and not to move, find out who screamed "Fire!", and reprimand that person publicly
   D. jump on top of a counter, obtain the attention of the crowd, direct the crowd to walk to the nearest stairway, and announce that there is no immediate danger
   E. communicate with the store manager, direct him to sound a fire alarm, find the woman who shouted "Fire!", obtain help in handling the crowd

7. In entering a building charged with smoke, it is BEST to
   A. keep as low as practicable
   B. keep the head as high as possible
   C. keep the hands moving
   D. keep the left shoulder forward and the head slanted over as near to the shoulder as practicable
   E. take quick, deep breaths

8. Suppose that you are employed as a firefighter. A new man is appointed to your company. This man has red hair. It is MOST probable that this man will
   A. have a fiery, uncontrollable temper
   B. be very aggressive
   C. be very intelligent
   D. be much like the other firefighters in your company
   E. be unusually obstinate

9. Of the following, the CHIEF advantage of having firefighters under competitive civil service is that
   A. fewer fires tend to occur
   B. fire prevention becomes a reality instead of a distant goal
   C. the efficiency level of the personnel tends to be raised
   D. provision may then be made for training by the municipality
   E. responsibility is necessarily centralized

10. Of the following, it is LEAST likely that fire will be caused by
    A. arson
    B. poor building construction
    C. carelessness
    D. inadequate supply of water
    E. explosives

11. The lever on fire alarm boxes for use by citizens of New York City should be
    A. very, very easy to manipulate
    B. just a little difficult to manipulate
    C. very difficult to manipulate
    D. constructed without regard to ease of manipulation
    E. constructed with regard only to ease of manipulation

12. It is desirable that the fire department have ladders of varying lengths MAINLY because some
    A. fires occur at greater distances from the ground than others
    B. firefighters are more agile than others
    C. firefighters are taller than others
    D. fires are harder to extinguish than others
    E. buildings are not fireproof

13. The PRIMARY function of a city fire department is to
    A. maintain the peace
    B. reduce industrial conflict
    C. improve the governmental machinery
    D. preserve life and property
    E. promote good citizenship

14. "It is said that in New York City, a fire alarm box can be seen from any corner." This is a desirable condition MAINLY because
    A. several alarms may be sounded by one person by running from one box to another
    B. little time is lost in sounding an alarm
    C. an alarm may be sounded from a different box if the nearest one is out of order
    D. fire apparatus can quickly reach any box
    E. the number of fires is reduced

15. The problem of determining the relative importance of brain and brawn in the equipment of a firefighter may BEST be settled by
    A. quantitative investigation
    B. securing the opinions of prominent educators
    C. ascertaining the attitude of the average citizen
    D. flipping a coin or by lot
    E. averaging both so that neither has any weight

16. The principal value of prompt, accurate, and complete reports is that such reports 16.____
    A. impress superior officers with the necessity for immediate action
    B. are good training and discipline for the writer
    C. mark the efficient person
    D. provide excellent reference material
    E. expedite official business

17. The LEAST important requisite for a ladder to be used by firefighters is 17.____
    A. visibility of color   B. strength
    C. lightness of weight   D. durability
    E. resistivity to fire

18. Of the following, the MAIN reason for regular cleaning of fire apparatus is that 18.____
    A. cleanliness is worthwhile in and of itself
    B. firefighters should always be busy performing useful operations
    C. deterioration is avoided
    D. the rules demand that firefighters demonstrate their awareness of their responsibilities
    E. this reduces the possibility of fires resulting from spontaneous combustion

19. "A firefighter does not have time to read engineering books when human life is in 'jeopardy'" means MOST NEARLY that 19.____
    A. preparation for an emergency cannot be made at the particular instant when the emergency arises
    B. the technique of firefighting bears no relation to engineering findings
    C. life is more important than property
    D. firefighters do not have enough time to read books
    E. reading is a useless pastime for a firefighter

20. "It used to be quite the common thing for firefighters to use large streams of water to extinguish small fires, and in some cases where the contents of the building were not entirely ruined by fire, the damage by water exceeded the fire damage as such." 20.____
    This statement illustrates the fact that
    A. considerable water is vitally necessary to extinguish fires
    B. water should be available near the scene of a fire
    C. water without hose is of little use
    D. courage is a greater asset to firefighters than modern apparatus
    E. fire losses are not always the consequence of flames

21. The statement "Municipal inspections should be coordinated" suggests MOST NEARLY that 21.____
    A. fire hazards are dangerous
    B. the detection of fire hazards is connected with other problems such as sanitation
    C. the various problems to be found in a municipality are of unequal importance

D. municipal inspections are closely tied up with non-inspectional services
E. municipal inspectors should cooperate with members of the community

22. "With fireproof schools, it would appear that drills are unnecessary."
The MAIN reason for believing this statement to be false is that
   A. panics sometimes occur
   B. fire extinguishers are available in every school
   C. fire alarms are easily sounded
   D. children are accustomed to drilling
   E. children should be taught that fireproofing is desirable

23. "Flame is of varying heat according to the nature of the substance producing it" means MOST NEARLY that
   A. some fires are larger than others
   B. the best measure of the heat produced by a particular substance is its temperature
   C. there can be no fire without flame or flame without fire
   D. inflammable substances should not be used in building construction
   E. the degree of heat evolved by the combustion of different materials is not identical

24. Of the following, the BEST action to take when small amounts of water have collected on a floor after a fire is to
   A. use a vacuum cleaner
   B. sprinkle with sawdust
   C. apply heat
   D. cover with asbestos
   E. use a hand fire extinguisher

25. When a firefighter must render first aid in the case of a simple fracture, his MAIN object should be to
   A. make sure that no infection sets in
   B. stop the flow of blood
   C. draw the broken bones together
   D. expose the fracture to the fresh air by cutting the clothing
   E. prevent movement of the ends of the broken bone

26. Constipation is relieved by
   A. cold water
   B. a solution of Epsom salts
   C. warm water
   D. a solution of arnica
   E. a solution of witch hazel

27. Of the following, the BEST treatment for a part of the body which has been frostbitten is
   A. rubbing with warm water
   B. brisk slapping of the affected part
   C. gentle massaging of the affected part
   D. applying heat
   E. rubbing with snow

28. A man's clothes begin to burn rather strongly. The BEST thing for this man to do, if possible, is to
    A. wrap himself in a rug of wool
    B. run to a doctor
    C. apply oil to his body
    D. shout in order to obtain assistance
    E. wrap himself in a rug of cotton

29. It is LEAST characteristic of the large, modern corporation that
    A. ownership is divorced from control
    B. liability of stockholders is limited
    C. it derives its powers from the state
    D. it is free from taxation
    E. the use of proxies in voting is almost universal

30. The zero point of a centigrade scale is equivalent to 32 degrees on a Fahrenheit scale and 100 degrees of the Centigrade is equal to 180 of the Fahrenheit scale.
    If a centigrade thermometer reads 15 degrees, the equivalent reading in degrees on a Fahrenheit thermometer is
    A. 32
    B. 27
    C. 40
    D. 59
    E. impossible to compute without additional data

31. With an increase in the diameter of a pipe, the cross-sectional area
    A. increases at a lesser rate than the frictional resistance to flow
    B. decreases in proportion to the square of the radius
    C. decreases in proportion to the square foot of the radius
    D. becomes equal to the circumference
    E. increases in greater proportion than the circumference

32. "The frictional resistance of water pipes and consequent loss of pressure become relatively less as the size of the pipe is increased." It follows that
    A. the longer the pipe the more efficient is its performance
    B. the loss of pressure in a given length of 2-inch pipe is greater than that occurring when the same amount of water flows through an equal length of 6-inch pipe
    C. pressure loss due to friction may be reduced by reducing the length of the pipe
    D. pressure in a length of 6-inch pipe is about half that of a 3-inch pipe
    E. the pressure in a length of pipe is equal to the reciprocal of its friction

33. The usual rule, satisfactory for most applications, to find the discharge at a given pump pressure is
   A. divide the pressure at which the pump is rated by the rated discharge and multiply by the pressure at which you desire to find the discharge
   B. divide rated discharge by rated pressure
   C. multiply rated pressure by the reciprocal of the rated discharge
   D. multiply the pressure at which the pump is rated by the discharge at that pressure and divide by the pressure at which you desire to find the discharge
   E. multiply the rated pressure by the square of the rated discharge

34. The tension per inch of length under which hose is placed is found by
   A. multiplying the diameter in inches by the pressure in pounds per square inch
   B. dividing the diameter in inches by the pressure in pounds per square inch
   C. multiplying the diameter in inches by the pressure in pounds per square inch and dividing the product by two
   D. squaring the sum of the diameter in inches and the pressure in pounds per square inch
   E. squaring the difference between the diameter in inches and the pressure in pounds per square inch

35. A tank is 10 feet high and 10 feet long. The pressure in pounds per square inch due to one foot elevation of water is .434. When the tank is full of water, the average pressure in pounds per square inch against the side of the tank is
   A. 31,248   B. 2.17   C. 43.40   D. 4.34   E. 8.68

36. If K fires break out during a given month and result in P dollars of loss, the average loss per fire, in dollars, is
   A. K multiplied by P   B. P divided by K
   C. K divided by P   D. 12 times K divided by 2 times P
   E. none of the above

37. The annual salary of firefighter I is R dollars less than that of firefighter II. The second firefighter earns V dollars annually. The amount in monthly salary by which the second firefighter exceeds the first is given by
   A. V minus R divided by 12   B. R times V divided by 12
   C. V minus R   D. 12 times V minus R
   E. R divided by 12

38. The distributor of an automobile is a
   A. device which supplies current while the machine is in motion in order to keep the battery charged
   B. motor which, by drawing a heavy current from the battery, is able to turn the crankshaft to which all the pistons are connected
   C. coil which distributes electrical energy to the various parts of the engine

D. chamber for mixing air and gasoline vapor in order to provide power
E. turning device which makes electric connection between the source of current and the spark plug of each cylinder just at the moment when that cylinder should be exploded

39. The difference between non-inflammable and incombustible substances is
    A. that the latter explode more readily
    B. that the latter have specific gravities near zero
    C. that the latter combine more quickly with gases
    D. that the latter respond more readily to chemical action
    E. none of the above

40. The exit doors in a theatre should swing out in the direction of the street MAINLY because
    A. panics should be avoided
    B. people should walk, not run, to the nearest exit
    C. the doors may catch fire
    D. exits are then more readily seen
    E. audiences can then get out easier

KEY (CORRECT ANSWERS)

1.	E	11.	B	21.	B	31.	E
2.	A	12.	A	22.	A	32.	B
3.	E	13.	D	23.	E	33.	D
4.	D	14.	B	24.	B	34.	A
5.	E	15.	A	25.	E	35.	B
6.	D	16.	E	26.	B	36.	B
7.	A	17.	A	27.	E	37.	E
8.	D	18.	C	28.	A	38.	E
9.	C	19.	A	29.	D	39.	E
10.	D	20.	E	30.	D	40.	E

TEST 2

DIRECTIONS: Each question or incomplete statement is followed by several suggested answers or completions. Select the one that BEST answers the question or completes the statement. *PRINT THE LETTER OF THE CORRECT ANSWER IN THE SPACE AT THE RIGHT.*

1. Of the following, the PRINCIPAL advantage of the automatic sprinkler is that it
   A. requires no chemical assistance
   B. discharges water under pressure on a fire at or near the point of flame
   C. does not necessitate the use of water
   D. discharges water on a fire under greater pressure than can be secured through the use of other devices
   E. sounds an alarm which can be heard at a great distance

   1.____

2. Rate of combustion is MOST probably increased by
   A. lowering temperature
   B. the addition of virtually any chemical
   C. the use of water
   D. the introduction of more oxygen
   E. the use of soda-acid

   2.____

3. The one of the following which is NOT a fire resister is
   A. asbestos
   B. tungstate of soda
   C. borax
   D. Sulphur
   E. phosphate of ammonia

   3.____

4. A volatile liquid is one which
   A. vaporizes readily
   B. resists oxidation
   C. heats very slowly
   D. is not a compound
   E. extinguishes fire

   4.____

5. The one of the following which is a gas and is not inert is
   A. neon
   B. nitrogen
   C. fluorine
   D. iodine
   E. bromine

   5.____

6. Elements of illuminating gas are
   A. carbon and hydrogen
   B. silicon and chlorine
   C. sodium and potassium
   D. oxygen and calcium
   E. magnesium and phosphorus

   6.____

7. The one of the following which is NOT an irritating gas when heated is
   A. sulphur dioxide
   B. carbon monoxide
   C. ammonia
   D. bromine gas
   E. vaporized nitric acid

   7.____

2 (#2)

8. The value of carbon tetrachloride in extinguishing fires consists in the fact that it
   A. is lighter than air
   B. is lighter than carbon dioxide
   C. liquefies at high pressures and forms a thin mist
   D. evaporates when sprayed on a fire and forms a heavy gas
   E. liquefies at low pressures and units with hydrogen

8._____

9. "A soft, wax-like metal, which rapidly decomposes water on which it floats. It is inflammable and may explode spontaneously on contact with water. It is used in chemical laboratories and is kept under oil, or paraffin in glass bottles, tin cans, and iron drums."
   This description BEST applies to
   A. picric acid   B. formic acid   C. nitro aniline
   D. chloride of lime E. potassium

9._____

10. "It ignites organic matter and explodes when brought in contact with alcohol or acetic acid. It is a strong oxidizing agent and should be isolated in storage, for when involved in fire it may cause an explosion."
    This description BEST applies to
    A. chromic acid   B. charcoal   C. celluloid
    D. barium dioxide   E. borneol

10._____

Questions 11-20.
DIRECTIONS: In Column I are listed a number of substances. Column II gives four classifications of these substances at ordinary temperatures. For each substance in Column I, print in the space at the right the description of the substances.

COLUMN I	COLUMN II	
11. Carbon dioxide	A. Gas	11._____
	B. Liquid	
12. Sulphuric acid	C. Metal	12._____
	D. Non-metallic solid	
13. Nitrogen		13._____
14. Sulphur		14._____
15. Magnesium		15._____
16. Calcium		16._____
17. Carbon		17._____
18. Hydrogen chloride		18._____
19. Hydrogen oxide		19._____
20. Chlorine		20._____

3 (#2)

Questions 21-50.

DIRECTIONS: Each group of five words contains two words which are the same or almost the same in meaning. Print in the space at the right the letters of the two words in each group which MOST NEARLY have the same meaning.

21.	A. covenant	B. astringency	C. counterpoise	21.____
	D. foible	E. equilibrium		
22.	A. tedium	B. calmness	C. calumny	22.____
	D. weariness	E. forgetfulness		
23.	A. ladder	B. hutch	C. coop	23.____
	D. stick	E. hydraulics		
24.	A. disparage	B. contemplate	C. levy	24.____
	D. assess	E. assuage		
25.	A. mauve	B. color	C. dark	25.____
	D. purple	E. musty		
26.	A. infinite	B. immeasurable	C. pervasive	26.____
	D. temporal	E. incendiary		
27.	A. categorize	B. adjudicate	C. support	27.____
	D. enjoin	E. try		
28.	A. collective	B. corruptible	C. sinuous	28.____
	D. collateral	E. subsidiary		
29.	A. enervate	B. enliven	C. emancipate	29.____
	D. produce	E. debilitate		
30.	A. globular	B. glib	C. violent	30.____
	D. voluminous	E. voluble		
31.	A. munificent	B. chary	C. frugal	31.____
	D. gratuitous	E. carious		
32.	A. province	B. structure	C. demeanor	32.____
	D. carriage	E. parsimony		
33.	A. brink	B. wedge	C. chasm	33.____
	D. edge	E. niche		
34.	A. disapprove	B. derive	C. deprecate	34.____
	D. felicitate	E. fulminate		

35. A. wreckage   B. responsibility   C. disfranchisement   35._____
    D. dereliction   E. neglect

36. A. coffer   B. authority   C. judgment   36._____
    D. extenuation   E. jurisdiction

37. A. normal   B. diverse   C. panoramic   37._____
    D. reversible   E. mean

38. A. rescission   B. abrogation   C. revulsion   38._____
    D. reversion   E. fillip

39. A. hydrant   B. water   C. plug   39._____
    D. fire   E. engine

40. A. awareness   B. idiom   C. dialect   40._____
    D. illiteracy   E. percussion

41. A. sift   B. sign   C. simmer   41._____
    D. weave   E. separate

42. A. within   B. posterior   C. beside   42._____
    D. anterior   E. prior

43. A. glean   B. gloss   C. gaze   43._____
    D. gather   E. glide

44. A. jocund   B. ruddy   C. hollow   44._____
    D. febrile   E. merry

45. A. harpy   B. precursor   C. endorser   45._____
    D. harbinger   E. juggler

46. A. insecure   B. insensate   C. devoid   46._____
    D. brutal   E. animate

47. A. leucocytic   B. fatal   C. mammoth   47._____
    D. portable   E. lethal

48. A. elementary   B. tertiary   C. didactical   48._____
    D. perceptive   E. diffident

49. A. abolition   B. abstention   C. abstract   49._____
    D. abundance   E. abridgment

50. A. blatant   B. docile   C. valiant   50._____
    D. obtrusive   E. brisk

KEY (CORRECT ANSWERS)

1.	B	11.	A	21.	CE	31.	BC	41.	AE
2.	D	12.	B	22.	AD	32.	CD	42.	DE
3.	D	13.	A	23.	BC	33.	AD	43.	AD
4.	A	14.	D	24.	CD	34.	AC	44.	AE
5.	C	15.	C	25.	AD	35.	DE	45.	BD
6.	A	16.	C	26.	AB	36.	BE	46.	BD
7.	B	17.	D	27.	BE	37.	AE	47.	BE
8.	D	18.	A	28.	DE	38.	AB	48.	CD
9.	E	19.	B	29.	AE	39.	AC	49.	CE
10.	A	20.	A	30.	BE	40.	BC	50.	AD

EXAMINATION SECTION
TEST 1

DIRECTIONS: Each question or incomplete statement is followed by several suggested answers or completions. Select the one that BEST answers the question or completes the statement. *PRINT THE LETTER OF THE CORRECT ANSWER IN THE SPACE AT THE RIGHT.*

1. Each year many children die in fires which they have started while playing with matches.
   Of the following measures, the one that would be MOST effective in preventing such tragedies is to
   A. warn the children of the dangers involved
   B. punish parents who are found guilty of neglecting their children
   C. keep matches out of the reach of children
   D. use only safety matches

   1.____

2. Holding a fire drill during the performance in a theatre would be ineffective MAINLY because
   A. the audience is in the theatre for pleasure and would resent interruption of the performance
   B. the members of the audience are transients who do not return to this theatre regularly
   C. the members of the audience have easy access to many exits in the theatre permitting speedy and safe evacuation of the building
   D. theatres are usually of fireproof construction and unlikely to catch fire

   2.____

3. The same care should be taken to avoid damage when extinguishing a fire in the home of a poor family as would be taken in the home of a wealthy family.
   The BEST justification for this statement is that the possessions of a poor family
   A. probably are not covered by fire insurance
   B. sometimes include items of great monetary value
   C. may be very precious to the family
   D. may contain valuable or irreplaceable documents, such as birth certificates, military discharge certificates, etc.

   3.____

4. Smoking in bed is considered to be an unsafe practice MAINLY because the smoker may
   A. become drowsy and carelessly discard smoldering matches or cigarettes
   B. fall asleep and burn his fingers or lips
   C. fall asleep and set fire to his clothing, the bedding, or furniture
   D. fall asleep and choke from the tobacco smoke and fumes

   4.____

5. At a fire in a rooming house, the manager tells the officer in command that all the roomers have evacuated the building.
   The one of the following actions which would be MOST proper for the officer to take in the situation is to
   A. order a search of the building for possible victims
   B. question the manager closely to make certain that everybody has in fact been evacuated
   C. question the roomers to obtain confirmation that all the occupants have been evacuated
   D. obtain a list of the roomers and then verify that each one of them is outside of the building

6. An elevator in a large apartment house became stuck between floors and the fire department was called to remove the trapped passengers. Soon after arriving, the officer in command informed the passengers that the fire department was present and would start rescue operations immediately.
   The MAIN reason for informing the passengers of their arrival was to reduce the chances that
   A. another agency would receive credit for the rescue
   B. the fire department would be criticized for being slow in responding
   C. the passengers would not cooperate with the rescuers
   D. the passengers would become panic-stricken

7. The election laws of many states require that general elections are to take place on the first Tuesday following the first Monday in November.
   The one of the following statements that is MOST accurate is that elections in those states
   A. in some years may be held on November 1st and in other years on November 8th
   B. may not be held on either November 1st or November 8th
   C. in some years may be held on November 1st but never on November 8th
   D. in some years may be held on November 8th but never on November 1st

8. At a smoky fire in a hotel, members of a ladder company are ordered to search all rooms and remove any persons they find remaining in the area threatened by fire or smoke. While performing this duty, a firefighter is prevented from entering a room by a ferocious dog standing in the doorway.
   In this situation, the BEST of the following actions for the firefighter to take is to
   A. look into the room without entering and, if no person can be seen inside, assume that the room is empty
   B. obtain assistance from other firefighters, subdue the dog, enter, and search the room
   C. attempt to find the dog's owner so that the dog can be removed and the room entered and searched
   D. call for assistance of the ASPCA in removing the dog and then enter and search the room

9. Sparks given off by welding torches are a serious fire hazard.
The BEST of the following methods of dealing with this hazard is to conduct welding operations only
   A. in fireproof buildings protected by sprinkler systems
   B. out-of-doors on a day with little wind blowing
   C. on materials certified to be non-combustible by recognized testing laboratories
   D. after loose combustible materials have been cleared from the area and with a man standing by with a hose line

10. A firefighter on his way to report for work early one evening noticed a man loitering near a fire alarm box. The man appeared to be touching the alarm box handle but withdrew his hand as the firefighter approached. When asked by the firefighter to explain his actions, the man denied touching the handle.
In this situation, the firefighter should
   A. summon a police officer and have the man arrested
   B. ignore the incident since no crime has been committed
   C. keep the man under surveillance until the man returns to his home
   D. locate the police officer on the beat and inform him of the incident

11. In a city, schools are required to hold at least 12 fire drills each school year, 8 of which must be conducted between September first and December first.
Of the following, the BEST justification for holding most fire drills during September 1 – December 1 period is that
   A. most fires occur during that period
   B. pupils are trained in evacuation of their schools at the beginning of the school year
   C. the weather is milder during that period
   D. school attendance is higher at the beginning of the school year

12. Following a severe smoky fire in the lobby of a hotel, a dead body was found in a room on the eighth floor. The coroner who examined the body found that the victim died from the inhalation of toxic gases and smoke.
The one of the following that is the MOST probable explanation of this occurrence is that
   A. the coroner made an error in his findings
   B. the victim inhaled the gases and smoke in the lobby, fled to the eighth floor to escape the fire, and collapsed there
   C. the gases and smoke traveled through vertical openings to the upper stories where they were inhaled by the victim
   D. a second fire occurred simultaneously in the upper stories of the hotel

13. The basic assumption of fire prevention educational programs is that people frequently
   A. must be forced into obeying fire laws
   B. are unaware of the dangers involved in some of their actions
   C. don't care whether or not their actions are dangerous
   D. assume that fire insurance protects them against all fire loss

14. The one of the following statements that is MOST accurate is that visibility in buildings on fire is
    A. not a serious problem mainly because fires give off sufficient light to enable firefighters to see clearly
    B. a serious problem mainly because fires often knock out the electrical system of the building
    C. not a serious problem mainly because most fires occur during daylight hours
    D. a serious problem mainly because smoke conditions often are encountered

15. While operating at a five-alarm fire, a firefighter is approached by an obviously intoxicated man who claims to be a former firefighter and who offers to help put out the fire.
    In this situation, the BEST of the following courses of action for the firefighter is to
    A. give the man some easy task to perform
    B. refer the man to the officer in command of the fire
    C. decline the offer of help and ask the man to remain outside of the fire lines
    D. ask to see the man's credentials and if he is a former firefighter as he claims, put him to work stretching hose lines

16. A civilian came into the firehouse to report that some adolescents had turned on a hydrant in the neighborhood. After getting the location of the hydrant, the firefighter on house watch asked the civilian for his name and was told *Smith*. The firefighter then thanked the civilian and proceeded to process the report.
    The firefighter's actions in this situation were
    A. *proper*
    B. *proper*, except that he should not have wasted time asking for the civilian's name
    C. *proper*, except that he should have attempted to find out whether the civilian's name really was *Smith*
    D. *proper*, except that he should have obtained the civilian's first name and address as well as his family name

17. Fire apparatus are not permitted to use their sirens when returning to quarters.
    Of the following, the MAIN justification for this restriction is that
    A. the chances of being involved in traffic accidents are reduced
    B. there is no need for prompt return to quarters after a fire has been extinguished
    C. apparatus return to quarters by less crowded streets than are used when responding to alarms
    D. the officer in command is better able to exchange radio messages with the fire alarm dispatcher

18. A fire escape platform is attached to a building flush with the window sill leading onto it.
    The MOST important reason for this arrangement is that it reduces the chance that
    A. intruders will utilize the fire escapes for illegal purposes since they will be visible from inside the apartment
    B. tenants will place garbage or other obstructions on the platform since these objects will be visible from inside the apartment
    C. persons using the fire escape in an emergency will trip as they leave the apartment
    D. sagging or loosening of the supports will occur without coming to the attention of persons occupying the apartment

19. A civilian, on his way home from work one evening, hears an alarm ringing and sees water running out of a sprinkler discharge pipe on the side of a building. No smoke or other indications of fire are seen. There is a padlock on the entrance to the building, no fire alarm box is in sight, and a firehouse is located 1½ blocks away.
    In this situation, it would be MOST proper for the civilian to
    A. take no action since there is no evidence of fire or other emergency
    B. attempt to ascertain the name of the building's owner and notify him of the situation
    C. send an alarm from the closest fire alarm box
    D. go to the firehouse and inform the man at the desk of the situation

20. Running a hose line between two rungs of a ladder into a building on fire is generally considered to be a
    A. *good* practice, mainly because resting the hose on the rungs of the ladder reduces the load that must be carried by the firefighters
    B. *poor* practice, mainly because the maneuverability of the ladder is reduced
    C. *good* practice, mainly because the weight of the hose line holds the ladder more securely against the side of the building
    D. *poor* practice, mainly because the ladder may be damaged by the additional weight of the hose line filled with water

21. Suppose that you are the firefighter on housewatch duty when a woman rushes into the firehouse and reports that a teenage gang is assaulting a man on the street several blocks away.
    In this situation, the BEST of the following courses of action for you to take FIRST is to
    A. notify the police department of the reported incident
    B. go to the scene of the disturbance and verify the woman's report
    C. suggest to the woman that she report the matter to the police department
    D. notify your fellow firefighters of the incident and all go to the aid of the man being assaulted

22. A firefighter on his way to work is standing on a subway platform waiting for his train. Suddenly a man standing beside him collapses to the floor, showing no sign of breathing.
    In this situation, the firefighter should
    A. run to the nearest telephone and summon an ambulance
    B. designate a responsible person to look after the victim and then continue on his way to the firehouse
    C. administer first aid measures to restore breathing
    D. take no action since the victim is obviously dead

23. Fire companies often practice methods of firefighting and lifesaving in public places.
    The one of the following which is the BEST justification for this practice is that it
    A. provides facilities for practicing essential operations which are not readily available in fire department installations
    B. impresses the taxpaying public that they are getting their money's worth
    C. attracts youngsters and interests them in firefighting as a career
    D. makes certain that all company equipment is in the best possible working condition

24. The one of the following fires which would generally present the GREATEST danger to surrounding buildings from flying sparks or brands is a fire in a(n)
    A. warehouse storing paper products
    B. factory manufacturing plastics
    C. outdoor lumberyard
    D. open-type parking lot

25. A fire marshal, questioning firefighters at the scene of a suspicious fire, obtains some conflicting statements about details of the fire situation present upon their arrival.
    The MOST likely explanation of this conflict is that
    A. the firefighters have not been properly trained to carry out their part in arson investigations
    B. the fire marshal did not give the firefighters time to collect and organize their impressions of the fire scene
    C. witnesses to an event see the situation from their own point of view and seldom agree on all details
    D. details are of little importance if there is general agreement on major matters

26. *His garden contained a profusion of flowers, shrubs, and bushes.*
    As used in this sentence, profusion means MOST NEARLY
    A. abundance   B. display
    C. representation   D. scarcity

27. *The inspector would not approve of the work because it was out of plumb.*
    As used in this sentence, out of plumb means MOST NEARLY
    A. not properly seasoned   B. not of the required strength
    C. not vertical   D. not fireproof

28. *The judge <u>admonished</u> the witness for his answer.*
    As used in this sentence, the word <u>admonished</u> means MOST NEARLY
    A. complimented   B. punished   C. questioned   D. warned

29. *A <u>millimeter</u> is a measure of length.*
    The length represented by one <u>millimeter</u> is _____ meter(s).
    A. one-thousandth of a   B. one thousand
    C. one-millionth of a   D. one million

30. *It is not possible to <u>misconstrue</u> his letter.*
    As used in this sentence, the word <u>misconstrue</u> means MOST NEARLY
    A. decipher   B. forget   C. ignore   D. misinterpret

31. *The man was <u>cajoled</u> into signing the contract.*
    As used in this sentence, the word <u>cajoled</u> means MOST NEARLY
    A. bribed   B. coaxed   C. confused   D. forced

32. *The announcement was met with general <u>derision</u>.*
    As used in this sentence, the word <u>derision</u> means MOST NEARLY
    A. anger   B. applause   C. disbelief   D. ridicule

33. *The speaker's words were moving but <u>irrelevant</u>.*
    As used in this sentence, the word <u>irrelevant</u> means MOST NEARLY
    A. insincere
    B. not based upon facts
    C. not bearing upon the subject under discussion
    D. self-contradictory

34. *The breakdown of the machine was due to a defective <u>gasket</u>.*
    As used in this sentence, the word <u>gasket</u> means MOST NEARLY
    A. filter   B. piston   C. sealer   D. transmission

35. *The noise of the <u>pneumatic</u> drill disturbed the teacher.*
    As used in this sentence, the word <u>pneumatic</u> means MOST NEARLY
    A. air pressure   B. electricity
    C. internal combustion   D. water pressure

36. *He exercised the <u>prerogatives</u> of his office with moderation.*
    As used in this sentence, the word <u>prerogatives</u> means MOST NEARLY
    A. burdens   B. duties
    C. opportunities   D. privileges

37. *He made his decisions after a <u>cursory</u> examination of the facts.*
    As used in this sentence, the word <u>cursory</u> means MOST NEARLY
    A. biased   B. critical   C. exhaustive   D. hasty

38. *John was appointed <u>provisional</u> chairman of the arrangements committee.*
    As used in this sentence, the word <u>provisional</u> means MOST NEARLY
    A. official   B. permanent   C. temporary   D. unofficial

39. *After the bush is planted, the ground around it should be <u>tamped</u>.*   39.____
    As used in this sentence, the word <u>tamped</u> means MOST NEARLY
    A. loosened   B. packed   C. raked   D. watered

40. *The volcano was <u>dormant</u> during the time I visited the island.*   40.____
    As used in this sentence, the word <u>dormant</u> means MOST NEARLY
    A. erupting   B. extinct   C. inactive   D. threatening

41. *A starter's gun is not considered to be a <u>lethal</u> weapon.*   41.____
    As used in this sentence, the word <u>lethal</u> means MOST NEARLY
    A. criminal   B. deadly   C. offensive   D. reliable

42. *At the crucial moment, the <u>seismograph</u> failed to function.*   42.____
    As used in this sentence, the word <u>seismograph</u> means MOST NEARLY an instrument for measuring
    A. earthquakes   B. heartbeats
    C. humidity   D. nuclear radiation

Questions 43-45.

DIRECTIONS: Questions 43 through 45, inclusive, contain words, one of which in each group is misspelled. Indicate the MISSPELLED word.

43. A. beneficial   B. diasterous   C. incredible   D. miniature   43.____

44. A. auxilliary   B. hypocrisy   C. phlegm   D. vengeance   44.____

45. A. aisle   B. cemetary   C. courtesy   D. extraordinary 45.____

Questions 46-47.

DIRECTIONS: Questions 46 and 47 consist of four sentences lettered A, B, C, and D. One sentence in each group contains an error in grammar or punctuation. Indicate the INCORRECT sentence in each group.

46. A. Ham and eggs is the specialty of the house.   46.____
    B. He is one of the students who are on probation.
    C. Do you think that either one of us have a chance to be nominated for president of the class?
    D. I assume that either he was to be in charge or you were.

47. A. Its a long road that has no turn.   47.____
    B. To run is more tiring than to walk.
    C. We have been assigned three new reports: namely, the statistical summary, the narrative summary and the budgetary summary.
    D. Had the first payment been made in January, the second would be due in April.

Questions 48-50.

DIRECTIONS: Questions 48 through 50 are based upon the following paragraphs.

The sizes of living rooms shall meet the following requirements:

1. In each apartment there shall be at least one living room containing at least 120 square feet of clear floor area, and every other living room except a kitchen shall contain at least 70 square feet of clear floor area.
2. Every living room which contains less than 80 square feet of clear floor area or which is located in the cellar or basement shall be at least 9 feet high and every other living room 8 feet high.

Apartments containing three or more rooms may have dining bays, which shall not exceed 55 square feet in floor surface area and shall not be deemed separate rooms or subject to the requirements for separate rooms. Every such dining bay shall be provided with at least one window containing an area at least one-eighth of the floor surface area of such dining bay.

48. The MINIMUM volume of a living room, other than a kitchen, which meets the minimum requirements of the above paragraphs is one that measures _____ cubic feet.
    A. 70 B. 80 C. 630 D. 640

49. A builder proposes to construct an apartment house containing an apartment consisting of a kitchen which measures 10 feet by 6 feet, a room 12 feet by 12 feet, and one 11 feet by 7 feet.
    This apartment
    A. *does not comply* with the requirements of the paragraph
    B. *complies* with the requirements of the paragraph provided that it is not located in the cellar or basement
    C. *complies* with the requirements of the paragraph provided that the height of the smaller rooms is at least 9 feet
    D. *may or may not comply* with the requirements of the paragraph, depending upon the clear floor area of the kitchen

50. The one of the following definitions of the term *living room* which is MOST in accord with its meaning in the above paragraphs is
    A. a sitting room or parlor
    B. the largest room in the apartment
    C. a room used for living purposes
    D. any room in an apartment containing 120 square feet of clear floor area

KEY (CORRECT ANSWERS)

1.	C	11.	B	21.	A	31.	B	41.	B
2.	B	12.	C	22.	C	32.	D	42.	A
3.	C	13.	B	23.	A	33.	C	43.	B
4.	C	14.	D	24.	C	34.	C	44.	A
5.	A	15.	C	25.	C	35.	A	45.	B
6.	D	16.	D	26.	A	36.	D	46.	C
7.	D	17.	A	27.	C	37.	D	47.	A
8.	B	18.	C	28.	D	38.	C	48.	C
9.	D	19.	C	29.	A	39.	B	49.	C
10.	D	20.	B	30.	D	40.	C	50.	C

TEST 2

DIRECTIONS: Each question or incomplete statement is followed by several suggested answers or completions. Select the one that BEST answers the question or completes the statement. *PRINT THE LETTER OF THE CORRECT ANSWER IN THE SPACE AT THE RIGHT.*

Questions 1-2.

DIRECTIONS: Questions 1 and 2 are based upon the following paragraphs.

The sizes of living rooms shall meet the following requirements:

1. In each apartment there shall be at least one living room containing at least 120 square feet of clear floor area, and every other living room except a kitchen shall contain at least 70 square feet of clear floor area.
2. Every living room which contains less than 80 square feet of clear floor area or which is located in the cellar or basement shall be at least 9 feet high and every other living room 8 feet high.

Apartments containing three or more rooms may have dining bays, which shall not exceed 55 square feet in floor surface area and shall not be deemed separate rooms or subject to the requirements for separate rooms. Every such dining bay shall be provided with at least one window containing an area at least one-eighth of the floor surface area of such dining bay.

1. Assume that one room in a four-room apartment measures 20 feet by 10 feet and contains a dining bay 8 feet by 6 feet.
   According to the above paragraphs, the dining bay MUST be provided with a window measuring AT LEAST _____ square feet.
   A. 6   B. 7   C. 25   D. 55

   1.____

2. Kitchens, according to the above paragraphs, are
   A. *not considered* living rooms
   B. *considered* living rooms and must, therefore, meet the height and area requirements of the paragraph
   C. *considered* living rooms but they need not meet either the height or area requirements of the paragraphs
   D. *considered* living rooms but they need meet only the height requirements, not the area requirements, of the paragraphs

   2.____

Questions 3-7.

DIRECTIONS: Questions 3 through 7 are based upon the following paragraph.

Cotton fabrics treated with the XYZ Process have features which make them far superior to any previously known flame-retardant treated cotton fabrics. XYZ are glow resistant, when exposed to flames or intense heat form tough, pliable, and protective chars, are inert physiologically to persons handling or exposed to the fabric; are only slightly heavier than untreated fabrics; and are susceptible to further wet and dry finishing treatments. In addition, the treated fabrics exhibit little or no adverse change in feel, texture, and appearance, and are shrink-, rot- and mildew-resistant. The treatment reduces strength only slightly. Finished fabrics have "easy care" properties in that they are wrinkle-resistant and dry rapidly.

3. It is MOST accurate to state that the author, in the above paragraph, presents
   A. facts but reaches no conclusion concerning the value of the process
   B. his conclusion concerning the process and facts to support his conclusion
   C. his conclusion concerning the value of the process unsupported by facts
   D. neither facts nor conclusions, but merely describes the process

4. The one of the following articles for which the XYZ Process would be MOST suitable is
   A. nylon stockings
   B. woolen shirt
   C. silk tie
   D. cotton bedsheet

5. The one of the following aspects of the XYZ Process which is NOT discussed in the above paragraph is its effects on
   A. costs
   B. washability
   C. wearability
   D. the human body

6. The MAIN reason for treating a fabric with the XYZ Process is to
   A. prepare the fabric for other wet and dry finishing treatments
   B. render it shrink-, rot-, and mildew-resistant
   C. increase its weight and strength
   D. reduce the chance that it will catch fire

7. The one of the following which would be considered a minor drawback of the XYZ Process is that it
   A. forms chars when exposed to flame
   B. makes fabrics mildew-resistant
   C. adds to the weight of fabrics
   D. is compatible with other finishing treatments

Questions 8-11.

DIRECTIONS: Questions 8 through 11 are based upon the following paragraph.

Language performs an essentially social function; it helps us to get along together, to communicate and achieve a great measure of concerted action. Words are signs which have significance by convention, and those people who do not adopt the conventions simply fail to communicate. They do not "get along" and a social force arises which encourages them to achieve the correct associations. "Correct" means as used by other members of the social group. Some of the vital points about language are brought home to an Englishman when visiting America, and vice versa, because our vocabularies are nearly the same—but not quite.

8. *Communicate*, as that word is used in the above paragraph, means to
   A. make ourselves understood
   B. send written messages
   C. move other persons to concerted action
   D. use language in its traditional or conventional sense

9. Usage of a word is *correct*, as that term is defined in the above paragraph, when the word is used as it is
   A. defined in standard dictionaries
   B. used by the majority of persons throughout the world who speak the same language
   C. used by the majority of educated persons who speak the same language
   D. used by other persons with whom we are associating

9.____

10. In the above paragraph, the author is concerned PRIMARILY with the
    A. meaning of words
    B. pronunciation of words
    C. structure of sentences
    D. origin and development of language

10.____

11. According to the above paragraph, the main language problem of an Englishman, while visiting America, stems from the fact that an Englishman
    A. uses some words that have different meanings for Americans
    B. has different social values than the Americans
    C. has had more exposure to non-English speaking persons than Americans have had
    D. pronounces words differently than Americans do

11.____

Questions 12-15.

DIRECTIONS: Questions 12 through 15 are based upon the following paragraph.

Whenever a social group has become so efficiently organized that it has gained access to an adequate supply of food and has learned to distribute it among its members so well that wealth considerably exceeds immediate demands, it can be depended upon to utilize its surplus energy in an attempt to enlarge the sphere in which it is active. The structure of ant colonies renders them particularly prone to this sort of expansionist policy. With very few exceptions, ants of any given colony are hostile to those of any other community, even of the same species, and this condition is abound to produce preliminary bickering among colonies which are closely associated.

12. According to the above paragraph, a social group is wealthy when it
    A. is efficiently organized
    B. controls large territories
    C. contains energetic members
    D. produces and distributes food reserves

12.____

13. According to the above paragraph, the structure of an ant colony is its
    A. social organization
    B. nest arrangement
    C. territorial extent
    D. food-gathering activities

13.____

14. It follows from the preceding paragraph that the LEAST expansionist society would be one that has
    A. great poverty generally
    B. more than sufficient wealth to meet its immediate demands
    C. great wealth generally
    D. wide inequality between its richest and poorest members

14.____

15. According to the preceding paragraph, an ant generally is hostile EXCEPT to other
    A. insects
    B. ants
    C. ants of the same species
    D. ants of the same colony

16.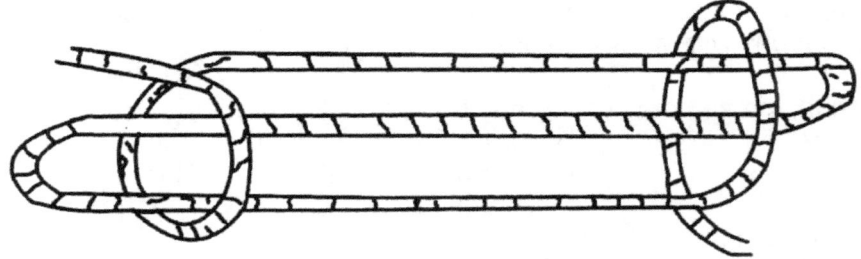

    The knot shown in the above diagram would BEST be used to
    A. form a noose for hoisting tools
    B. wrap around fire victims to lower them to the ground
    C. shorten the effective length of a piece of rope
    D. lash two ladders together to extend their lengths

17.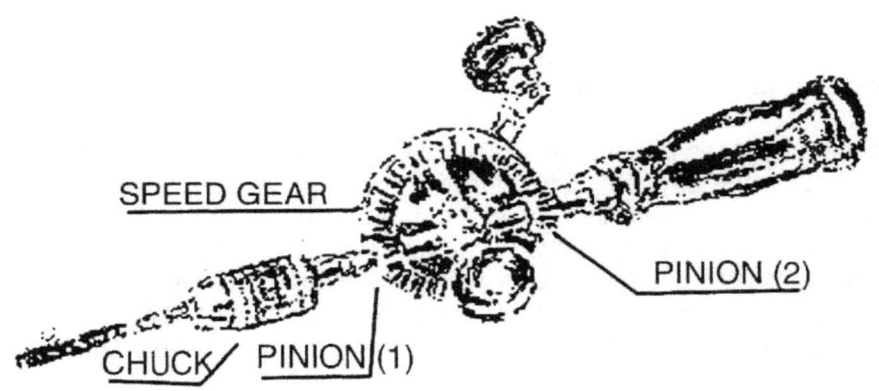

    The function of pinion gear (2) in the hand drill shown in the above diagram is to
    A. increase the speed of the chuck
    B. keep the speed gear from wobbling
    C. double the turning force on the chuck
    D. allow reverse rotation of the speed gear

18. Assume that two identical insulated jugs are filled with equal quantities of water from a water tap. A block of ice is placed in one jug, and the same quantity of ice, chopped in small cubes, is placed in the other jug.
    The one of the following statements that is MOST accurate is that the water in the jug containing the chopped ice, compared to the water in the other jug, will be chilled _____ temperature.
    A. *faster* but to a substantially higher
    B. *faster* and to approximately the same
    C. *slower* but to a substantially higher
    D. *slower* and to approximately the same

Questions 19-21.

DIRECTIONS: Questions 19 through 21 relate to the following diagrams of the dials of a water meter which registers water consumption in cubic feet

19. The MAXIMUM quantity that can be registered directly by the above dials is MOST NEARLY _____ cubic feet.
    A. 9,000   B. 10,000   C. 99,000   D. 100,000

    19._____

20. The one of the following readings of the meter, as shown above, that is MOST accurate is _____ cubic feet.
    A. 1465   B. 9047   C. 90,465   D. 91,475

    20._____

21. The one of the following systems of gears which could be used to drive the meter shown above is

    21._____

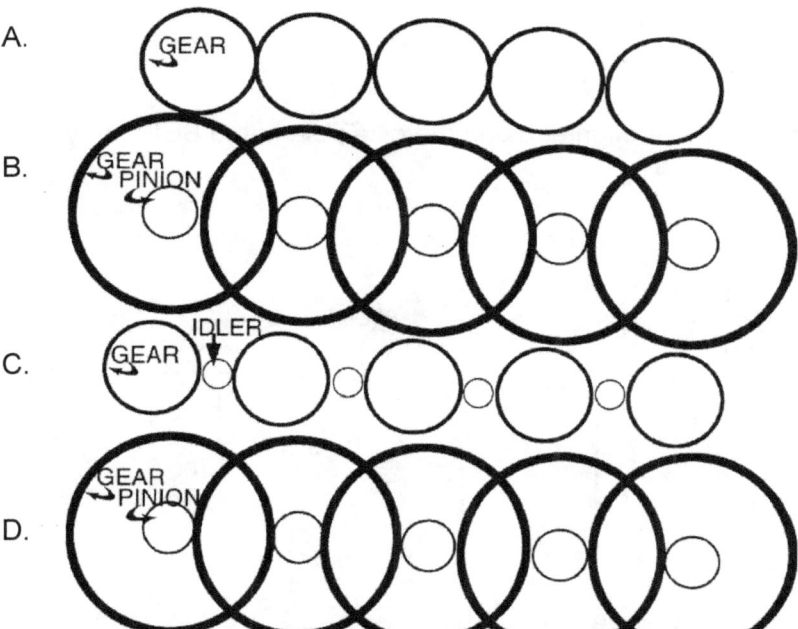

22.

The long pole and hook shown in the above sketch is called a pike pole. Firefighters sometimes push the point and hook through plaster ceilings and then pull the ceiling down.
Of the following, the MOST likely reason for this practice is to
A. let heat and smoke escape from the room
B. trace defective electric wiring through the house
C. see if hidden fire is burning above the ceiling
D. remove combustible material which will provide fuel

23.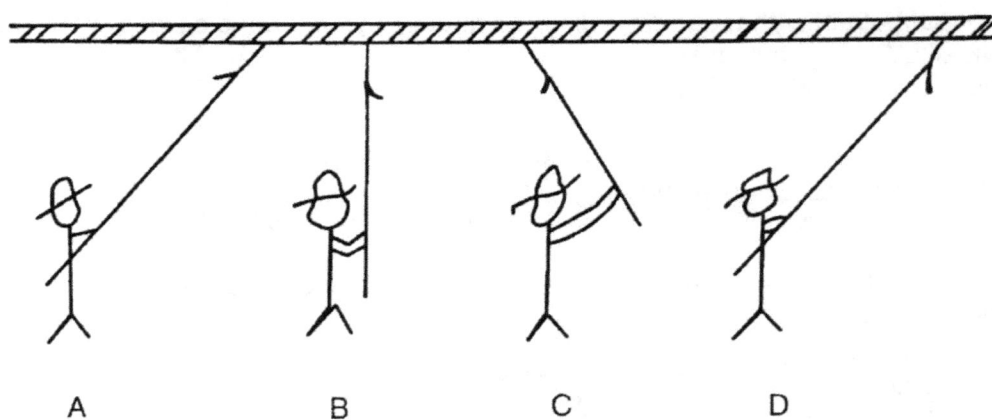

In the figures shown above, the firefighter using the pike pole in the BEST way is Firefighter
A. A   B. B   C. C   D. D

24.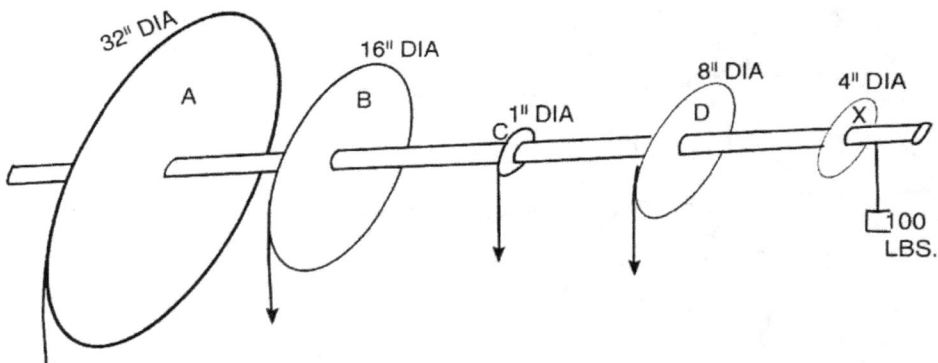

In the above diagram illustrating a gang of pulleys, all of which are fixed to the common shaft, the 100 lbs. weight attached to pulley X will be balanced by a weight of 25 lbs. properly attached to pulley
A. A   B. B   C. C   D. D

25.

Suppose that the same quantity of water is placed in the cup and bowl pictured above and both are left on a table. The time required for the water to evaporate completely from the cup, compared to the bowl, would be
   A. longer
   B. shorter
   C. equal
   D. longer or shorter, depending upon the temperature and humidity in the room

26.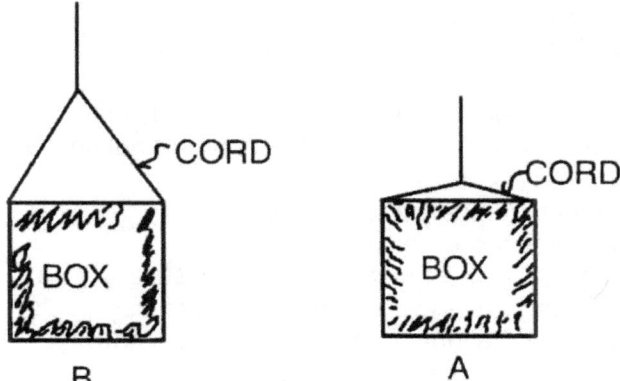

Two packages, identical in size, shape, and contents, are tied by identical pieces of cord. One package (A) is tied tightly and the other (B) is tied loosely. If the packages are held by the cord and handled in the same manner, the cord on the package that is held tightly (A) is
   A. more likely to snap
   B. less likely to snap
   C. equally likely to snap
   D. more or less likely to snap, depending upon the quality of the cord, the number of ply, and other factors not given

27. Some tools are known as all-purpose tools because they may be used for a great variety of purposes; others are called special purpose tools because they are suitable only for a particular purpose.
Generally, an all-purpose tool, compared to a special tool for the same purpose, is
   A. cheaper
   B. less efficient
   C. safer to use
   D. simpler to operate

28. During a snowstorm, a passenger car gets stuck in the snow. It is observed that the rear wheels are spinning in the snow and the front wheels are not turning.
The one of the following statements which BEST explains why the car is NOT moving is that
   A. moving parts of the motor are frozen or blocked by the ice and snow
   B. the front wheels are not receiving power because of a defective or malfunctioning transmission
   C. the rear wheels are not obtaining sufficient traction because of the snow
   D. the distribution of the power to the front and rear wheels is not balanced

29. When the inside face of a rubber suction cup is pressed against a smooth wall, it USUALLY remains in place because of the
   A. force of molecular attraction between the rubber and the wall
   B. pressure of the air on the rubber cup
   C. suction caused by the elasticity of the rubber
   D. static electricity generated by friction between rubber and the wall

30. An observation balloon is filled with just sufficient helium to inflate fully its gas bag. A second identical balloon is filled with twice the amount of helium as the first.
The lifting power of the second balloon, compared to the first, is
   A. *greater*, mainly because it contains more helium
   B. *greater*, mainly because it contains helium under higher pressure
   C. *equal*, mainly because the gas bag has the same cubic capacity
   D. *less*, mainly because the additional helium adds to the weight of the balloon without increasing the cubic capacity of the gas bag

31. When a standing subway passenger pulls the metal *safety hand strap* onto which he is holding, it swings toward him. When he releases it, it swings back to its original position.
The MOST accurate explanation of why the handle returns to its original position is that it is
   A. counterweighted
   B. responding to centrifugal forces acting upon it
   C. spring actuated
   D. well-balanced

32. The self-contained gas mask consists of a tank containing breathable air which is supplied to the user by means of flexible tubes.
This type of gas mask would be LEAST effective in an atmosphere containing
   A. insufficient oxygen to sustain life
   B. gases irritating to the skin
   C. gases which cannot be filtered
   D. a combination of toxic gases

33. At a fire during very cold weather, a firefighter who was ordered to shut down a hose line left it partly open so that a small amount of water continued to flow out of the nozzle.
Leaving the nozzle partially opened in this situation was a
    A. *good* practice, mainly because the hose line can be put back into action more quickly
    B. *poor* practice, mainly because the escaping water will form puddles which will freeze on the street
    C. *good* practice, mainly because the water in the hose line will not freeze
    D. *poor* practice, mainly because unnecessary water damage to property will result

34. Some sprinkler systems are supplied by water from a single source; others are supplied by water from two different sources.
Generally, firefighters consider the two source system preferable to the single source system because the two source system
    A. is cheaper to install
    B. is less likely to be put out of operation
    C. is capable of delivering water at higher pressures
    D. goes into operation faster

35. Firefighters must often chop holes in roof planking to let smoke escape from burning buildings. When chopping these holes, they try to place their axe-cuts just alongside the heavy supporting beams underneath the planking.
Of the following, the MOST likely reason for positioning the cut just to the side of such beams is that
    A. the planking is thinnest at this point
    B. there are no nails in this area to dull the axe
    C. the axe is less likely to bounce
    D. the beam provides a strong support for the firefighters using the axe

36. The function of the flat surface machined into the shaft in the above diagram is to
    A. prevent slippage of a pulley positioned at this end of the shaft
    B. provide a non-skid surface to hold the shaft steady as it is machined
    C. prevent the shaft from rolling about when it is placed on a flat workbench
    D. reveal sub-surface defects in the shaft

37.

A chain consists of 5" long and ¼" thick alternating with links 2" long and ¼" thick as shown in the above diagram. (Length is measured end-to-end.)
If the chain is to be attached to hooks at both ends, the maximum distance that can be spanned by a chain consisting of 20 links is MOST NEARLY
   A. a distance which cannot be determined unless it is known whether the chain starts with a large link or small link.
   B. 70 inches
   C. 65 inches
   D. 60 inches

38.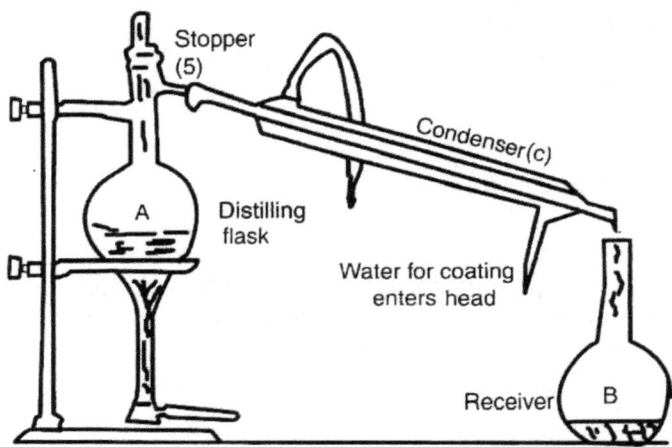

The above diagram shows a system for distilling pure water (flask B) from a salt water solution (flask A).
The one of the following statements that BEST explains why there is no salt in the water in flask B is that
   A. water, but not salt, is vaporized
   B. the salt is absorbed when it passes through condenser (C)
   C. the salt is filtered at the stopper (S)
   D. only pure water is used in the condenser

39. The diagram shown at the right represents the storage space of a fire engine.
The amount of space available for the storage of hose in the fire engine is MOST NEARLY _____ cubic feet.
   A. 40
   B. 75
   C. 540
   D. 600

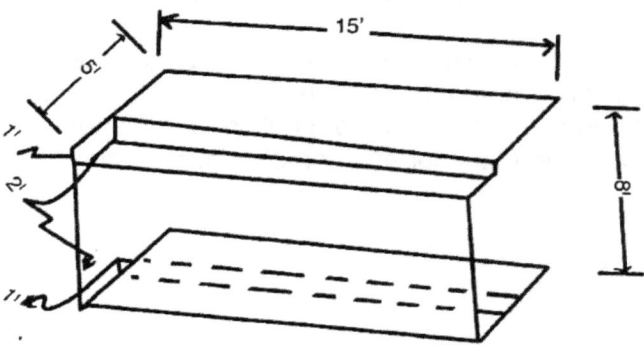

11 (#2)

40. If a piece of rope 100 feet long is cut so that one piece is ²/₃ as long as the other piece, the length of the longer piece must be _____ feet.
A. 60 B. 66²/₃ C. 70 D. 75

40._____

41. A water tank has a discharge valve which is capable of emptying the tank when full in two hours. It also has an inlet valve which can fill the tank, when empty, in four hours and a second inlet valve which can fill the tank, when empty, in six hours.
If the tank is full, and all three valves are opened fully, with water flowing through each valve to capacity, the tank will be emptied in
A. 2 hours
B. 6 hours
C. 12 hours
D. a period of time which cannot be determined from the information given

41._____

42. Final grades in a history course are determined as follows:
Class recitations – weight 50
Weekly quizzes - weight 25
Final examination – weight 25
A student has an average of 60 on a class recitation and 80 on weekly quizzes. In order to receive a final grade of 75, he must obtain on his final examination a grade of
A. 75 B. 80 C. 90 D. 100

42._____

43. Suppose that 8 inches of snow contribute as much water to the reservoir system as one inch of rain.
If, during a snowstorm, an average of 12 inches of snow fell during a six-hour period, with drifts as high as three feet, the addition to the water supply as a result of this snowfall ultimately will be the equivalent of
A. 1 ½ inches of rain
B. 3 inches of rain
C. 4 ½ inches of rain
D. an amount of rain which cannot be determined from the information given

43._____

44. If the pay period of an employee is changed from every two weeks to twice a month, his gross pay (before deductions) from each pay period will
A. *increase* by one-tenth   B. *increase* by one-twelfth
C. *decrease* by one-thirteenth D. *decrease* by one-fifteenth

44._____

45. In a certain state, the automobile license tags consist of two letters followed by three digits, e.g., AA-122.
The MAXIMUM number of different combinations of numbers and letters which can be obtained under this system is MOST NEARLY
A. 13,500 B. 75,000 C. 325,000 D. 675,000

45._____

12 (#2)

KEY (CORRECT ANSWERS)

1. A	11. A	21. D	31. C	41. C
2. D	12. D	22. C	32. B	42. D
3. B	13. A	23. D	33. C	43. A
4. D	14. A	24. B	34. B	44. B
5. A	15. D	25. A	35. C	45. D
6. D	16. C	26. A	36. A	
7. C	17. B	27. B	37. D	
8. A	18. B	28. C	38. A	
9. D	19. D	29. B	39. C	
10. A	20. C	30. D	40. A	

EXAMINATION SECTION
TEST 1

DIRECTIONS: Each question or incomplete statement is followed by several suggested answers or completions. Select the one that BEST answers the question or completes the statement. *PRINT THE LETTER OF THE CORRECT ANSWER IN THE SPACE AT THE RIGHT.*

1. While performing a routine inspection of a factory building, a firefighter is asked a question by the plant manager about a matter which is under the control of the Health Department and about which the firefighter has little knowledge.
   In this situation, the BEST of the following courses of action for the firefighter to take is to
   A. answer the question to the best of his ability
   B. tell the manager that he is not permitted to answer the question because it does not relate to a fire department matter
   C. tell the manager that he will refer the question to the Health Department
   D. suggest to the manager that he communicate with the Health Department about the matter

1.____

2. A firefighter on duty who answers a departmental telephone should give his name and rank
   A. at the start of the conversation, as a matter of routine
   B. only if asked for this information by the caller
   C. only if the caller is a superior officer
   D. only if the telephone message requires the firefighter to take some action

2.____

3. At a recent five-alarm fire in Area A, several companies from Area B were temporarily assigned to occupy the quarters and take over the duties of companies engaged in fighting the fire.
   The MAIN reason for relocating the Area B companies was to
   A. protect the firehouses from robbery or vandalism which might occur if they were left vacant for a long period
   B. provide for speedy response to the fire if additional companies are required
   C. give the Area B companies an opportunity to become familiar with the problems of the A area
   D. provide protection to the A area in the event other fires should occur

3.____

4. Two firefighters, on their way to report for duty early one morning, observe a fire in a building containing a supermarket on the street level and apartments on the upper stories. One firefighter runs into the building to spread the alarm to the tenants. The other firefighter runs to a street alarm box two blocks away and sends an alarm.
   The latter firefighter should then
   A. return to the building which is on fire and help evacuate the tenants

4.____

B. remain at the fire alarm box in order to direct the first fire company that arrives to the location of the fire
C. look for a telephone in order to call his own fire company and explain that he and his companion will be late in reporting for duty
D. look for a telephone in order to call the Health Department and request that an inspector be sent to the supermarket to examine the food involved in the fire

5. A man found an official fire department badge and gave it to his young son to use as a toy.
   The man's action was improper MAINLY because
   A. it is disrespectful to the fire department to use the badge in this manner
   B. the boy may injure himself playing with the badge
   C. an effort should have been made first to locate the owner of the badge before giving it to the boy
   D. the badge should have been returned to the fire department

6. In case of a fire in a United States mail box, the fire department recommends that an extinguishing agent which smothers the fire, such as carbon tetrachloride, should be used.
   Of the following, the MOST likely reason for NOT recommending the use of water is that
   A. water is not effective on fires in small tightly enclosed spaces
   B. someone might have mailed chemicals that could explode in contact with water
   C. water may damage the mail untouched by fire so that it could not be delivered
   D. the smothering agent can be put on the fire faster than water can be

7. Of the following, the MAIN difficulty in the way of obtaining accurate information about the causes of fires is that
   A. firefighters are too busy putting out fires to have time for investigation of the causes of fires
   B. most people have little knowledge about fire hazards
   C. fires destroy much of the evidence which would indicate the causes of the fires
   D. fire departments are more interested in fire prevention than in investigating fires that have already occurred

8. In an effort to discourage the sending of false alarms and to help apprehend those guilty of this practice, it is suggested that the handles of fire alarm boxes be covered with a dye which would stain the hand of a person sending an alarm, and which would not wash off for 24 hours. The dye would be visible only under an ultraviolet light.
   Of the following, the CHIEF objection to such a device is that it would
   A. require funds that can be better used for other purposes
   B. have no effect on false alarms transmitted by telephone
   C. discourage some persons from sending alarms for real fires
   D. punish the innocent as well as the guilty

9. Automatic fire extinguishing sprinkler systems sometimes are not effective on fires accompanied by explosions, CHIEFLY because
   A. these fires do not generate enough heat to start sprinkler operation
   B. the pipes supplying the sprinklers are usually damaged by the explosion
   C. fires in explosive materials usually cannot be extinguished by water
   D. sprinkler heads are usually clogged by dust created by the explosion

10. When a fire occurs in the vicinity of a subway system, there is the possibility that water from the firefighter's hose streams will flood underground portions of the subway lines through sidewalk gratings.
    Of the following methods of reducing this danger, the one that would generally be MOST suitable is for the officer in command to order his fire fighters to
    A. use fewer hose lines and smaller quantities of water than they would ordinarily
    B. attack the fire from positions which are distant from the sidewalk gratings
    C. cover the sidewalk gratings with canvas tarpaulins
    D. advise the subway dispatcher to re-route the subway trains

11. When responding to alarms, fire department apparatus generally follow routes established in advance.
    The one of the following which would be LEAST valid justification for this practice is that
    A. motorists living in the area become familiar with these routes and tend to avoid them
    B. the likelihood of collision between two pieces of fire department apparatus is reduced
    C. the fastest response generally is obtained
    D. road construction, road blocks, and detours and similar conditions can be avoided

12. An off-duty firefighter sees, from a distance, a group of teenage boys set fire to a newspaper and toss the flaming pages into an open window of a building which is being torn down.
    In this situation, the FIRST action which should be taken by the firefighter is to
    A. send a fire alarm from the closest street alarm box
    B. chase the boys and attempt to catch one of them
    C. investigate whether a fire has been started
    D. call the police from the closest police alarm box or telephone

13. When responding to an alarm, officers are not to talk to the chauffeur driving the apparatus except to give orders or directions.
    Of the following, the BEST justification for this rule is that it
    A. gives the officer an opportunity to make preliminary plans for handling the fire problem
    B. enables the chauffeur to concentrate on driving the apparatus
    C. maintains the proper relationship between the ranks while on duty
    D. permits the officer to observe the chauffeur's skill, or lack of skill, in driving the apparatus

14. The approved method of reporting a fire by telephone is FIRST to dial the
    A. central headquarters of the fire department
    B. borough headquarters of the fire department
    C. local fire station house
    D. telephone operator

15. Door in theatres and other places of public assembly usually open outward.
    The MAIN reason for this requirement is, in the event of a fire, to
    A. provide the widest possible passageway for escape of the audience
    B. prevent panic-stricken audiences from jamming the doors in a closed position
    C. indicate to the audience the safe direction of travel
    D. prevent unauthorized persons from entering the building

16. Fire prevention inspections should be conducted at irregular hours or intervals.
    The BEST justification for this *irregularity* is that it permits the firefighters to
    A. make inspections when they have free time
    B. see the inspected establishments in their normal condition and not in their *dressed-up* condition
    C. avoid making inspections at times which would be convenient for the inspected establishments
    D. concentrate their inspectional activities on those establishments which present the greatest fire hazard

17. Some gas masks provide protection to the user by filtering out from the air certain harmful gases present in the atmosphere.
    A mask of this type would NOT be suitable in an atmosphere containing
    A. heavy, black smoke
    B. a filterable gas under pressure
    C. insufficient oxygen to sustain life
    D. more than one filterable harmful gas

18. Firefighters are instructed never to turn on the gas supply to a house, which was turned off by them during a fire.
    Of the following, the MOST important reason for this prohibition is that
    A. the fire may have made the gas meters inaccurate
    B. unburned gas may escape from open gas jets
    C. the utility company's employees may object to firefighters performing their work
    D. firefighters should not do anything which is not directly related to extinguishing fires

19. A firefighter in uniform, performing inspectional duty, comes upon a group of young men assaulting a police officer. The firefighter goes to the aid of the police officer and, in the course of the struggle, receives some minor injuries.
    The action of the firefighter in this situation was
    A. *proper*, chiefly because members of the uniform forces must stick together

B. *improper*, chiefly because people in the neighborhood, as a result, might refuse to cooperate with the fire department's various programs
C. *proper*, chiefly because all citizens have an obligation to assist police officers in the performance of their duty
D. *improper*, chiefly because the fire department lost the services of the firefighter while he was recovering from his injuries

20. Members of the fire department may not make a speech on fire department matters without the approval of the fire commissioner. Requests for permission must be accompanied by a copy or summary of the speech.
    The MAIN reason for this requirement is to
    A. determine whether the member is engaged in political activities which are forbidden
    B. reduce the chance that the public will be misinformed about fire department policies or procedures
    C. provide the department with a lists of members who can serve in the department's speakers' bureau
    D. provide the department with information about the off-duty activities of members

21. For a firefighter to straddle a hose line while holding the nozzle and directing water on fires is a
    A. *good* practice, mainly because better balance is obtained by the firefighter
    B. *poor* practice, mainly because the firefighter directing the hose may trip over the hose
    C. *good* practice, mainly because better control over the hose line is obtained
    D. *poor* practice, mainly because the hose might whip about and injure the firefighter

22. Firefighters are required to wear steel-reinforced inner-soles inside their rubber boots.
    The MAIN purpose of these inner-soles is to
    A. make the boots more durable and long-lasting
    B. protect the firefighter's feet from burns from smoldering objects or embers
    C. protect the firefighter's feet from injury from falling objects
    D. protect the firefighter's feet from nails or other sharp objects

23. Promoting good relations with the public is an important duty of every member of the fire department.
    Of the following, the BEST way for a firefighter to promote good public relations generally is to
    A. become active in civic and charitable organizations
    B. be well-dressed, clean, and neat on all occasions
    C. write letters to newspapers explaining the reasons for departmental procedures
    D. perform his duties with efficiency, consideration, and courtesy

24. Firefighters are advised to avoid wearing rings on their fingers.
The MAIN reason for this advice is that the rings have a tendency to
    A. be damaged during operations at fires
    B. scratch persons receiving first aid treatment
    C. catch on objects and injure the wearer
    D. scratch furniture and/or other valuable objects

25. Suppose that you are a firefighter on housewatch duty when a civilian enters the firehouse. He introduces himself as a British firefighter visiting the country to study American firefighting methods. He asks your permission to ride on the fire apparatus when it responds to alarms in order to observe operations at first hand. You know that it is against departmental policy to permit civilians to ride apparatus without written permission from headquarters.
In this situation, you should
    A. refuse the request but suggest that he follow the apparatus in his own car when it responds to an alarm
    B. call headquarters and request permission to permit the visitor to ride the apparatus
    C. refuse the request and suggest that he apply to headquarters for permission
    D. refuse the request and suggest that he should return the next time that the fire department holds open house

26. *The cause of the emergency was a defective gas flue.*
As used in this sentence, the word flue means MOST NEARLY
    A. burner   B. duct   C. jet   D. supply

27. *The crux of the matter is finding the right man for the job.*
As used in this sentence, the word crux means MOST NEARLY
    A. obvious solution   B. neglected consideration
    C. final step   D. decisive port

28. *His assistance in this project was invaluable*
As used in this sentence, the word invaluable means MOST NEARLY
    A. worthless   B. priceless
    C. inconspicuous   D. difficult to evaluate

29. *There are many facets to this problem.*
As used in this sentence, the word facets means MOST NEARLY
    A. alternatives   B. aspects   C. difficulties   D. solutions

30. *The map clearly indicated the contour of the lake.*
As used in this sentence, the word contour means MOST NEARLY
    A. composition   B. location   C. outline   D. source

31. *The hot weather made him lethargic.*
As used in this sentence, the word lethargic means MOST NEARLY
    A. drowsy   B. perspire   C. tense   D. thirsty

32. *The arrangements for the meeting were haphazard.*
    As used in this sentence, the word haphazard means MOST NEARLY
    A. according to a plan
    B. determined by mere chance
    C. overly detailed
    D. disregarded

33. *The committee could not agree on an agenda for the conference.*
    As used in this sentence, the word agenda means MOST NEARLY
    A. rules of procedure
    B. meeting place
    C. qualifications of delegates
    D. things to be done

34. *The population of the province is fairly homogeneous.*
    As used in this sentence, the word homogeneous means MOST NEARLY
    A. devoted to agricultural pursuits
    B. conservative in outlook
    C. essentially alike
    D. sophisticated

35. *The reports of injuries during the past month are being tabulated.*
    As used in this sentence, the word tabulated means MOST NEARLY
    A. analyzed
    B. placed in a file
    C. put in the form of a table
    D. verified

36. *The terms offered were tantamount to surrender.*
    As used in this sentence, the word tantamount means MOST NEARLY
    A. equivalent   B. opposite   C. preferable   D. preliminary

37. *The firefighter's injuries were superficial.*
    As used in this sentence, the word superficial means MOST NEARLY
    A. on the surface
    B. not fatal
    C. free from infection
    D. not painful

38. *This experience warped his outlook on life.*
    As used in this sentence, the word warped means MOST NEARLY
    A. changed
    B. improved
    C. strengthened
    D. twisted

39. *Hotel guests usually are transients.*
    As used in this sentence, the word transients means MOST NEARLY
    A. persons of considerable wealth
    B. staying for a short time
    C. visitors from other areas
    D. untrustworthy persons

40. *The pupil's work specimen was considered unsatisfactory because of his failure to observe established tolerances.*
    As used in this sentence, the word tolerances means MOST NEARLY
    A. safety precautions
    B. regard for the rights of others
    C. allowable variations in dimensions
    D. amount of waste produced in an operation

41. *Punishment was severe because the act was considered willful.* 41._____
   As used in this sentence, the word willful means MOST NEARLY
   A. brutal   B. criminal   C. harmful   D. intentional

42. *The malfunctioning of the system was traced to a defective thermostat.* 42._____
   As used in this sentence, the word thermostat means MOST NEARLY a device that reacts to changes in
   A. amperage   B. water pressure
   C. temperature   D. atmospheric pressure

Questions 43-45.

DIRECTIONS: Questions 43 through 45, inclusive, contain words, one of which is misspelled. Indicate the MISPELLED word.

43. A. calendar   B. desirable   C. familar   D. vacuum   43._____

44. A. deteriorate   B. elligible   C. liable   D. missile   44._____

45. A. amateur   B. competent   C. mischeivous   D. occasion   45._____

Questions 46-47.

DIRECTIONS: Questions 46 and 47 consist of four sentences lettered A, B, C, and D. One of the sentences in each group contains an error in grammar or punctuation. Indicate the INCORRECT sentence in each group.

46. A. Give the message to whoever is on duty.   46._____
   B. The teacher who's pupil won first prize presented the award.
   C. Between you and me, I don't expect the program to succeed.
   D. His running to catch the bus caused the accident.

47. A. The process, which was patented only last year is already obsolete.   47._____
   B. His interest in science (which continues to the present) led him to convert his basement into a laboratory.
   C. He described the book as "verbose, repetitious, and bombastic".
   D. Our new director will need to possess three qualities: vision, patience, and fortitude.

Questions 48-50.

DIRECTIONS: Questions 48 through 50 are based on the following paragraph.

A plastic does not consist of a single substance, but is a blended combination of several. In addition to the resin, it may contain various fillers, plasticizers, lubricants, and coloring material. Depending upon the type and quantity of substances added to the binder, the properties, including combustibility, may be altered considerably. The flammability of plastics depends upon the composition and, as with other materials, upon their physical size and condition. Thin sections, sharp edges, or powdered plastics will ignite and burn more readily than the same amount of identical material in heavy sections with smooth surfaces.

48. According to the above paragraph, all plastics contain a
    A. resin
    B. resin and a filler
    C. resin, filler, and plasticizer
    D. resin, filler, plasticizer, lubricant, and coloring material

49. The one of the following conclusions that is BEST supported by the above paragraph is that the flammability of plastics
    A. generally is high
    B. generally is moderate
    C. generally is low
    D. varies considerably

50. According to the above paragraph, *plastics* can BEST be described as
    A. a trade name
    B. the name of a specific product
    C. the name of a group of products which have some similar and some dissimilar properties
    D. the name of any substance which can be shaped or molded during the production process

KEY (CORRECT ANSWERS)

1.	D	11.	A	21.	D	31.	A	41.	D
2.	A	12.	C	22.	D	32.	B	42.	C
3.	D	13.	B	23.	D	33.	D	43.	C
4.	B	14.	D	24.	C	34.	C	44.	B
5.	D	15.	B	25.	C	35.	C	45.	C
6.	C	16.	B	26.	B	36.	A	46.	B
7.	C	17.	C	27.	D	37.	A	47.	A
8.	C	18.	B	28.	B	38.	D	48.	A
9.	B	19.	C	29.	B	39.	B	49.	D
10.	C	20.	B	30.	C	40.	C	50.	C

TEST 2

DIRECTIONS: Each question or incomplete statement is followed by several suggested answers or completions. Select the one that BEST answers the question or completes the statement. *PRINT THE LETTER OF THE CORRECT ANSWER IN THE SPACE AT THE RIGHT.*

Questions 1-4.

DIRECTIONS: Questions 1 through 4 are based on the following paragraph.

To guard against overheating of electrical conductors in buildings, an overcurrent protective device is provided for each circuit. This device is designed to open the circuit and cut off the flow of current whenever the current exceeds a predetermined limit. The fuse, which is the most common form of overcurrent protection, consists of a fusible metal element which when heated by the current to a certain temperature melts and opens the circuit.

1. According to the above paragraph, a circuit which is NOT carrying an electric current is a(n)
    A. open circuit
    B. closed circuit
    C. circuit protected by a fuse
    D. circuit protected by an overcurrent protective device other than a fuse

1.____

2. As used in the above paragraph, the one of the following which is the BEST example of a *conductor* is a(n)
    A. metal table which comes in contact with a source of electricity
    B. storage battery generating electricity
    C. electrical wire carrying an electrical current
    D. dynamo converting mechanical energy into electrical energy

2.____

3. A fuse is NOT
    A. an overcurrent protective device
    B. the most common form of overcurrent production
    C. dangerous because it allows such a strong flow of electricity that the wires carrying it may become heated enough to set fire to materials in contact with them
    D. a safety valve

3.____

4. According to the above paragraph, the MAXIMUM number of circuits that can be handled by a fuse box containing 6 fuses
    A. is 3
    B. is 6
    C. is 12
    D. cannot be determined from the information given in the above paragraph

4.____

Questions 5-7.

DIRECTIONS: Questions 5 through 7 are based on the following paragraph.

Unlined linen hose is essentially a fabric tube made of closely woven linen yarn. Due to the natural characteristics of linen, very shortly after water is introduced, the threads swell after being wet, closing the minute spaces between them making the tube practically water-tight. This type of hose tends to deteriorate rapidly if not thoroughly dried after use or if installed where it will be exposed to dampness or the weather. It is not ordinarily built to withstand frequent service or for use where the fabric will be subjected to chafing from rough or sharp surface.

5. Seepage of water through an unlined linen hose is observed when the water is first turned on.
   From the above paragraph, we may conclude that the seepage
   A. indicates that the hose is defective
   B. does not indicate that the hose is defective provided that the seepage is proportionate to the water pressure
   C. does not indicate that the hose is defective provided that the seepage is greatly reduced when the hose becomes thoroughly wet
   D. does not indicate that the hose is defective provided that the seepage takes place only at the surface of the hose

6. Unlined linen hose is MOST suitable for use
   A. as a garden hose
   B. on fire department apparatus
   C. as emergency fire equipment in buildings
   D. in fire department training schools

7. The use of unlined linen hose would be LEAST appropriate in a(n)
   A. outdoor lumber yard
   B. non-fireproof office building
   C. department store
   D. cosmetic manufacturing plant

Questions 8-15.

DIRECTIONS: Each of Questions 8 through 15 consists of a statement which contains one word that is INCORRECTLY used because it is not in keeping with the meaning that the statement is evidently intended to convey. Determine which word is incorrectly used. Then, select from among the words, lettered A, B, C, or D, the word which, when substituted for the incorrectly used word, would BEST help to convey the meaning of the statement.

8. The lack of emphasis upon fire prevention has helped to promote the purpose for which the department exists—that of preventing loss of life and property from fire.
   A. defeat
   B. disaster
   C. extinguishment
   D. excess

9. A general rule when discovering a fire is to call the fire department at once, simultaneously with the use of extinguishers so that in case the fire is not promptly reported the fire department will be available for such rescues and major firefighting operations as may be necessary.
   A. extinguished   B. preparatory   C. tactics   D. training

10. Considerable research by psychologists indicates that rest periods and uniformity in work assignments tend to reduce the harmful effects of fatigue and monotony.
    A. cause   B. morale   C. stimulating   D. variations

11. The advantage of the automatic fire detection system is that although it gives warning of fire, it does nothing toward checking it.
    A. alarm   B. emergency   C. manual   D. shortcoming

12. Unfortunately, we have become accustomed to letters which are unclear, pamphlets which are models of concise prose and books which do everything except illuminate their subject.
    A. clarify   B. muddled   C. poetic   D. to

13. Large fires are seldom destructive enough to enable a fire department officer to develop, through experience alone, real proficiency in handling them.
    A. frequent   B. planning   C. preventing   D. study

14. In this modern age, progress and growth of our communities have been most rapid and counterbalanced by vast industrial, commercial, and residential expansion.
    A. accompanied   B. economy   C. deterioration   D. technology

15. Often a fire investigator has been encouraged to introduce evidence he obtained at the fire scene because the courts have held that the premises were not guarded; and that anyone could have entered after the fire was extinguished and before the investigators arrived.
    A. cross-examine   B. police   C. unable   D. witnesses

16. Axe handles are usually made of wood rather than steel PRIMARILY because wooden handles _____ steel handles.
    A. can be manufactured at a lower cost than
    B. do not become hot when used near fires as do
    C. cushion the impact to the user more than
    D. do not rust as do

17. Modern firehouses have automatic hose dryers for drying rubber-lined hose after use. The controls are usually set to provide heat no higher than 25°F above room temperature.
    Of the following, the MOST important reason for NOT using more heat is that the
    A. wear and tear on the dryers would become excessive
    B. hose dries more thoroughly if it dries slowly
    C. hose would be too hot to handle
    D. rubber lining would deteriorate too rapidly

18. The one of the following which BEST explains why smoke usually rises from a fire is that
    A. cooler, heavier air displaces lighter, warm air
    B. heat energy of the fire propels the smoke upward
    C. suction from the upper air pulls the smoke upward
    D. burning matter is chemically changed into heat energy

18.____

19. The above diagram shows various types of ramps leading to a loading platform. The ramp which would permit the load to be moved up to the platform with the LEAST amount of force is
    A. 1   B. 2   C. 3   D. 4

19.____

20. The practice of racing a car engine to warm it up in cold weather generally is
    A. *good*, mainly because repeated stalling of the engine and drain on the battery is avoided
    B. *bad*, mainly because too much gas is used to get the engine heated
    C. *good*, mainly because the engine becomes operational in the shortest period of time
    D. *bad*, mainly because proper lubrication is not established rapidly enough

20.____

21. Ice on sidewalks often can be melted by sprinkling salt on it.
    The melting of the ice results from
    A. a chemical reaction between the salt and ice which produces heat
    B. attraction of sun rays by the salt to the ice
    C. lowering of the freezing point of water by the salt
    D. heat of friction caused by persons walking on the salt

21.____

22. Only one of the following four statements relating to the temperature at which water will boil is correct.
    The CORRECT statement is that
    A. water always boils at the same temperature regardless of pressure
    B. water heated slowly by a low lame will boil at a higher temperature than water heated quickly by a high flame
    C. a large quantity of water will boil at a higher temperature than a small quantity
    D. water heated at sea level will boil at a higher temperature than water heated on the top of a mountain

22.____

23. A substance which is a good conductor of heat is MOST likely to be a poor
    A. conductor of electricity
    B. insulator of heat
    C. vibrator of sound
    D. reflector of light

24. The above diagram shows what happens to a bar consisting of iron on one side fastened to brass on the other when it is heated in the flame of a burner.
    The BEST explanation of the curvature of the bar in diagram 2 is that
    A. iron expands more than brass when heated
    B. brass expands more than iron when heated
    C. the iron side of the bar was in the hottest part of the flame
    D. the brass side of the bar was in the hottest part of the flame

25. A load is to be supported from a steel beam by a chain consisting of 20 links and a hook. If each link of the chain weighs 1 pound and can support a weight of 1,000 pounds, and the hook weighs 5 pounds and can support a weight of 5,000 pounds, the MAXIMUM load that can be supported from the hook is MOST NEARLY _____ lbs.
    A. 25,000   B. 5,000   C. 1,000   D. 975

26. Ice formation in water pipes often causes the bursting of the pipes because
    A. the additional weight of ice overloads the pipes
    B. water cannot pass the ice block and builds up great pressure on the pipes
    C. the cold causes contraction of the pipes and causes them to pull apart
    D. water expands upon freezing and builds up great pressure on the pipes

27. Ocean shore areas tend to have less temperature variation between winter and summer extremes than inland areas.
    Of the following, the BEST explanation for this observation is that generally
    A. prevailing winds are from the ocean to land in the summer and from land to the ocean in the winter
    B. inland areas have natural vegetation which absorbs summer heat and then releases it in the winter
    C. water adjacent to shoreline areas absorbs summer heat and then releases it in the winter
    D. warm water ocean currents moderate the temperature of land adjacent to the shoreline

28.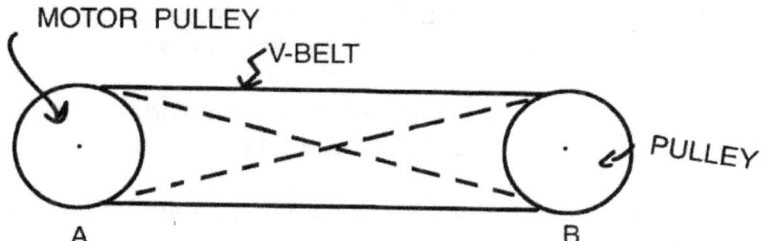

In the above diagram, crossing the V belt as shown by dotted lines will result in
A. pulley A reversing direction
B. no change in the direction of either pulley
C. pulley B reversing direction
D. stoppage of motor

Questions 29-31.

DIRECTIONS: Questions 29 through 31 are based on the following diagram.

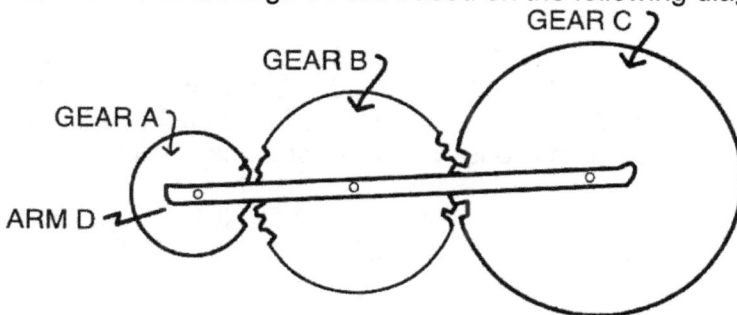

(Assume that the teeth of the gears are continuous all the way around each gear.)

29. Fastening gear A to arm D at another point in addition to its shaft will result in
    A. gear B rotating on its shaft in a direction opposite to gear A
    B. gear C rotating on its shaft in a direction opposite to gear A
    C. arm D rotating around the shaft of gear C
    D. locking of all gears

30. If gear C is fastened to a supporting frame, not shown, so that it cannot rotate and gear A turns clockwise on its shaft, then gear B will turn _____ around the shaft of gear C.
    A. counterclockwise and arm D will turn clockwise
    B. counterclockwise and arm D will turn counterclockwise
    C. clockwise and arm D will turn clockwise
    D. clockwise and arm D will turn counterclockwise

31. If gear B is fastened to a supporting frame, not shown, so that it cannot rotate and arm D rotates clockwise around the shaft of gear B, then for each complete revolution arm D makes, gear A will make _____ than one turn _____ about its own shaft.
    A. more; clockwise   B. less; clockwise
    C. more; counterclockwise   D. less; counterclockwise

32. As a ship sails away from shore, it appears to go below the horizon. The one of the following that BEST explains this observation is that it results from the
    A. rise and fall of tides
    B. curvature of the earth's surface
    C. refraction of light
    D. effect of gravity on moving bodies

33. Of the following, the MOST important reason for lubricating moving parts of machinery is to
    A. reduce friction
    B. prevent rust formation
    C. increase inertia
    D. reduce the accumulation of dust and dirt on the parts

34. A canvas tarpaulin measures 6 feet by 9 feet.
    The largest circular area that can be covered completely by this tarpaulin is a circle with a diameter of _____ feet.
    A. 9   B. 8   C. 7   D. 6

35. The population of Maple Grove was 1,000 in 2015. In 2016, the population increased 40 percent but in 2017, 2018, and 2019, the population decreased 20 percent, 10 percent, and 25 percent, respectively. (For each year, the percentage change in population is based upon a comparison with the preceding year.)
    At the end of this period, the population was MOST NEARLY
    A. 900   B. 850   C. 800   D. 750

Questions 36-38.

DIRECTIONS: Questions 36 through 38 are to be answered on the basis of the diagram that appears below. In this diagram, pulley A and pulley B are both firmly attached to shaft C so that both pulleys and the shaft can turn only as a single unit. The radius of pulley A is 4 inches and that of pulley B is 1 inch.

36. If the weight WA weighs 20 lbs., the system will be in balance if the weight WB weighs _____ lbs.
    A. 5   B. 10   C. 20   D. 80

37. If the rope on pulley A is pulled downward so that it unwinds, the rope on pulley B will
    A. wind slower
    B. wind faster
    C. unwind slower
    D. unwind faster

37.____

38. When pulley A makes one complete revolution, pulley B will make
    A. one-quarter of a revolution
    B. one revolution
    C. four revolutions
    D. a number of revolutions which cannot be determined from the information given

38.____

39. For combustion to take place, the atmosphere must contain at least 12 percent oxygen.
    The MAXIMUM percent of oxygen in an atmosphere which can support combustion is
    A. 21%   B. 25%   C. 50%   D. 100%

39.____

40. The ratio of boys to girls in one school is 6 to 4. A second school contains half as many boys and twice as many girls as the first.
    The one of the following statements that is MOST accurate is that
    A. both schools have the same number of pupils
    B. the first school has 10 percent more pupils than the second
    C. the second school has 10 percent more pupils than the first
    D. there is not sufficient information to reach any conclusion about which school has more pupils

40.____

41. In a certain city, X number of cases of malaria have occurred over a 10-year period, resulting in Y number of deaths.
    The average annual death rate from malaria in this city is
    A. $\dfrac{Y}{10}$ B. $\dfrac{10}{X}$ C. $10 - \dfrac{X}{Y}$ D. $\dfrac{Y(10X)}{X+Y}$

41.____

42. A firefighter's softball team wins 6 games out of the first 9 games. They go on to win all their remaining games and finish the season with a final average of games won of .750.
    The total number of games they played that season was
    A. 10   B. 12   C. 15   D. 18

42.____

Questions 43-45.

DIRECTIONS: Questions 43 through 45 are based on the following diagram.

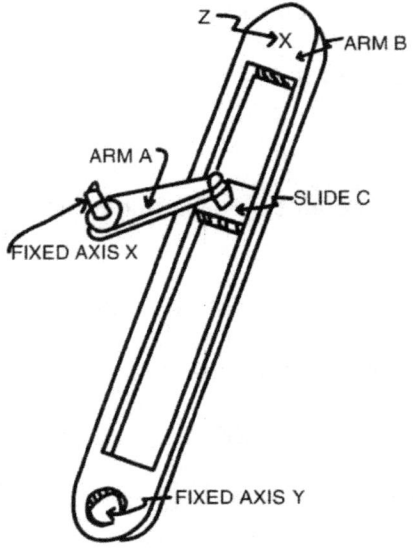

43. If arm A should rotate in a circle, arm B will MOST likely
    A. rotate in a larger circle
    B. move back and forth in an arc
    C. follow an unpredictable eccentric motion
    D. drop to the horizontal and lock

43.____

44. Points X, Y, and Z will be in a straight line _____ of the slot.
    A. only when slide C is at the top
    B. only when slide C is at the bottom
    C. only when slide C is at the mid-point
    D. when slide C is at either the top or the bottom

44.____

45. If arm A should rotate at a constant speed, arm B will MOST likely move at _____ speed(s).
    A. an increasing
    B. a decreasing
    C. a constant
    D. varying

45.____

KEY (CORRECT ANSWERS)

1. A	11. D	21. C	31. A	41. A
2. A	12. B	22. D	32. B	42. B
3. C	13. A	23. B	33. A	43. B
4. B	14. A	24. B	34. D	44. D
5. C	15. C	25. C	35. D	45. D
6. C	16. C	26. D	36. D	
7. A	17. D	27. C	37. A	
8. A	18. A	28. C	38. B	
9. A	19. C	29. D	39. D	
10. D	20. D	30. B	40. C	

EXAMINATION SECTION
TEST 1

DIRECTIONS: Each question or incomplete statement is followed by several suggested answers or completions. Select the one that BEST answers the question or completes the statement. *PRINT THE LETTER OF THE CORRECT ANSWER IN THE SPACE AT THE RIGHT.*

1. A problem which is likely to be found in a hotel fire which is NOT usually found in fires involving other types of residences, such as apartment houses, is
    A. obstructions in hallways and other passageways
    B. large numbers of persons in relation to the number of rooms
    C. delay in the transmission of the fire alarm
    D. many occupants who don't know the location of exits

1.____

2. On his way to work one morning, a firefighter noticed a high tension wire which had been blown down and was lying across the sidewalk and into the road. The one of the following which would be the MOST appropriate course of action for him to take would be to
    A. move the wire to one side by means of a stick or branch of a tree and continue on his way
    B. continue on his way to his firehouse and report the situation to the officer on duty
    C. call the public utility company from the first public telephone which he passes on his way to the firehouse
    D. stand by the wire to warn away passersby and ask one of them to call the public utility company

2.____

3. Generally, firefighters on fire prevention inspection duty do not inspect the living quarters of private dwellings unless the occupants agree to the inspection.
   The BEST of the following explanations of why private dwellings are excluded from compulsory inspections is that
    A. private dwellings seldom catch fire
    B. fires in private dwellings are more easily extinguished than other types of fires
    C. people may resent such inspections as an invasion of privacy
    D. the monetary value of private dwellings is lower than that of other types of occupancies

3.____

4. Fire lines are usually established by the police in order to keep bystanders out of the immediate vicinity while firefighters are fighting the fire.
   Of the following, the BEST justification for the establishment of these fire lines is to
    A. prevent theft of property from partially destroyed apartments or stores
    B. prevent interference with operations of the firefighters
    C. give privacy to the victims of the fire
    D. help apprehend arsonists in the crowd

4.____

5. All probationary firefighters are trained in both engine company and ladder company operations.
   The MOST important reason for training in both types of organizations is that
   A. at any fire it may be necessary for engine company firefighters to perform ladder company duties and vice versa
   B. engine company firefighters can better perform their own functions if they are also trained in ladder company functions and vice versa.
   C. after such training, the probationary firefighters can better decide which type of company he prefers
   D. after such training, the fire department can better decide which firefighters are best suited for each type of company

5.____

6. While on inspection duty, a firefighter discovers the superintendent of a tenement just starting to remove boxes and other material which are blocking hallways. Apparently, the superintendent started removal as soon as he saw the firefighter approach.
   In this situation, it is MOST important that the firefighter
   A. warn the superintendent of the penalties for violation of the Fire Prevention Code
   B. help the superintendent remove the material blocking the hallways
   C. commend the superintendent for his efforts to maintain a safe building
   D. check again, after completing the inspection, to see whether the material has been removed completely

6.____

7. Loss of an official department badge by a firefighter is a serious offense for which disciplinary action may be taken against the member.
   Of the following, the MAIN reason that the fire department regards this loss so seriously is that
   A. badges are expensive and difficult to replace
   B. loss of a badge usually is an indication of poor morale
   C. the person finding any badge might use it for improper purposes
   D. a firefighter must at all times wear proper identification

7.____

8. At 2 A.M. in the morning, a passerby observes a fire in an office building. He immediately starts to run to a nearby corner in order to look for a fire alarm box. After running a few steps, he notices a police telephone box on a lamp post and uses it to report the fire.
   This action is
   A. *good*, chiefly because the police as well as the fire department, respond to fire alarms
   B. *bad*, chiefly because police telephone boxes are not to be used by civilians under any circumstances
   C. *good*, chiefly because the fire department will then receive prompt notification of the fire
   D. *bad*, chiefly because police telephone boxes may be used by the public only for police emergencies

8.____

9. A fire insurance inspector suggested to the manager of a fireproof warehouse that bags of flour be stacked on skids (wooden platforms 6" high, 6x6 feet in area).
   The BEST justification for this suggestion is that in the event of a fire, the bags on skids are less likely to
   A. topple
   B. be damaged by water used in extinguishment
   C. catch fire
   D. be ripped by fire equipment

10. Permitting piles of scrap paper cuttings to accumulate in a factory building is a bad practice CHIEFLY because they may
    A. ignite spontaneously
    B. interfere with fire extinguishment operations
    C. catch fire from a spark or smoldering match
    D. interfere with escape of occupants if a fire occurs

11. High grass and weeds should not be permitted to grow near a building CHIEFLY because, in the event of a grass fire, the weeds and grass may
    A. give off toxic fumes
    B. limit maneuverability of firefighters
    C. interfere with the escape of occupants from the building
    D. bring the fire to the building and set it on fire

12. Visitors near patients in oxygen tents are not permitted to smoke.
    The BEST of the following reasons for this prohibition is that
    A. the flame of the cigarette or cigar may flare dangerously
    B. smoking tobacco is irritating to persons with respiratory disease
    C. smoking in bed is one of the major causes of fires
    D. diseases may be transmitted by means of tobacco smoke

13. At a hot and smoky fire, a lieutenant ordered the members of his company to work in pairs. Of the following, the BEST justification of this order is that
    A. better communications result since one firefighter can bring messages back to the lieutenant
    B. more efficient operation results since many vital activities require two firefighters
    C. better morale results since firefighters are more willing to face danger in pairs
    D. safer operations result since one can help the other if he is disabled

14. Firefighters frequently open windows, doors, and skylights of a building on fire in a planned or systematic way in order to ventilate the building.
    The one of the following which is LEAST likely to be accomplished by ventilation is the
    A. increase in visibility of firefighters
    B. slowdown in the rate of burning of the building
    C. reduction in the danger from toxic gases
    D. control the direction of travel of the fire

15. At the first sign of a fire, the manager of a motion picture theatre had the lights turned on and made the following announcement: *Ladies and gentlemen, the management has found it necessary to dismiss the audience. Please remain seated until it is time for our aisle to file out. In leaving the theatre, follow the directions of the ushers. There is no danger involved.*
    The manager's action in this situation was
    A. *proper*
    B. *improper*, chiefly because he did not tell the audience the reason for the dismissal
    C. *improper*, chiefly because he did not permit members of the audience to leave at once
    D. *improper*, chiefly because he misled the audience by saying that there was no danger

15.____

16. Generally, sprinkler heads must be replaced each time they are used.
    The BEST explanation of why this is necessary is that the sprinkler heads
    A. are subject to rusting after discharging water
    B. may become clogged after discharging water
    C. have a distorted pattern of discharge of water after use
    D. are set off by the effect of heat on metal and cannot be reset

16.____

17. After a fire in an apartment had been brought under control, firefighters were engaged in extinguishing the last traces of the fire. A firefighter who noticed an expensive vase in the room in which activities were concentrated moved it to an empty closet in another room.
    The firefighter's action was
    A. *proper*, chiefly because the owners would realize that extreme care was taken to avoid damage to their possessions
    B. *improper*, chiefly because disturbance of personal possession should be kept to a minimum
    C. *proper*, chiefly because the chance of damage is reduced
    D. *improper*, chiefly because the firefighter should have devoted his efforts to putting out the fire

17.____

18. While standing in front of a firehouse, a firefighter is approached by a woman with a baby carriage. The woman asks the firefighter if he will keep an eye on the baby while she visits a doctor in a nearby building.
    In this situation, the BEST course of action for the firefighter is to
    A. agree to the woman's request but warn her that it may be necessary for him to answer an alarm
    B. refuse politely after explaining that he is on duty and may not become involved in other activities
    C. refer the woman to the officer on duty
    D. ask the officer on duty for permission to grant the favor

18.____

19. Suppose that, while cooking, a pan of grease catches fire.
The one of the following methods which would be MOST effective, if available, in putting out the fire is to
   A. dash a bucket of water on the fire
   B. direct a stream of water on the fire from a fire extinguisher
   C. pour a bottle of household ammonia on the fire
   D. empty a box of baking soda on the fire

19.____

20. Persons engaged in certain hazardous activities are required to obtain a fire department permit or certificate for which a fee is charged.
The MAIN reason for requiring permits or certificates is to
   A. obtain revenue for the city government
   B. prevent unqualified persons from engaging in these activities
   C. obtain information about these activities in order to plan for fire emergencies
   D. warn the public of the hazardous nature of these activities

20.____

21. A firefighter, on his way to work, is stopped by a citizen who complains that the employees of a nearby store frequently pile empty crates and boxes in a doorway, blocking passage.
The one of the following which would be the MOST appropriate action for the firefighter to take is to
   A. assure the citizen that the fire department's inspectional activities will eventually catch up with the store
   B. obtain the address of the store and investigate to determine whether the citizen's complaint is justified
   C. obtain the address of the store and report the complaint to his superior officer
   D. ask the citizen for specific dates on which this practice has occurred to determine whether the complaint is justified

21.____

22. The crime of arson is defined as the malicious burning of a house or property.
The one of the following which is the BEST illustration of arson is a fire in a(n)
   A. apartment started by a four-year-old boy playing with matches
   B. barn started by a drunken man who overturns a lantern
   C. store started by the bankrupt owner in order to collect insurance
   D. house started by a neighbor who carelessly burned leaves in his garden

22.____

23. The fire department now uses companies on fire duty, with their apparatus, for fire prevention inspection in commercial buildings.
The one of the following changes which was MOST important in making this inspection procedure practicable was the
   A. reduction of hours of work of firefighters
   B. use of two-way radio equipment
   C. use of enclosed cabs on fire apparatus
   D. increase in property values during the post-war period

23.____

24. Many fires are caused by improper use of oxy-acetylene torches.
The MAIN cause of such fires is the
    A. high pressure under which the gases are stored
    B. failure to control or extinguish sparks
    C. high temperatures generated by the equipment
    D. explosive nature of the gases used

25. Members of the fire department are permitted to engaged in outside employment during their off-duty time under certain conditions.
However, members are not permitted to work as carpenters specializing in the elimination of violations of the fire prevention code because such work
    A. requires great skill and knowledge
    B. might be inspected by them or other firefighters
    C. may cause injury to the firefighters
    D. would deprive a worker of his means of earning a living

26. *Easily broken or snapped* defines the word
    A. brittle   B. pliable   C. cohesive   D. volatile

27. *At right angles to a given line or surface* defines the word
    A. horizontal   B. oblique
    C. perpendicular   D. adjacent

28. *Tools with cutting edges for enlarging or shaping holes* are
    A. screwdrivers   B. pliers   C. reamers   D. nippers

29. *An instrument used for measuring very small distances* is called a
    A. gage   B. compass   C. slide ruler   D. micrometer

30. When the phrase *acrid smoke* is used, it refers to smoke that is
    A. irritating   B. dense   C. black   D. very hot

31. *The officer gave explicit directions on how the work was to be done.*
As used in this sentence, the word explicit means MOST NEARLY
    A. implied   B. clear   C. vague   D. brief

32. *After the fire had been extinguished, the debris was taken outside and soaked.*
As used in this sentence, the word debris means MOST NEARLY
    A. wood   B. rubbish   C. couch   D. paper

33. *The trapped man blanched when he saw the life net below him.*
As used in this sentence, the word blanched means MOST NEARLY
    A. turned pale   B. sprang forward
    C. flushed   D. fainted

34. *The firefighter and his officer discussed the problem candidly.*
As used in this sentence, the word candidly means MOST NEARLY

35. *The fire truck came <u>careening</u> down the street.* 35.____
 As used in this sentence, the word <u>careening</u> means MOST NEARLY
 A. with sirens screaming
 B. at a slow speed
 C. swaying from side to side
 D. out of control

Question 36.

DIRECTIONS: Question 36 consists of four sentences lettered A, B, C, and D. One of the sentences contains a grammatical error. Indicate the INCORRECT sentence.

36. A. The length of ladder trucks varies considerably. 36.____
 B. The probationary firefighter reported to the officer to whom he was assigned.
 C. The lecturer emphasized the need for we firefighter to be punctual.
 D. Neither the officers nor the members of the company knew about the new procedure.

37. *There are three principal elements, determining the hazard of buildings: the contents hazard, the fire resistance of the structure, and the character of the interior finish, concluded the speaker.* 37.____
 The one of the following statements that is MOST acceptable is that in the above passage
 A. the comma following the word *elements* is incorrect
 B. the comma following the word *buildings* is incorrect
 C. the comma following the word *finish* is incorrect
 D. there is no error in the punctuation of the sentence

Questions 38-40.

DIRECTIONS: Questions 38 through 40, inclusive, contains lists of words, one of which is misspelled. Indicate the MISSPELLED word in each group.

38. A. felony B. lacerate C. cancellation D. seperate 38.____

39. A. battallion B. beneficial 39.____
 C. miscellaneous D. secretary

40. A. camouflage B. changeable C. embarass D. inoculate 40.____

Questions 41-44.

DIRECTIONS: Questions 41 through 44 are based on the following paragraph.

    The canister type gas mask consists of a tight-fitting face piece connected to a canister containing chemicals which filter toxic gases and smoke from otherwise breathable air. These masks are of value when used with due regard to the fact that two or three percent of gas in air is about the highest concentration that the chemicals in the canister will absorb and that these masks do not provide the oxygen which is necessary for the support of life. In general, if flame is visible, there is sufficient oxygen for firefighters although toxic gases may be present. Where there is heavy smoke and no flame, an oxygen deficiency may exist. Fatalities have occurred where filter type canister masks have been used in attempting rescue from manholes, wells, basements, or other locations deficient in oxygen.

41. If the mask described above is used in an atmosphere containing oxygen, nitrogen, and carbon monoxide, we would expect the mask to remove from the air breathed
    A. the nitrogen only
    B. the carbon monoxide only
    C. the nitrogen and the carbon monoxide
    D. none of these gases

42. According to this paragraph, when a firefighter is wearing one of these masks at a fire where flame is visible, he can generally feel that as far as breathing is concerned, he is
    A. *safe*, since the mask will provide him with sufficient oxygen to live
    B. *unsafe*, unless the concentration is below 2 or 3 percent
    C. *safe*, provided the gas concentration is above 2 or 3 percent
    D. *unsafe*, since the mask will not provide him with sufficient oxygen to live

43. According to this paragraph, fatalities have occurred to persons using this type gas mask in manholes, wells, and basements because
    A. the supply of oxygen provided by the mask ran out
    B. the air in those places did not contain enough oxygen to support life
    C. heavy smoke interfered with the operation of the mask
    D. the chemicals in the canister did not function properly

44. The following short-hand formula may be used to show, in general, the operation of the gas mask described in the preceding paragraph:
    (Chemicals in canister) $\rightarrow$ (Air + gases) = Breathable Air.
    The arrow in the formula, when expressed in words, means MOST NEARLY
    A. replace
    B. are changed into
    C. act upon
    D. give off

Questions 45-47.

DIRECTIONS: Questions 45 through 47, inclusive, are based on the following paragraph.

The only openings permitted in fire partitions except openings for ventilating ducts shall be those required for doors. There shall be but one such door opening unless the provision of additional openings would not exceed in total width of all doorways 25 percent of the length of the wall. The minimum distance between openings shall be three feet. The maximum area for such a door opening shall be 80 square feet, except that such openings for the passage of motor trucks may be a maximum of 140 square feet.

45. According to the above paragraph, openings in fire partitions are permitted only for
    A. doors
    B. doors and windows
    C. doors and ventilation ducts
    D. doors, windows, and ventilation ducts

46. In a fire partition 22 feet long and 10 feet high, the MAXIMUM number of doors 3 feet wide and 7 feet high is
    A. 1   B. 2   C. 3   D. 4

47.

    The one of the following statements about the layout shown above that is MOST accurate is that the
    A. total width of the openings is too large
    B. truck opening is too large
    C. truck and door openings are too close together
    D. layout is acceptable

48. At a given temperature, a wet hand will freeze to a bar of metal, but not to a piece of wood, because the
    A. metal expands and contracts more than the wood
    B. wood is softer than the metal
    C. wood will burn at a lower temperature than the metal
    D. metal is a better conductor of heat than the wood

49. Of the following items commonly found in a household, the one that uses the MOST electric current is a(n)
    A. 150 watt light bulb   B. toaster
    C. door buzzer   D. 8" electric fan

50. Sand and ashes are frequently placed on icy pavement to prevent skidding. The effect of the sand and ashes is to increase
    A. inertia   B. gravity   C. momentum   D. friction

KEY (CORRECT ANSWERS)

1. D	11. D	21. C	31. B	41. B
2. D	12. A	22. C	32. B	42. B
3. C	13. D	23. B	33. A	43. B
4. B	14. B	24. B	34. B	44. C
5. A	15. A	25. B	35. C	45. C
6. D	16. D	26. A	36. C	46. A
7. C	17. C	27. C	37. A	47. B
8. C	18. B	28. C	38. D	48. D
9. B	19. D	29. D	39. A	49. B
10. C	20. B	30. A	40. C	50. D

TEST 2

DIRECTIONS: Each question or incomplete statement is followed by several suggested answers or completions. Select the one that BEST answers the question or completes the statement. *PRINT THE LETTER OF THE CORRECT ANSWER IN THE SPACE AT THE RIGHT.*

1. *The suspect was <u>detained</u> until a witness proved he could not have committed the crime.*
   As used in this sentence, the word <u>detained</u> means MOST NEARLY
   A. suspected   B. accused   C. held   D. observed

2. *The firefighter's <u>equilibrium</u> improved shortly after he had stumbled out of the smoke-filled building.*
   As used in this sentence, the word <u>equilibrium</u> means MOST NEARLY
   A. breathing   B. balance   C. vision   D. vigor

3. *The water supply in the tank began to <u>dwindle</u> soon after the pumps were turned on.*
   As used in this sentence, the word <u>dwindle</u> means MOST NEARLY
   A. grow smaller   B. whirl about
   C. become muddy   D. overflow

4. *They thought his illness was <u>feigned</u>.*
   As used in this sentence, the word <u>feigned</u> means MOST NEARLY
   A. hereditary   B. contagious   C. pretended   D. incurable

5. *The officer <u>corroborated</u> the information given by the firefighter.*
   As used in this sentence, the word <u>corroborated</u> means MOST NEARLY
   A. questioned   B. confirmed   C. corrected   D. accepted

6. *Only after an inspection were they even able to <u>surmise</u> what caused the fire.*
   As used in this sentence, the word <u>surmise</u> means MOST NEARLY
   A. guess   B. discover   C. prove   D. isolate

7. *Officers shall report all <u>flagrant</u> violations of regulations or laws by subordinates.*
   As used in this sentence, the word <u>flagrant</u> means MOST NEARLY
   A. glaring   B. accidental   C. habitual   D. minor

Questions 8-10.

DIRECTIONS: Questions 8 through 10, inclusive, are based on the following paragraph.

The average daily flow of water through public water systems in American cities ranges generally between 40 and 250 gallons per capita, depending upon the underground leakage in the system, the amount of waste in domestic premises, and the quantity used for industrial purposes. The problem of supplying this water has become serious in many cities. Supplies, once adequate, in many cases have become seriously deficient, due to greater demands with increased population, and growing industrial use of water. Water works, operating on fixed schedules of water charges, have in many cases not been able to afford the heavy capital expenditures necessary to provide adequate supply, storage, and distribution facilities. Thus, the adequacy of a public water supply for fire protection in any given location cannot properly be taken for granted.

8. The four programs listed below are possible ways by which American communities might try to reduce the seriousness of the water shortage problem. The one of the four programs which does NOT directly follow from the paragraph above is the program of
   A. regular replacement of old street water mains by new ones
   B. inspection and repair of leaky plumbing fixtures
   C. fire prevention inspection and education to reduce the amount of water used to extinguish fires
   D. research into industrial processes to reduce the amount of water used in those processes

8._____

9. The MAIN conclusion reached by the above paragraph is
   A. there is a waste of precious natural resources in America
   B. communities have failed to control the industrial use of water
   C. a need exists for increasing the revenue of water works to build up adequate supplies of water
   D. fire departments cannot assume that they will always have the necessary supply of water available to fight fires

9._____

10. Per capita consumption of water of a community is determined by the formula:

   A. $\dfrac{\text{population}}{\text{total consumption in gallons}}$ = per capita consumption in gallons

   B. $\dfrac{\text{total consumption in gallons}}{\text{population}}$ = per capita consumption in gallons

   C. Total consumption in gallons x population = per capita consumption in gallons
   D. Total consumption in gallons − population = per capita consumption in gallons

10._____

Questions 11-14.

DIRECTIONS: Questions 11 through 14 are based upon the following paragraph.

An annual leave allowance, which combines leaves previously given for vacation, personal business, family illness, and other reasons shall be granted members. Calculation of credits for such leave shall be on an annual basis beginning January 1st of each year. Annual leave credits shall be based on time served by members during preceding calendar year. However, when credits have been accrued and member retires during current year, additional annual leave credits shall in this instance be granted at accrual rate of three days for each completed month of service, excluding terminal leave. If accruals granted for completed months of service extend into the following month, member shall be granted an additional three days accrual for completed month. This shall be the only condition where accruals in a current year are granted for vacation period in such year.

11. According to the above paragraph, if a firefighter's wife were to become seriously seriously ill so that he would take time off from work to be with her, such time off would be deducted from his _____ leave allowance.   11._____
    A. annual
    B. vacation
    C. personal business
    D. family illness

12. Terminal leave means leave taken   12._____
    A. at the end of the calendar year
    B. at the end of the vacation year
    C. immediately before retirement
    D. before actually earned, because of an emergency

13. A firefighter appointed on July 1, 2018 will be able to take his first full or normal annual leave during the period   13._____
    A. July 1, 2018 to June 30, 2019
    B. January 1, 2019 to December 31, 2019
    C. July 1, 2019 to June 30, 2020
    D. January 1, 2020 to December 31, 2020

14. According to this paragraph, a member who retires on July 15 of this year will be entitled to receive leave allowance based on this year of _____ days.   14._____
    A. 15
    B. 18
    C. 22
    D. 24

Questions 11-14.

DIRECTIONS: Questions 15 through 18 are based upon the following paragraph.

During fire operations all members shall be constantly alert to possibility of the crime of arson. In the event conditions indicate this possibility, the officer in command shall promptly notify the Fire Marshal. Unauthorized persons shall be prohibited from entering premises and actions of those authorized carefully noted. Members shall refrain from discussion of the fire and prevent disturbance of essential evidence. If necessary, the officer in command shall detail one or more members at location with information for the Fire Marshal upon his arrival.

15. From the above paragraph, it may be inferred that the reason for prohibiting unauthorized persons from entering the fire premises when arson is suspected is to prevent such persons from   15._____
    A. endangering themselves in the fire
    B. interfering with the firefighters fighting the fire
    C. disturbing any evidence of arson
    D. committing acts of arson

16. The one of the following titles which BEST describes the subject matter of the above paragraph is:
    A. TECHNIQUES OF ARSON DETECTION
    B. THE ROLE OF THE FIRE MARSHAL IN ARSON CASES
    C. FIRE SCENE PROCEDURES IN CASES OF SUSPECTED ARSON
    D. EVIDENCE IN ARSON INVESTIGATIONS

16._____

17. The one of the following statements that is MOST correct and complete is that the responsibility for detecting signs of arson at a fire belongs to the
    A. Fire Marshal
    B. Fire Marshal and officer in command
    C. Fire Marshal, officer in command, and any members detailed at location with information for the Fire Marshal
    D. members present at the scene of the fire regardless of their rank or position

17._____

18. From the above paragraph, it may be inferred that the Fire Marshal usually arrives at the scene of a fire _____ the fire companies.
    A. before
    B. simultaneously with
    C. immediately after
    D. some time after

18._____

19. The air near the ceiling of a room usually is warmer than the air near the floor because
    A. there is better air circulation at the floor level
    B. warm air is lighter than cold air
    C. windows usually are nearer the floor than the ceiling
    D. heating pipes usually run along the ceiling

19._____

20.

DIA. 1   DIA. 2

It is safer to use the ladder positioned as shown in Diagram 1 than as shown in Diagram 2 because in Diagram 1
    A. less strain is placed upon the center rungs of the ladder
    B. it is easier to grip and stand on the ladder
    C. the ladder reaches a lower height
    D. the ladder is less likely to tip over backwards

20._____

21.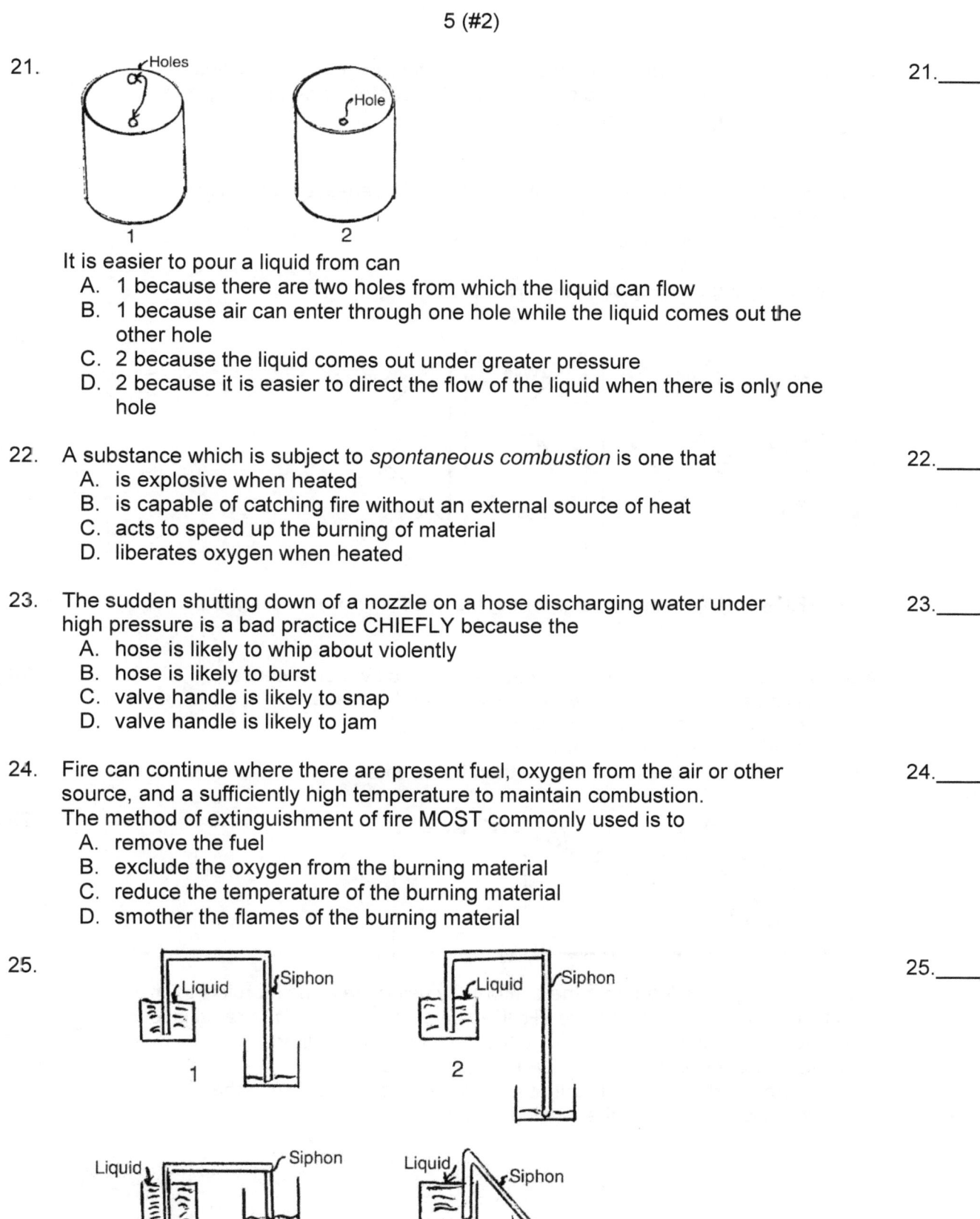

It is easier to pour a liquid from can
- A. 1 because there are two holes from which the liquid can flow
- B. 1 because air can enter through one hole while the liquid comes out the other hole
- C. 2 because the liquid comes out under greater pressure
- D. 2 because it is easier to direct the flow of the liquid when there is only one hole

21.____

22. A substance which is subject to *spontaneous combustion* is one that
- A. is explosive when heated
- B. is capable of catching fire without an external source of heat
- C. acts to speed up the burning of material
- D. liberates oxygen when heated

22.____

23. The sudden shutting down of a nozzle on a hose discharging water under high pressure is a bad practice CHIEFLY because the
- A. hose is likely to whip about violently
- B. hose is likely to burst
- C. valve handle is likely to snap
- D. valve handle is likely to jam

23.____

24. Fire can continue where there are present fuel, oxygen from the air or other source, and a sufficiently high temperature to maintain combustion.
The method of extinguishment of fire MOST commonly used is to
- A. remove the fuel
- B. exclude the oxygen from the burning material
- C. reduce the temperature of the burning material
- D. smother the flames of the burning material

24.____

25.

25.____

The one of the siphon arrangements shown on the preceding page which would MOST quickly transfer a solution from the container on the left side to the one on the right side is numbered
  A. 1   B. 2   C. 3   D. 4

26. Static electricity is a hazard in industry CHIEFLY because it may cause
    A. dangerous or painful burns
    B. chemical decomposition of toxic elements
    C. sparks which can start an explosion
    D. overheating of electrical equipment

27.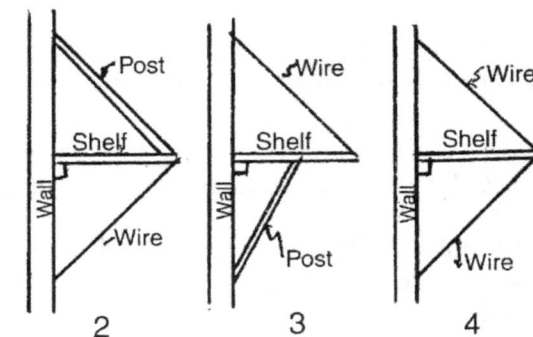

    The STRONGEST method of supporting the shelf is shown in Diagram
      A. 1   B. 2   C. 3   D. 4

28. A rowboat will float deeper in fresh water than in salt water because
    A. in the salt water, the salt will occupy part of the space
    B. fresh water is heavier than salt water
    C. salt water is heavier than fresh water
    D. salt water offers less resistance than fresh water

29.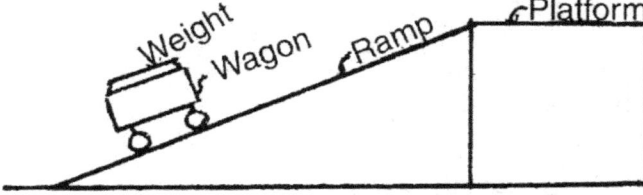

    It is easier to get the load onto the platform by using the ramp than it is to lift it directly onto the platform. This is TRUE because the effect of the ramp is to
    A. reduce the amount of friction so that less force is required
    B. distribute the weight over a larger area
    C. support part of the load so that less force is needed to move the wagon
    D. increase the effect of the moving weight

30.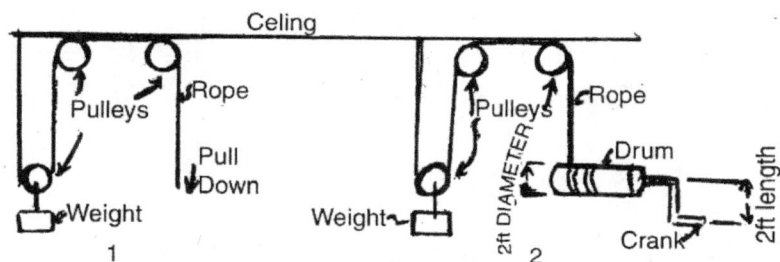

More weight can be lifted by the method shown in Diagram 2 than as shown in Diagram 1 because
- A. it takes less force to turn a crank than it does to pull in a straight line
- B. the drum will prevent the weight from falling by itself
- C. the length of the crank is larger than the radius of the drum
- D. the drum has more rope on it easing the pull

31. As the endless chain is pulled down in the direction shown, the weight will move _____ than the endless chain is pulled down.
- A. up faster
- B. up slower
- C. down faster
- D. down slower

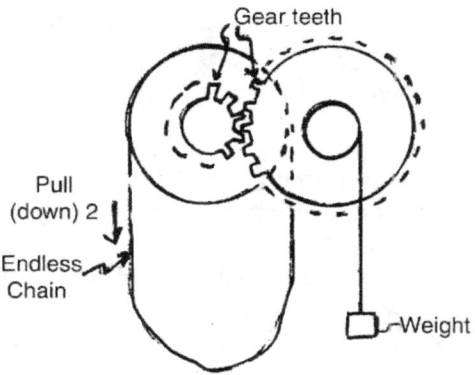

32. Two balls of the same size, but different weights, are both dropped from a 10-foot height.
The one of the following statements that is MOST accurate is that
- A. both balls will reach the ground at the same time because they are the same size
- B. both balls will reach the ground at the same time because the effect of gravity is the same on both balls
- C. the heavier ball will reach the ground first because it weighs more
- D. the lighter ball will reach the ground first because air resistance is greater on the heavier ball

33. It is considered poor practice to increase the leverage of a wrench by placing a pipe over the handle of the wrench.
This is TRUE principally because
- A. the wrench may break
- B. the wrench may slip off the handle
- C. it is harder to place the wrench on the nut
- D. the wrench is more difficult to handle

34.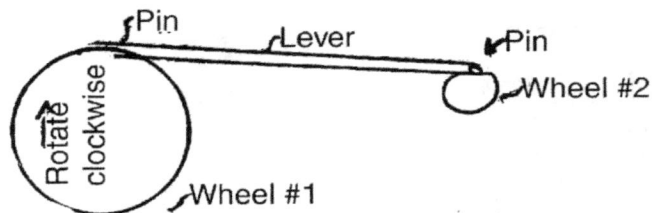

If Wheel #1 is turned in the direction shown, Wheel #2 will
A. turn continuously in a clockwise direction
B. turn continuously in a counterclockwise direction
C. move back and forth
D. become jammed and both wheels will stop

35.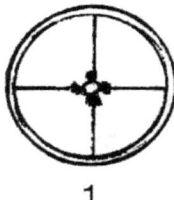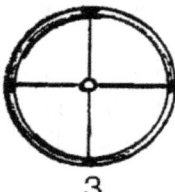

The above diagrams are of flywheels made of the same material with the same dimensions and attached to similar engines. The solid areas represent equal weights attached to the flywheel.
If all three engines are running at the same speed for the same length of time, and the power to the engines is shut off simultaneously,
A. Wheel 1 will continue turning longest
B. Wheel 2 will continue turning longest
C. Wheel 3 will continue turning longest
D. all three wheels will continue turning for the same time

36. The one of the following substances which expands when freezing is
A. alcohol B. ammonia C. mercury D. water

Questions 37-38.

DIRECTIONS: Questions 37 through 38 are to be answered upon the information in the following statement.

The electrical resistance of copper wires varies directly with their lengths and inversely with their cross-section areas.

37. A piece of copper wire 30 feet long is cut into two pieces, 20 feet and 10 feet. The resistance of the longer piece, compared to the shorter, is _____ as much.
A. one-half
B. two-thirds
C. one and one-half
D. twice

38. Two pieces of copper wire are each 10 feet long but the cross-section area of one is 2/3 that of the other.
The resistance of the piece with the larger cross-section area is _____ the resistance of the smaller.
   A. one-half
   B. two-thirds
   C. one and one-half times
   D. twice

39. When drilling a hole through a piece of wood with an auger bit, it is considered good practice to clamp a piece of scrap wood to the underside of the piece through which the hole is being drilled.
The MAIN reason for this is to
   A. direct the auger bit
   B. speed up the drilling operation
   C. prevent the drill from wobbling
   D. prevent splintering of the wood

40.

The arrangement of the lever which would require the LEAST amount of force to move the weight is shown in the diagram numbered
   A. 1   B. 2   C. 3   D. 4

41. A man and boy working together complete a job in 8 hours.
If a boy does half as much work as a man, two men working together can complete the job in _____ hours.
   A. 7½   B. 7   C. 6½   D. 6

42. In a yard 100 feet by 60 feet, a dog is tied by a leash to a stake driven into the ground in the center of the yard.
If the dog is to be kept from going off the property, the MAXIMUM acceptable length of the leash is _____ feet.
   A. 60   B. 50   C. 30   D. 28

43. From a length of pipe 10 feet long, a 3⅓ foot piece is to be cut.
If the diameter of the 10-foot length is 5 inches, the diameter of the piece to be cut will be _____ inches.
   A. 5   B. 2⅓   C. 2   D. 1⅔

10 (#2)

44. A certain crew consists of one foreman who is paid $20.00 per hour, 2 carpenters who are paid $16.80 per hour, 4 helpers who are paid $14.00 per hour, and 10 laborers who ae paid $10.00 per hour.
The average hourly earnings of the members of the crew is MOST NEARLY
   A. $15.20   B. $14.00   C. $13.40   D. $12.40

44._____

45. The fraction which is equivalent to the sum of .125, .25, .375, and .0625 is
   A. 5/8   B. 13/16   C. 7/8   D. 15/15

45._____

KEY (CORRECT ANSWERS)

1. C	11. A	21. B	31. D	41. D
2. B	12. C	22. B	32. B	42. C
3. A	13. D	23. B	33. A	43. A
4. C	14. B	24. C	34. D	44. D
5. B	15. C	25. B	35. C	45. B
6. A	16. C	26. C	36. D	
7. A	17. D	27. A	37. D	
8. C	18. D	28. C	38. B	
9. D	19. B	29. C	39. D	
10. B	20. D	30. C	40. A	

EXAMINATION SECTION
TEST 1

DIRECTIONS: Each question or incomplete statement is followed by several suggested answers or completions. Select the one that BEST answers the question or completes the statement. *PRINT THE LETTER OF THE CORRECT ANSWER IN THE SPACE AT THE RIGHT.*

1. The MOST important reason for having members of the fire department wear uniforms is to
   A. indicate the semi-military nature of the fire department
   B. build morale and esprit de corps of members
   C. identify members on duty to the public and other members
   D. provide clothing suitable for the work performed

   1.____

2. Of the following types of fires, the one which is likely to have the LEAST amount of damage from water used in extinguishment is a fire in a(n)
   A. rubber toy factory
   B. retail hardware store
   C. outdoor lumber yard
   D. furniture warehouse

   2.____

3. When fighting fires involving unevenly piled goods, it is particularly important that the water streams penetrate all parts of the goods exposed to the fire. The position of hose nozzle which will provide MAXIMUM water penetration is
   A. above the fire
   B. to the side away from the wind
   C. on level with the fire
   D. to the side facing the wind

   3.____

4. In cases of suspected arson, it is important that firefighters engaged in fighting the fire remember conditions that existed at the time of their arrival. Particular attention should be given to all doors and windows.
   The MAIN justification for this statement is that knowledge of the condition of the doors and windows may indicate
   A. where the fire started
   B. who set the fire
   C. the best way to ventilate the building
   D. that someone wanted to prevent extinguishment

   4.____

5. While visiting the lounge of a hotel, a firefighter discovers a fire which apparently has been burning for some time and is rapidly spreading.
   Of the following, the FIRST action for him to take is to
   A. find the nearest fire extinguisher and attempt to put out the fire
   B. notify the desk clerk of the fire
   C. send an alarm from the nearest street alarm box
   D. run throughout the hotel and warn all occupants to evacuate the building

   5.____

6. A firefighter inspecting buildings in a commercial area came to one whose outside surface appeared to be of natural stone. The owner told the firefighter that it was not necessary to inspect his building as it was fireproof. The firefighter, however, completed his inspection of the building.
Of the following, the BEST reason for continuing the inspection is that
    A. stone buildings catch fire as readily as wooden buildings
    B. the fire department cannot make exceptions in its inspection procedures
    C. the building may have been built of imitation stone
    D. interiors and contents of stone buildings can catch fire

7. The one of the following which is LEAST valid as a reason for the fire department to investigate the causes of fire is to
    A. determine whether the fire was the result of arson
    B. estimate the amount of loss for insurance purposes
    C. gather information useful in fire prevention
    D. discover violations of the Fire Prevention Code

8. While on duty at a fire, a probationary firefighter receives an order from his lieutenant which appears to conflict with the principles of firefighting taught at the fire school.
Of the following, the BEST course of action for the firefighter to take is to follow the order and at a convenient time, after the fire, to
    A. discuss the apparent inconsistency with his lieutenant
    B. discuss the apparent inconsistency with another officer
    C. mention this apparent inconsistency in an informal discussion group
    D. ask a more experienced firefighter about the apparent inconsistency

9. When fighting fires on piers, the fire department frequently drafts salt water from the harbor.
The CHIEF advantage of using harbor water instead of relying on water from street mains is that harbor water is
    A. less likely to cause water damage
    B. available in unlimited quantities
    C. more effective in extinguishing fires due to its salt content
    D. less likely to freeze in low temperatures due to its salt content

10. Firefighters always try to keep to a minimum the amount of water used in extinguishing a fire without reducing the effectiveness of their operation.
Of the following reasons for firefighters using water sparingly, the LEASE valid is that the use of excess water may
    A. dangerously overload a building and cause its collapse
    B. flood the subway system or damage other public utilities
    C. damage the contents of the building on fire
    D. dangerously reduce the water supply of the city

11. A firefighter on duty at a theatre who discovers standees obstructing aisles should immediately
    A. report the situation to his superior officer
    B. order the standees to move out of the aisles
    C. ask the theatre manager to correct the situation
    D. issue a summons to the usher assigned to that area

12. At a fire on the fourth floor of an apartment house, the first engine company to arrive advanced a hose line up the stairway to the third floor before charging the hose with water.
    The MAIN reason that the firefighter delayed charging their line is that an empty line
    A. is less likely to whip about and injure firefighters
    B. is easier to carry
    C. won't leak water
    D. is less subject to damage

13. Suppose the owner of a burning tenement building complains that, although the fire is located on the first floor, firefighters are chopping holes in the roof. Of the following, the MOST appropriate reason you can give for their action is that the fire can be fought most effectively by permitting
    A. smoke and hot gases to escape
    B. firefighters to attack the fire from above
    C. firefighters to gain access to the building through the holes
    D. immediate inspection of the roof area for extension of the fire

14. The fire department always endeavors to purchase the best apparatus and equipment and maintain them in the best condition.
    The MAIN justification for this policy is that
    A. public confidence in the department is increased
    B. failure of equipment at a fire may have serious consequences
    C. replacement of worn-out parts is often difficult
    D. the dollar cost to the department is less in the long run

15. The one of the following statements about smoke which is MOST accurate is that smoke is
    A. irritating but not dangerous in itself
    B. irritating and dangerous only because it may reduce the oxygen content of the air breathed
    C. dangerous because it may reduce the oxygen content of the air breathed and often contains toxic gases
    D. dangerous because it supports combustion

16. Suppose that you are a firefighter making a routine inspection of a rubber goods factory. During the inspection, you discover some minor violation of the Fire Prevention code. When you call these violations to the attention of the factory owner, he becomes annoyed and tells you that he is the personal friend of high officials in the fire department and the city government.

Under these circumstances, the BEST of the following courses for you to follow is to
- A. summon a police officer to arrest the owner for attempting to intimidate a public official performing his duty
- B. make a very thorough inspection and serve summonses for every possible violation of the Fire Prevention Code
- C. ignore the owner's remarks and continue the inspection in your usual manner
- D. try to obtain from the owner the names and positions of his friends

17. It has been suggested that property owners should be charged a fee each time the fire department is called to extinguish a fire on their property.
Of the following, the BEST reason for rejecting this proposal is that
    - A. delay in calling the fire department may result
    - B. many property owners don't occupy the property they own
    - C. property owners may resent such a charge as they pay real estate taxes
    - D. it may be difficult to determine on whose property a fire started

18. Standpipe systems of bridges in the city all are the dry pipe type. A dry pipe system has no water in the pipes when not in use; when water is required, it is necessary first to pump water into the system.
The MAIN reason for using a dry standpipe system is to prevent
    - A. corrosion of the pipes
    - B. freezing of water in the pipes
    - C. waste of water through leakage
    - D. strain on the pumps

19. Assume that you are a firefighter on your way home after completing your tour of duty. Just as you are about to enter the subway, a man runs up to you and reports a fire in a house located five blocks away. You recognize the man as a simple-minded but harmless person who frequently loiters around firehouses and at fires.
Of the following, the BEST action for you to take is to
    - A. run to the house to see is there really is a fire
    - B. call in an alarm from a nearby telephone
    - C. ignore the report because of the man's mental condition
    - D. call the police and ask that a radio patrol car investigate the report

20. Sometimes a piece of apparatus is ready to leave the fire station before all members are completely dressed and equipped. In order to avoid delay, these firefighters finish dressing on the way to the fire.
This practice, although sometimes necessary, is undesirable MAINLY because
    - A. a poor impression is made on the public
    - B. the firefighters are not able to size up the situation as they approach the fire
    - C. the possibility of dropping equipment from the moving apparatus is increased
    - D. the danger of injury to the firefighters is increased

21. When operating at a pier fire, firefighters usually avoid driving their apparatus onto the pier itself.
    The MAIN reason for this precaution is to reduce the possibility that the apparatus will be
    A. delayed in returning to quarters
    B. driven off the end of the pier
    C. destroyed by a fire that spreads rapidly
    D. in the way of the firefighters

22. Pumpers recently purchased by the fire department are equipped with enclosed cabs. In the past, fire department apparatus was the open type, with no cab or roof.
    The MAIN advantage of the enclosed cab is that it provides
    A. additional storage space for equipment
    B. a place of shelter for firefighters operating in an area of radioactivity
    C. protection for firefighters from weather conditions and injury
    D. emergency first aid and ambulance facilities

23. Heavy blizzards greatly increase the problems and work of the fire department. When such a situation occurs, the fire commissioner could reasonably expected to
    A. order members of the fire department to perform extra duty
    B. limit parking on city streets
    C. station firefighters at fire alarm boxes to prevent the sending of false alarms
    D. prohibit the use of kerosene heaters

24. Regulations of the fire department require that when placing hose on a fire wagon, care should be taken to avoid bending the hose at places where it had been bent previously.
    The MOST important reason for this requirement is that repeated bending of the hose at the same place will cause _____ the hose at those places.
    A. kinks in   B. weakening of
    C. discoloration of   D. dirt to accumulate and clog

25. While fighting a fire in an apartment when the occupants are not at home, a firefighter finds a sum of money in a close.
    Under these circumstances, the firefighter should turn over the money to
    A. a responsible neighbor
    B. the desk sergeant of the nearest police station
    C. the superintendent of the apartment house
    D. his superior officer

26. *When necessary to remove a cornice, every effort should be made to pull it back on the roof.*
    The MOST important reason for the direction in the above quotation is that pulling the cornice on the roof rather than dropping it to the street below
    A. requires less time
    B. is safer for the people on the street

C. makes it possible to re-use the cornice
D. is less dangerous to firefighters working on the roof

27. After a fire has been extinguished, a firefighter often remains at the scene after the others have left.
Of the following, the MAIN reason for this practice is that this firefighter can
   A. prevent looters from stealing valuables
   B. watch for any rekindling of the fire
   C. search the area for lost valuables
   D. examine the premises for evidence of arson

27.____

28. Firefighters usually attempt to get as close as possible to the seat of a fire so that they can direct their hose streams with accuracy. However, intense heat sometimes keeps them at a distance.
The one of the following which is NOT a satisfactory method of overcoming this problem is to
   A. have firefighters use some solid object, such as a wall, as a shield
   B. keep firefighters cool by wetting them with small streams of water
   C. use large high pressure streams and operate at a great distance from the fire
   D. use a water spray to break down the heat waves coming from the fire

28.____

29. Suppose that you are an off-duty firefighter driving your car in the downtown area. As you cross an intersection, you hear sirens and, looking back, see fire apparatus approaching.
In this situation, the BEST action for you to take is to
   A. attempt to clear a path for the fire apparatus by driving rapidly and sounding your horn
   B. drive to the next intersection and direct traffic until the apparatus has passed
   C. permit the apparatus to pass, then follow it closely to the fire, sounding your horn as you drive
   D. pull to the curb, permit the apparatus to pass, then continue on your way

29.____

30. Whenever a public performance is given in a theatre involving the use of scenery or machinery, a firefighter is assigned to be present.
The MAIN reason for this assignment is that
   A. theatres are located in high property value districts
   B. the use of scenery and machinery increases the fire hazard
   C. theatrical districts have heavy traffic, making for slow response of apparatus
   D. emergency exits may be blocked by the scenery or machinery

30.____

Questions 31-46.

DIRECTIONS: Questions 31 through 46, inclusive, test your knowledge of the meaning of words. For each definition, select the word which fits it BEST. Indicate the word in each group.

31. A man who builds with stone, brick, or similar materials is called a(n) 31.____
    A. artisan   B. journeyman   C. laborer   D. mason

32. The path followed by one heavenly body in its revolution about another is called a(n) 32.____
    A. comet   B. meteor   C. orbit   D. satellite

33. To swing backward and forward defines the word 33.____
    A. alternate   B. gesticulate   C. oscillate   D. procrastinate

34. Sphere of authority is called 34.____
    A. constituency   B. dictatorial   C. jurisdiction   D. vassal

35. Gradual decrease in the width of an elongated object is called a 35.____
    A. bevel   B. slope   C. spiral   D. taper

36. To make rows of small holes through a substance defines the word 36.____
    A. penetrate   B. perforate   C. permeate   D. pulsate

37. A situation involving choices between equally unsatisfactory alternatives is called a 37.____
    A. crisis   B. deadlock   C. dilemma   D. farce

38. A statement of self-evident truth is called a(n) 38.____
    A. adage   B. axiom   C. hypothesis   D. theory

39. *The wire connecting the two terminals must be kept taut.* 39.____
As used in this sentence, the word taut means MOST NEARLY without
    A. defects   B. slack
    C. electrical charge   D. pressure

40. *Reaching the summit appeared beyond the capacity of the hikers.* 40.____
As used in this sentence, the word summit means MOST NEARLY
    A. canyon   B. peak   C. plateau   D. ravine

41. *The plot was thwarted by the quick action of the police.* 41.____
As used in this sentence, the word thwarted means MOST NEARLY
    A. blocked   B. discovered   C. punished   D. solved

42. *An abrasive was required by the machinist to complete his task.* 42.____
As used in this sentence, the word abrasive means MOST NEARLY

8 (#1)

43. *The facades of the building were dirty and grimy.*   43.____
    As used in this sentence, the word facades means MOST NEARLY
    A. cellars   B. fronts   C. residents   D. surroundings

44. *Several firefighters were injured by the detonation.*   44.____
    As used in this sentence, the word detonation means MOST NEARLY
    A. accident   B. collapse   C. collision   D. explosion

45. *The foreman was ordered to expedite production of the vital part.*   45.____
    As used in this sentence, the word expedite means MOST NEARLY
    A. accelerate   B. control   C. improve   D. revise

46. *Religious bigotry is repugnant to all true democrats.*   46.____
    As used in this sentence, the word repugnant means MOST NEARLY

Questions 47-50.

DIRECTIONS: Questions 47 through 50, inclusive, relate to the information given in the
              following paragraph and are to be answered in accordance with this
              information.

Division commanders shall arrange and maintain a plan for the use of hose wagons to transport members in emergencies. Upon receipt of a call for members, the deputy chief of the division from whom the members are called shall have the designated hose wagon placed out of service and prepared for the transportation of members. Hose wagons shall be placed at central assembly points, and members detailed instructed to report promptly to such locations equipped for fire duty. Hose wagons designated shall remain at regular assignments when not engaged in the transportation of members.

47. Preparation of the hose wagon for this special assignment of transporting of   48.____
    members would MOST likely involve
    A. checking the gas and oil, air in tires, and mechanical operation of the
       apparatus
    B. removal of hose lines to make room for the members being transported
    C. gathering of equipment which will be needed by the members being
       transported
    D. instructing the driver on the best route to be used

48. Hose wagons used for emergency transportation of members are placed out of   48.____
    service because they are
    A. not available to respond to alarms in their own district
    B. more subject to mechanical breakdown while on emergency duty
    C. engaged in operations which are not the primary responsibility of their
       division
    D. considered reserve equipment

49. Of the following, the BEST example of the type of emergency referred to in the above paragraph is a(n)
    A. firefighter injured at a fire and requiring transportation
    B. subway strike which prevents firefighters from reporting for duty
    C. unusually large number of false alarms occurring at one time
    D. need for additional manpower at a fire

50. A *central assembly point*, as used in the above paragraph, would MOST likely be a place
    A. close to the place of the emergency
    B. in the geographical center of the division
    C. easily reached by the members assigned
    D. readily accessible to the intersection of major highways

KEY (CORRECT ANSWERS)

1.	C	11.	C	21.	C	31.	D	41.	A
2.	C	12.	B	22.	C	32.	C	42.	D
3.	A	13.	A	23.	A	33.	C	43.	B
4.	D	14.	B	24.	B	34.	C	44.	D
5.	B	15.	C	25.	D	35.	D	45.	A
6.	D	16.	C	26.	B	36.	B	46.	B
7.	B	17.	A	27.	B	37.	C	47.	B
8.	A	18.	B	28.	C	38.	B	48.	A
9.	B	19.	B	29.	D	39.	B	49.	D
10.	D	20.	D	30.	B	40.	B	50.	C

TEST 2

DIRECTIONS: Each question or incomplete statement is followed by several suggested answers or completions. Select the one that BEST answers the question or completes the statement. *PRINT THE LETTER OF THE CORRECT ANSWER IN THE SPACE AT THE RIGHT.*

1. Steel supporting beams in buildings often are surrounded by a thin layer of concrete to keep the beams from becoming hot and collapsing during a fire. The one of the following statements which BEST explains how collapse is prevented by this arrangement is that concrete
   A. becomes stronger as its temperature is increased
   B. acts as an insulating material
   C. protects the beam from rust and corrosion
   D. reacts chemically with steel at high temperatures

   1.____

2. If boiling water is poured into a drinking glass, the glass is likely to crack. If, however, a metal spoon first is placed in the glass, it is much less likely to crack.
   The reason that the glass with the spoon is less likely to crack is that the spoon
   A. distributes the water over a larger surface of the glass
   B. quickly absorbs heat from the water
   C. reinforces the glass
   D. reduces the amount of water which can be poured into the glass

   2.____

3. It takes more energy to force water through a long pipe than through a short pipe of the same diameter.
   The PRINCIPAL reason for this is
   A. gravity   B. friction   C. inertia   D. cohesion

   3.____

4. A pump, discharging at 300 lbs. per square inch pressure, delivers water through 100 feet of pipe laid horizontally.
   If the valve at the end of the pipe is shut so that no water can flow, then the pressure at the valve is, for practical purposes,
   A. greater than the pressure at the pump
   B. equal to the pressure at the pump
   C. less than the pressure at the pump
   D. greater or less than the pressure at the pump, depending on the type of pump used

   4.____

5. The explosive force of a gas when stored under various pressures is given in the following table:

Storage Pressure	Explosive Force
10	1
20	8
30	27
40	64
50	125

   5.____

The one of the following statements which BEST expresses the relationship between the storage pressure and explosive force is that
A. there is no systematic relationship between an increase in storage pressure and an increase in explosive force
B. the explosive force varies as the square of the pressure
C. the explosive force varies as the cube of the pressure
D. the explosive force varies as the forth power of the pressure

6.

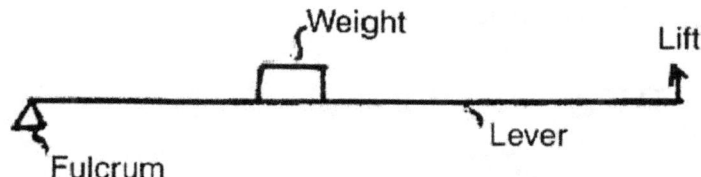

The leverage system in the above sketch is used to raise a weight.
In order to reduce the amount of force required to raise the weight, it is necessary to
A. decrease the length of the lever
B. place the weight closer to the fulcrum
C. move the weight closer to the person applying the force
D. move the fulcrum further from the weight

7. In the sketch shown at the right of a block and fall, if the end of the rope P is pulled so that it moves one foot, the distance the weight will be raised is _____ ft.
A. ½
B. 1
C. 1½
D. 2

8.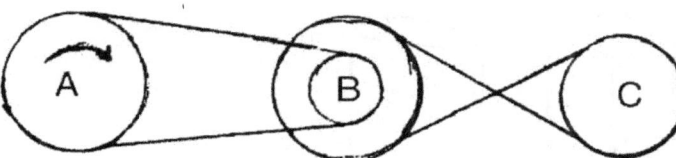

The above sketch diagrammatically shows a pulley and belt system.
If pulley A is made to rotate in a clockwise direction, then pulley C will rotate _____ than pulley A and in a _____ direction.
A. faster; clockwise   B. slower; clockwise
C. faster; counterclockwise   D. slower; counterclockwise

9.

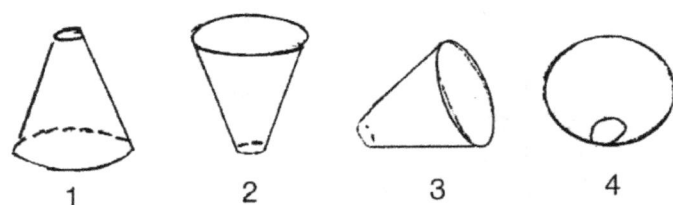

The above diagrams show four positions of the same object.
The position in which this object is MOST stable is
A. 1   B. 2   C. 3   D. 4

10.

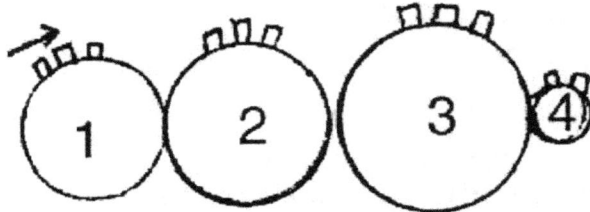

The above sketch diagrammatically shows a system of meshing gears with relative diameters as drawn.
If gear 1 is made to rotate in the direction of the arrow, then the gear that will turn FASTEST is numbered
A. 1   B. 2   C. 3   D. 4

11.

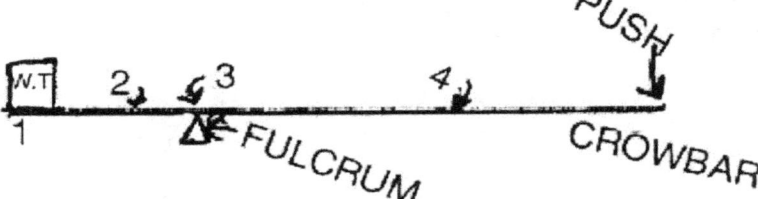

The above sketch shows a weight being lifted by means of a crowbar.
The point at which the tendency for the bar to break is GREATEST at
A. 1   B. 2   C. 3   D. 4

12.

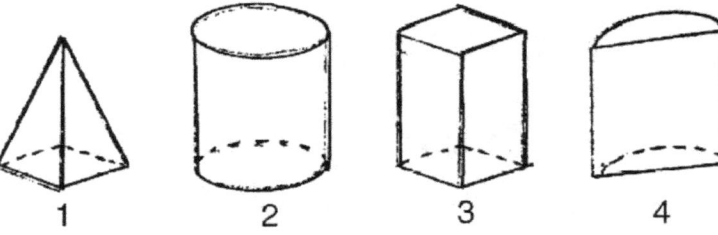

The above sketches show four objects which weigh the same but have different shapes.
The object which is MOST difficult to tip over is numbered
A. 1   B. 2   C. 3   D. 4

13.

An object is to be lifted by means of a system of lines and pulleys.
Of the systems shown above, the one which would require the GREATEST force to be used in lifting the weight is the one numbered
A. 1   B. 2   C. 3   D. 4

14. An intense fire develops in a room in which carbon dioxide cylinders are stored. The PRINCIPAL hazard in this situation is that
   A. the CO_2 may catch fire
   B. toxic fumes may be released
   C. the cylinders may explode
   D. released CO_2 may intensify the fire

15. At a fire involving the roof of a 5-story building, the firefighters trained their hose stream on the fire from a vacant lot across the street, aiming the stream at a point about 15 feet above the roof.
In this situation, water in the stream would be traveling at the GREATEST speed
   A. as it leaves the hose nozzle
   B. at a point midway between the ground and the roof
   C. at the maximum height of the stream
   D. as it drops on the roof

16. A principle of lighting is that the intensity of illumination at a point is inversely proportional to the square of the distance from a source of illumination.
Assume that a pulley lamp is lowered from a position of 6 feet to one of three feet above a desk.
According to the above principle, we would expect that the amount of illumination reaching the desk from the lamp in the lower position, as compared to the higher position, will be _____ as much.
   A. half   B. twice   C. four times   D. nine times

17. A firefighter searching an area after an explosion comes upon a man with a leg injury, bleeding severely and in great pain.
Under these circumstances, the FIRST action the firefighter should take is to attempt to
   A. immobilize the man's leg   B. cover the man with a blanket or coat
   C. stop the bleeding   D. make the man comfortable

18.

 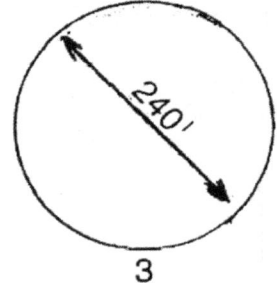 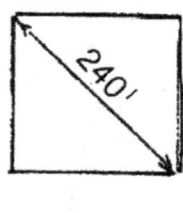

1   2   3   4

When standpipes are required in a structure, sufficient risers must be installed so that no point on the floor is more than 120 feet from a riser.
The one of the above diagrams which gives the MAXIMUM area which can be covered by one riser is
  A. 1   B. 2   C. 3   D. 4

Questions 19-21.

DIRECTIONS: Questions 19 through 21, inclusive, are to be answered on the basis of the following table. Data for certain categories have been omitted from the table. You are to calculate the missing numbers if needed to answer the questions.

	2016	2017	Increase
Firefighters	9,326	9,744	
Lieutenants	1,355	1,417	
Captains		443	107
Others			
	11,469	12,099	

19. The number in the *Others* group in 2016 was MOST NEARLY
    A. 450   B. 475   C. 500   D. 525

20. The group which had the LARGEST percentage increase was
    A. firefighters   B. lieutenants   C. captains   D. others

21. In 2017, the ratio between firefighters and all other ranks of the uniformed force was MOST NEARLY
    A. 5:1   B. 4:1   C. 2:1   D. 1:1

Questions 22-27.

DIRECTIONS: Questions 22 through 27, inclusive, consist of sentences which may be correct or they may contain errors in spelling, grammar, or punctuation. In the space at the right, print the letter
        A if the sentence is correct;
        B if the sentence contains an error in spelling
        C if the sentence contains an error in grammar; and
        D if the sentence contains an error in punctuation.

22. The performance of the apparatus, was evaluated by qualified engineers conducting exhaustive analyses. 22.____

23. The importance of the department's operations is not appreciated sufficiently by the legislative committee that controls appropriations. 23.____

24. Those who have the opportunity to observe and study the shifting scene in the nation's fire service had been aware of the necessity for more dynamic leadership. 24.____

25. The apprentice accidently turned the wrong knob; a violent explosion resulted. 25.____

26. "On this melancholy occasion, the minister said, we must dedicate ourselves anew to the prevention of wanton destruction of lives and property by fire." 26.____

27. Despite the heroic efforts of the volanteer firefighters, the conflagration raged out of control, consuming everything in its destructive path. 27.____

Questions 28-31.

DIRECTIONS: Questions 28 through 31, inclusive, are based on the information given in the following paragraph and are to be answered in accordance with this information.

The principal value of inspection work is in the knowledge obtained relating to the various structural features of the building and the protective features provided. Knowledge of the location of stairways and elevators, the obstruction provided by merchandise, the danger from absorption of water by baled stock, the potential hazard of rupture of containers such as drums or cylinders, and the location of protective equipment, all are essential features to be noted and later discussed in company school and officer's college.

28. According to the above paragraph, the CHIEF value of inspection work is to gather information which will aid in 28.____
    A. fixing responsibility for fires
    B. planning firefighting operations
    C. training new firefighters
    D. obtaining compliance with the Building Code

29. The one of the following objects which would be the MOST help in accomplishing the objective of the inspection as stated in the above paragraph is 29.____
    A. copy of the Building Code   B. chemical analysis kit
    C. plan of the building   D. list of the building's tenants

30. An example of a *structural feature* contained in the above paragraph is the 30.____
    A. location of stairways and elevators
    B. obstruction provided by merchandise
    C. danger of absorption of water by baled stock
    D. hazard of rupture of containers such as drums or cylinders

31. Of the following, the BEST example of what is meant by a *protective feature*, as used in the above paragraph, is 31._____
    A. a fire extinguisher
    B. a burglar alarm
    C. fire insurance
    D. a medical first-aid kit

Questions 32-35.

DIRECTIONS: Questions 32 through 35, inclusive, relate to the information given in the following paragraph and are to be answered in accordance with this information.

Old buildings are liable to possess a special degree of fire risk merely because they are old. Outmoded electrical wiring systems and installation of new heating appliances for which the building was not designed may contribute to the increased hazard. Old buildings have often been altered many times; parts of the structure may antedate building codes; dangerous defects may have been covered up. On the average, old buildings contain more lumber than comparable new buildings which, in itself, makes old buildings more susceptible to fire. It is not true, though, that sound lumber in old buildings is drier than new lumber. Moisture content of lumber varies with that of the atmosphere to which it is exposed.

32. According to the above paragraph, old buildings present a special fire hazard CHIEFLY because of the 32._____
    A. poor planning of the buildings when first designed
    B. haphazard alteration of the buildings
    C. failure to replace worn-out equipment
    D. inadequate enforcement of the building codes

33. We may conclude from the above paragraph that lumber 33._____
    A. should not be used in building unless absolutely necessary
    B. should not be used near electrical equipment
    C. is more inflammable than newer types of building materials
    D. tends to lose its moisture at a constant rate

34. According to the above paragraph, the amount of moisture in the wooden parts of a building depends upon the 34._____
    A. age of the building
    B. moisture in the surrounding air
    C. type of heating equipment used in the building
    D. quality of lumber used

35. In regard to building codes, the above paragraph implies that 35._____
    A. old buildings are exempt from the provisions of building codes
    B. some buildings now in use were built before building codes were adopted
    C. building codes usually don't cover electrical wiring systems
    D. building codes generally are inadequate

8 (#2)

Questions 36-38.

DIRECTIONS: Questions 36 through 38, inclusive, relate to the information given in the following paragraph and are to be answered in accordance with this information.

Fire records indicate that about 10 percent of the total value of fire loss in the United States is due to fires caused by heating equipment, and that insufficient clearance to combustible materials is an important factor in a large percentage of these fires. The need for adequate clearance is emphasized at periods of severe cold weather, when heating equipment is run at full capacity, by a marked increase in the number of fires.

36. In a given year in the United States, 2,000,000 fires caused 10,000 deaths and destroyed $500,000,000 worth of property.
We may conclude from the above paragraph that heating equipment caused
   A. 200,000 fires
   B. fires resulting in the death of 1,000 persons
   C. fire resulting in the destruction of $50,000,000 worth of property
   D. 200,000 fires resulting in the death of 1,000 persons and the destruction of $50,000,000 worth of property

36.____

37. By *clearance to combustible materials*, as used in the above paragraph, is meant
   A. testing laboratory approval for heating equipment
   B. maintaining heating equipment in clean condition
   C. keeping sufficient space between heating equipment and inflammable material
   D. obtaining appropriate permits before installing the heating equipment

37.____

38. The month-to-month changes in the number of fires caused by heating equipment is MOST affected by the
   A. season of the year
   B. amount of clearance to combustible materials
   C. condition of the equipment
   D. long-term trend in fire statistics

38.____

39. Two firehouses are located on the same avenue 10 miles apart. A house located on this avenue somewhere between the two companies catches fire and both companies respond, starting at exactly the same time and reaching the fire at exactly the same time. One engine traveled at an average speed of 20 miles per hour, and the other at an average speed of 30 miles per hour. The number of miles traveled by the faster engine was
   A. 5   B. 6   C. 7   D. 8

39.____

40. Assume that six firefighters are required to operate a piece of apparatus and that each firefighter is on duty 42 hours per week. Assume further that time lost from duty because of vacations, sick leave, and other reasons amounts to 10 percent of the company's manpower.

40.____

Under these conditions, the number of firefighters required to operate this apparatus at full strength around the clock is MOST NEARLY
A. 21 B. 24 C. 27 D. 30

KEY (CORRECT ANSWERS)

1. B	11. C	21. B	31. A
2. B	12. A	22. D	32. B
3. B	13. C	23. A	33. C
4. B	14. C	24. C	34. B
5. C	15. A	25. B	35. B
6. B	16. C	26. D	36. C
7. A	17. C	27. B	37. C
8. C	18. C	28. B	38. A
9. A	19. A	29. C	39. B
10. D	20. C	30. A	40. C

EXAMINATION SECTION
TEST 1

DIRECTIONS: Each question or incomplete statement is followed by several suggested answers or completions. Select the one that BEST answers the question or completes the statement. *PRINT THE LETTER OF THE CORRECT ANSWER IN THE SPACE AT THE RIGHT.*

1. When fighting fires in passenger airplanes, firefighters usually attempt to rescue passengers and crew before putting out the flame.
   To accomplish the rescue, it is usually BEST to approach the burning airplane from the side
   A. where the fire is hottest
   B. where the generators are located
   C. where the reserve gas tanks are located
   D. which is nearest the fire apparatus
   E. where the doors are located

   1.____

2. As soon as the engine pulled up to the scene of the fire, a firefighter, axe in hand, jumped off, ran to the door, and broke it in.
   The action of this firefighter was
   A. *wise*; he prepared the way for the hose firefighters to move in
   B. *unwise*; he should have broken a window
   C. *wise*; speed is important in the rescue of fire victims
   D. *unwise*; he should have tried the door first to see if it was unlocked
   E. *unwise*; he should have first tried to locate the owner

   2.____

3. Firefighters generally try to confine a fire to its point of origin.
   Of the following, the MOST important result of so doing is that
   A. property damage is minimized
   B. shorter hose lines are required
   C. immediate risks to fore forces are reduced
   D. fewer firefighters are needed on the firefighting forces
   E. damage to fire equipment is reduced

   3.____

4. Suppose you, a newly assigned firefighter, are shown how to do a certain task by our lieutenant. You start the job but as you progress you encounter many difficulties.
   Of the following, the MOST desirable step for you to take at this time is to
   A. ask your lieutenant to suggest an easier way of doing the job
   B. speak to your lieutenant about your difficulties
   C. continue the task as well as you can
   D. stop what you are doing and do something else
   E. ask one of the older members for instructions

   4.____

5. The one of the following statements about electric fuses that is MOST valid is that they
   A. should never be replaced by coins
   B. may be replaced by coins for a short time if there are no fuses available
   C. may be replaced by coins provided that the electric company is notified
   D. may be replaced by coins provided that care is taken to avoid overloading the circuit
   E. may be replaced only by a licensed electrician

6. A principal of an elementary school made a practice of holding fire drills on the last Friday of each month, just before normal dismissal.
   In general, conducting fire drills according to a regular schedule is
   A. *good*; pupils are more cooperative when fire drills result in early dismissal
   B. *bad*; fire drills should not be expected
   C. *good*; panic is avoided if the pupils know that there isn't a fire
   D. *bad*; holding fire drills once or twice a term is sufficient
   E. *good*; teachers can plan to finish their lessons before the fire drill

7. It has been observed that persons in a burning building generally attempt to escape through the means provided for normal entry and exit.
   Of the following, the MOST likely reason for this is that
   A. people generally feel safer in groups
   B. people usually don't know the location of fire exits
   C. emergency exits are not easily reached
   D. the use of emergency exits requires physical dexterity
   E. people tend to behave in accordance with their habits

8. A firefighter inspecting a small retail store for hazardous fire conditions is told by the owner that the whole inspection procedure is a waste of time and money.
   Of the following, the BEST action for the firefighter to take is to
   A. question the owner to prove to him how little he knows about the problem
   B. explain to the owner the benefits of the inspection program
   C. curtly tell the owner that he is entitled to his opinions and continue the inspection
   D. ask the owner if he can suggest a better way of preventing fires
   E. continue the inspection without answering the owner

9. The officer in charge of operations at a fire has the responsibility for *sizing up* or evaluating the fire situation.
   Of the following factors, the one which would have LEAST influence on the *size up* is the
   A. time of fire
   B. contents of the building on fire
   C. insurance coverage
   D. amount of smoke
   E. height of the building on fire

10. When searching burning houses, firefighters usually pay particular attention to closets and the space under beds and furniture.
    Of the following, the MOST important reason for this practice is that often

A. information about the cause of the fire may be found there
B. children try to hide from danger in those places
C. dogs and cats are forgotten in the excitement
D. people mistake closet doors for exits
E. valuable possessions may be found there

11. When fighting fires, it is MOST important for a firefighter to realize that in the winter
    A. the water supply is more plentiful
    B. cold water is more effective than warm water in putting out fires
    C. snow conditions may delay fire apparatus
    D. water in hose lines not in use may freeze
    E. many fires are caused by heating equipment

12. Suppose you are a firefighter making an inspection of a factory. During the inspection, the factory manager asks you a technical question which you cannot answer.
    Of the following, the BEST procedure for you to follow is to
    A. tell him you are not there to answer his questions but to make an inspection
    B. guess at the answer so he won't doubt your competence
    C. tell him you don't know the answer but that you will look it up and notify him
    D. give him the title of a textbook that probably would contain the information
    E. change the subject by asking him a question

13. While performing building inspections, a firefighter finds a janitor in the basement checking for a gas leak by holding a lighted match to the gas pipes.
    Of the following, the firefighter's FIRST action should be to
    A. reprimand the janitor for endangering life and property
    B. explain the hazards of this action to the janitor
    C. report the janitor to his superior as incompetent
    D. tell the janitor to put out the match
    E. issue a summons for this action

14. A firefighter has complained to his lieutenant about drafts from loosely fitting windows in the bunk area of the firehouse. Several weeks pass and the condition has not been corrected.
    Of the following, the MOST appropriate action for the firefighter to take at this time is to
    A. ask the captain if the lieutenant has reported his complaint
    B. ask his lieutenant how the matter is coming along
    C. circulate a petition among the other members of the company to have this condition corrected
    D. write to the office of the Chief of the Department about the matter
    E. write to the Uniformed Firefighter's Association about the matter

15. In answering an alarm, it is found that the fire has been caused by *smoking in bed*, setting fire to the mattress. The man is safe but the mattress is blazing. After putting out the flames, the mattress should be
    A. turned over and left on the bed
    B. immediately ripped open and the stuffing examined
    C. taken into the bathroom and soaked in the tub
    D. taken to the street below and the stuffing examined
    E. thoroughly soaked in place by means of a hose stream

16. As a probationary firefighter, you get an idea for improving equipment maintenance and mention it to an older member. At the next company inspection, your superior officer publicly praises this man for his excellent suggestion, but it is your idea.
    The action you should take in this situation is to
    A. tell the other members of the company the whole story after the inspection
    B. ask for advice from another older member
    C. forget about the incident since this man will probably be helpful to you in return
    D. do nothing about it but next time make your suggestions to your superior officer
    E. warn the older man that you won't permit him to get away with stealing your idea

17. The first rule of hose firefighters is to place themselves in the line of travel of a fire whenever possible.
    Of the following, the MOST valid reason for this rule is that
    A. danger to firefighters from heat and smoke is reduced
    B. shorter hose lines are necessary
    C. the opportunity to control the fire is increased
    D. danger to fire equipment is reduced
    E. life-saving rescues are facilitated

18. Of the following types of fires, the one which presents the GREATEST danger from poisonous gas fumes is a fire in a warehouse storing
    A. drugs   B. groceries
    C. cotton cloth   D. paper
    E. unfinished furniture

19. Fires in prisons and mental hospitals are particularly dangerous to life CHIEFLY because their inmates usually
    A. live under crowded conditions
    B. live in locked rooms
    C. ignore fire safety regulations
    D. deliberately start fires
    E. cannot be trusted with fire extinguishers

20. In fighting fires, use the smallest amount of water sufficient to put out the fire. In general, this advice is
    A. *good*, mainly because it will conserve the water supply
    B. *bad*, mainly because it will increase the danger of the fire spreading
    C. *good*, mainly because it will require the use of fewer hose lines
    D. *bad*, mainly because it will take longer to put out the fire
    E. *good*, mainly because it will reduce water damage

21. The fire department has criticized management of several hotels for failure to call the fire department promptly when fires are discovered.
    The MOST probable reason for this delay by the management is that
    A. fire insurance rates are affected by the number of fires reported
    B. most fires are extinguished by the hotels' staff before the fire department arrives
    C. hotel guests frequently report fires erroneously
    D. it is feared that hotel guests will be alarmed by the arrival of fire apparatus
    E. many fires smolder for a long time before they are discovered

22. A firefighter, taking some clothing to a dry cleaner in his neighborhood, noticed that inflammable cleaning fluid was stored in a way which created a fire hazard. The firefighter called this to the attention of the proprietor, explaining the danger involved.
    This method of handling the situation was
    A. *bad*; the firefighter should not have interfered in a matter which was not his responsibility
    B. *good*; the proprietor would probably remove the hazard and be more careful in the future
    C. *bad*; the firefighter should have reported the situation to the fire inspector's office without saying anything to the proprietor
    D. *good*; since the firefighter was a customer, he should treat the proprietor more leniently than he would treat other violators
    E. *bad*; the firefighter should have ordered the proprietor to remove the violation immediately and issued a summons

23. Traditionally, firefighters have attacked fires with solid streams of water from hose lines. A new development in firefighting is to break up the solid water stream as it leaves the hose nozzle into a large number of tiny droplets, called a fog stream.
    Of the following claimed advantages of a solid stream, as compared to a fog stream, the one that is MOST valid is that a solid stream
    A. has greater cooling effect per gallon of water
    B. causes less water damage
    C. results in less drain on the water supply
    D. involves less risk of walls collapsing
    E. can be used at a greater distance from the fire

24. A firefighter caught a civilian attempting to re-enter a burning building despite several warnings to stay outside of the fire lines. The civilian insisted frantically that he must save some very valuable documents from the fire. The firefighter then called a police officer to remove the civilian.
    The firefighter's action was
    A. *wrong*; it is bad public relations to order people about
    B. *right*; the firefighter is charged with the responsibility of protecting lives
    C. *wrong*; the firefighter should have explained to the civilian why he should not enter the building
    D. *right*; civilians must be excluded from the fire zone
    E. *wrong*; every person has a right to risk his own life as he sees it

25. A lieutenant orders a firefighter to open the windows in a room filled with smoke. He starts with the window nearest the entrance and follows the wall around the room until all the windows are opened.
    The MOST important reason for using this procedure is that he can
    A. avoid stumbling over furniture
    B. breathe the fresher air near the walls
    C. locate unconscious persons at the same time
    D. avoid the weakened floor in the middle of the room
    E. find his way back to the entrance

26. One purpose of building inspections is to enable the fire department to plan its operations before a fire starts.
    This statement is
    A. *incorrect*; no two fires are alike
    B. *correct*; many firefighting problems can be anticipated
    C. *incorrect*; fires should be prevented, not extinguished
    D. *correct*; the fire department should have detailed plans for every possible emergency
    E. *incorrect*; fires are not predictable

27. A recent study showed that false alarms occur mostly between Noon and 1 P.M., and between 3 and 10 P.M.
    The MOST likely explanation of these results is many false alarms are sent by
    A. school children   B. drunks
    C. mentally handicapped   D. arsonists
    E. accident victims

28. A superintendent of a large apartment house discovered a fire in a vacant apartment. After notifying the fire department, he went to the basement and shut off the central air conditioning system.
    In so doing, the superintendent acted
    A. *wisely*; escape of gas fumes from the air conditioning system was prevented
    B. *unwisely*; the fire would have been slowed down by the cooling effect of the air conditioning

C. *wisely*; the air conditioning system was protected from damage by the fire
D. *unwisely*; the air conditioning system would have expelled smoke from the building
E. *wisely*; spread of the fire by means of a force draft was prevented

29. Large woolen blankets are unsatisfactory as emergency life nets CHIEFLY because they usually are
    A. too small to catch a falling person
    B. difficult to grasp since they have no handles
    C. difficult to maneuver into position
    D. not circular in shape as are regular life nets
    E. not tensile enough to hold falling bodies

30. Fires can be fought most effectively from close range.
    Of the following, the CHIEF obstacle preventing firefighters from getting close to fires is the
    A. heat of the fire
    B. height of most city buildings
    C. distance from the hydrants of most fires
    D. inaccessible location of most fires
    E. wide area covered by the fire

31. While in training school, your class assists at a fire. After the fire is under control, an older firefighter, who has no authority over you, tells you that he was watching you perform your tasks. He suggests certain changes in your methods.
    Of the following, your BEST course of action is to
    A. thank him for his advice and tell him you will use it when you find yourself in difficulty
    B. discuss the changes he proposed with him and then take the action which seems best to you
    C. listen to his analysis of the situation and follow his advice
    D. thank him for his advice and bring up his suggestions at the next class session
    E. listen to him, thank him courteously, but ignore his suggestions

32. A member of a fire rescue company discovers an injured man at the foot of the stairway on the third floor of a burning building. The man, who fell down the stairs, complains of pains in his back. The fire is a considerable distance away, in the cellar, but the area is rapidly filling with smoke.
    Of the following, the BEST course for the firefighter to follow is to
    A. give the injured man first aid on the spot and leave him there
    B. carefully carry the injured man to safety
    C. stay with the injured man to make certain that the fire doesn't reach him
    D. find his officer and ask for instructions
    E. go for medical assistance

33. Listed below are five operating characteristics of most automatic sprinkler systems.
The one characteristic of those listed which is LEAST desirable is that automatic sprinkler systems
   A. operate only in the fire zone
   B. go into operation soon after a fire starts
   C. operate in the midst of high heat and smoke
   D. continue operating after the fire is extinguished
   E. operate in inaccessible places

34. *The extinguisher must be inverted before it will operate.*
As used in this sentence, the word inverted means MOST NEARLY
   A. turned over   B. completely filled   C. lightly shaken
   D. unhooked   E. opened

35. *Sprinkler systems in buildings can retard the spread of fires.*
As used in this sentence, the word retard means MOST NEARLY
   A. quench   B. outline   C. slow
   D. reveal   E. aggravate

36. *Although there was widespread criticism, the director refused to curtail the program.*
As used in this sentence, the word curtail means MOST NEARLY
   A. change   B. discuss   C. shorten
   D. expand   E. enforce

37. *Argon is an inert gas.*
As used in this sentence, the word inert means MOST NEARLY
   A. unstable   B. uncommon   C. volatile
   D. inferior   E. inactive

38. *The firefighters turned their hoses on the shed and the main building simultaneously.*
As used in this sentence, the word simultaneously means MOST NEARLY
   A. in turn   B. without hesitation
   C. with great haste   D. as needed
   E. at the same time

39. *The officer was rebuked for his failure to act promptly.*
As used in this sentence, the word rebuked means MOST NEARLY
   A. demoted   B. reprimanded   C. discharged
   D. reassigned   E. suspended

40. *Parkways in the city may be used to facilitate responses to alarms.*
As used in this sentence, the word facilitate means MOST NEARLY
   A. reduce   B. alter   C. complete
   D. ease   E. control

41. *Fire extinguishers are most effective when the fire is incipient.*
    As used in this sentence, the word incipient means MOST NEARLY
    A. accessible   B. beginning   C. red hot
    D. confined   E. smoky

42. *It is important to convey to new members the fundamental methods of firefighting.*
    As used in this sentence, the words convey to means MOST NEARLY
    A. inquire   B. prove for   C. confirm for
    D. suggest to   E. impart to

43. *The explosion was a graphic illustration of the effects of neglect and carelessness.*
    As used in this sentence, the word graphic means MOST NEARLY
    A. terrible   B. poor   C. typical
    D. unique   E. vivid

44. *The firefighter was assiduous in all things relating to his duties.*
    As used in this sentence, the word assiduous means MOST NEARLY
    A. aggressive   B. careless   C. persistent
    D. cautious   E. dogmatic

45. *A firefighter must be adept to be successful at his work.*
    As used in this sentence, the word adept means MOST NEARLY
    A. ambitious   B. strong   C. agile
    D. alert   E. skillful

46. *Officers shall see that parts are issued in consecutive order.*
    As used in this sentence, the word consecutive means MOST NEARLY
    A. objective   B. random   C. conducive
    D. effective   E. successive

47. *Practically every municipality has fire ordinances.*
    As used in this sentence, the word ordinances means MOST NEARLY
    A. drills   B. stations   C. engines
    D. laws   E. problems

48. *When the smoke cleared away, the firefighter's task was alleviated.*
    As used in this sentence, the word alleviated means MOST NEARLY
    A. lessened   B. visible   C. appreciated
    D. safer   E. accomplished

49. *The conflagration spread throughout the entire city.*
    As used in this sentence, the word conflagration means MOST NEARLY
    A. hostilities B. confusion   C. rumor
    D. epidemic   E. fire

10 (#1)

50. *The firefighter <u>purged</u> the gas tank after emptying its contents.*
    As used in this sentence, the word <u>purged</u> means MOST NEARLY
    A. sealed
    B. punctured
    C. exposed
    D. cleansed
    E. buried

50.____

KEY (CORRECT ANSWERS)

1.	E	11.	D	21.	D	31.	D	41.	B
2.	D	12.	C	22.	B	32.	B	42.	E
3.	A	13.	D	23.	E	33.	D	43.	E
4.	B	14.	B	24.	B	34.	A	44.	C
5.	A	15.	D	25.	E	35.	C	45.	E
6.	B	16.	D	26.	B	36.	C	46.	E
7.	E	17.	C	27.	A	37.	E	47.	D
8.	B	18.	A	28.	E	38.	E	48.	A
9.	C	19.	B	29.	E	39.	B	49.	E
10.	B	20.	E	30.	A	40.	D	50.	D

TEST 2

DIRECTIONS: Each question or incomplete statement is followed by several suggested answers or completions. Select the one that BEST answers the question or completes the statement. *PRINT THE LETTER OF THE CORRECT ANSWER IN THE SPACE AT THE RIGHT.*

1. Spontaneous combustion may be the reason for a pile of oily rags catching fire.
   In general, spontaneous combustion is the direct result of
   A. application of flame
   B. falling sparks
   C. intense sunlight
   D. chemical action
   E. radioactivity

   1.____

2. In general, firefighters are advised not to direct a solid stream of water on fres burning in electrical equipment.
   Of the following, the MOST logical reason for this instruction is that
   A. water is a conductor of electricity
   B. water will do more damage to the electrical equipment than the fire
   C. hydrogen in water may explode when it comes in contact with electric current
   D. water will not effectively extinguish fires in electrical equipment
   E. water may spread the fire to other circuits

   2.____

3. The height at which a fireboat will float in still water is determined CHIEFLY by the
   A. weight of the water displaced by the boat
   B. horsepower of the boat's engine
   C. number of propellers on the boat
   D. curve the bow has above the water line
   E. skill with which the boat is maneuvered

   3.____

4. When firefighters are working at the nozzle of a hose, they usually lean forward on the hose.
   The MOST likely reason for taking this position is that
   A. the surrounding air is cool, making the firefighters more comfortable
   B. a backward force is developed which must be counteracted
   C. the firefighters can better see where the stream strikes
   D. the firefighters are better protected from injury by falling debris
   E. the stream is projected further

   4.____

5. In general, the color and odor of smoke will BEST indicate
   A. the cause of the fire
   B. the extent of the fire
   C. how long the fire has been burning
   D. the kind of material on fire
   E. the exact seat of the fire

   5.____

6. As a demonstration, firefighters set up two hose lines identical in every respect except that one was longer than the other. Water was then delivered through these lines from one pump and it was seen that the stream from the longer hose line had a shorter *throw*.
Of the following, the MOST valid explanation of this difference in *throw* is that the
   A. air resistance to the water stream is proportional to the length of hose
   B. time required for water to travel through the longer hose is greater than for the shorter one
   C. loss due to friction is greater in the longer hose than in the shorter one
   D. rise of temperature is greater in the longer hose than in the shorter one
   E. longer hose line probably developed a leak at one of the coupling joints

6._____

7. Of the following toxic gases, the one which is MOST dangerous because it cannot be seen and has no odor is
   A. ether
   B. carbon monoxide
   C. chlorine
   D. ammonia
   E. cooking gas

7._____

8. You are visiting with some friends when their young son rushes into the room with his clothes on fire. You immediately wrap him in a rug and roll him on the floor.
The MOST important reason for your action is that the
   A. flames are confined within the rug
   B. air supply to the fire is reduced
   C. burns sustained will be third degree, rather than first degree
   D. whirling action will put out the fire
   E. boy will not suffer from shock

8._____

9. A firefighter discovers a man bleeding moderately from a gash wound about 1½" long in his right arm.
Of the following, the FIRST action this firefighter should take is to
   A. apply a tourniquet between the wound and the heart
   B. permit the bleeding to continue for a while in order to cleanse the wound
   C. give the injured man a blood transfusion
   D. apply pressure at the nearest pressure point between the wound and the heart
   E. apply pressure directly to the wound with compress

9._____

10. In treating burns, the LEAST important of the following goals is to
    A. prevent blistering
    B. prevent infection
    C. relieve pain
    D. prevent shock
    E. prevent tissue damage

10._____

11. The Battalion District in Manhattan is bounded on the north by Fifth Avenue, the west by the Hudson River, the south by 30th Street, and the east by Madison Avenue.
The above statement is WRONG in that
    A. none of the boundary lines intersect
    B. Fifth Avenue cannot be a northern boundary

11._____

C. the Hudson River cannot be a western boundary
D. 30th Street cannot be a southern boundary
E. Madison Avenue cannot be an eastern boundary

12. Of the following, the MAIN reason the Police Department is using some unmarked or unidentified patrol cars is to
    A. catch car thieves red-handed
    B. observe police officers in the performance of their duty
    C. reduce the expense of police equipment
    D. trap juvenile gangs
    E. reduce the number of traffic accidents

12.____

Questions 13-16.

DIRECTIONS: Questions 13 through 16, inclusive, are based upon the following paragraph.

Ventilation, as used in firefighting operations, means opening up a building or structure in which a fire is burning to release the accumulated heat, smoke, and gases. Lack of knowledge of the principles of ventilation on the part of firefighters may result in unnecessary punishment due to ventilation being neglected or improperly handled. While ventilation itself extinguishes o fires, when used in an intelligent manner, it allows firefighters to get at the fire more quickly, easily, and with less danger and hardship.

13. According to the above paragraph, the MOST important result of failure to apply the principles of ventilation at a fire may be
    A. loss of public confidence
    B. disciplinary action
    C. waste of water
    D. excessive use of equipment
    E. injury to firefighters

13.____

14. It may be inferred from the above paragraph that the CHIEF advantage of ventilation is that it
    A. eliminates the need for gas masks
    B. reduces smoke damage
    C. permits firefighters to work closer to the fire
    D. cools the fire
    E. enables firefighters to use shorter hose lines

14.____

15. Knowledge of the principles of ventilation, as defined in the above paragraph, would be LEAST important in a fire in a
    A. tenement house   B. grocery store   C. ship's hold
    D. lumberyard   E. office building

15.____

16. We may conclude from the above paragraph that for the well-trained and equipped firefighters, ventilation is
    A. a simple matter   B. rarely necessary
    C. relatively unimportant D. a basic tool
    E. sometimes a handicap

16.____

Questions 17-19.

DIRECTIONS: Questions 17 through 19 are based upon the following paragraph.

A fire of undetermined origin started in the warehouse shed of a flour mill. Although there was some delay in notifying the fire department, they practically succeeded in bringing the fire under control when a series of dust explosions occurred which caused the fire to spread and the main building was destroyed. The fire department's efforts were considerably handicapped because it was undermanned, and the water pressure in the vicinity was inadequate

17. From the information contained in the above paragraph, it is MOST accurate to state that the cause of the fire was
    A. suspicious
    B. unknown
    C. accidental
    D. arson
    E. spontaneous combustion

18. In the fire described above, the MOST important cause of the fire spreading to the main building was the
    A. series of dust explosions
    B. delay in notifying the fire department
    C. inadequate water pressure
    D. lack of manpower
    E. wooden construction of the building

19. In the fire described above, the fire department's efforts were handicapped CHIEFLY by
    A. poor leadership
    B. outdated apparatus
    C. uncooperative company employees
    D. insufficient water pressure
    E. poorly trained firefighters

Questions 20-22.

DIRECTIONS: Questions 20 through 22, inclusive, are based upon the following paragraph.

A flameproof fabric is defined as one which, when exposed to small sources of ignition such as sparks or smoldering cigarettes, does not burn beyond the vicinity of the source of the ignition Cotton fabrics are the materials commonly used that are considered most hazardous. Other materials, such as acetate rayons and linens, are somewhat less hazardous, and woolens and some natural silk fabrics, even when untreated, are about the equal of the average treated cotton fabric insofar as flame spread and ease of ignition are concerned. The method of application is to immerse the fabric in a flameproofing solution. The container used must be large enough so that all the fabric is thoroughly wet and there are no folds which the solution does not penetrate.

20. According to the above paragraph, a flameproof fabric is one which
    A. is unaffected by heat and smoke
    B. resists the spread of flames when ignited
    C. burns with a cold flame
    D. cannot be ignited by sparks or cigarettes
    E. may smolder but cannot burn

21. According to the above paragraph, woolen fabrics which have not been flameproofed are as likely to catch fire as _____ fabrics.
    A. treated silk
    B. treated acetate rayon
    C. untreated linen
    D. untreated synthetic
    E. treated cotton

22. In the method described above, the flameproofing solution is BEST applied to the fabric by _____ the fabric.
    A. sponging
    B. spraying
    C. dipping
    D. brushing
    E. sprinkling

Questions 23-26.

DIRECTIONS: Questions 23 through 26, inclusive, are based upon the following paragraph.

There is hardly a city in the country that is not short of fire protection in some areas within its boundaries. These municipalities have spread out and have re-shuffled their residential, business, and industrial districts without readjusting the existing protective fire forces, or creating new protection units. Fire stations are still situated according to the needs of earlier times and have not been altered or improved to house modern firefighting equipment. They are neither efficient for carrying out their tasks nor livable for the men who must occupy them.

23. Of the following, the title which BEST describes the central idea of the above paragraph is THE
    A. DYNAMIC NATURE OF CONTEMPORARY SOCIETY
    B. COST OF FIRE PROTECTION
    C. LOCATION AND DESIGN OF FIRE STATIONS
    D. DESIGN AND USE OF FIREFIGHTING EQUIPMENT
    E. GROWTH OF AMERICAN CITIES

24. According to the above paragraph, fire protection is inadequate in the United States in _____ areas _____ cities.
    A. most; of some
    B. some; of most
    C. some; in all
    D. all; in some
    E. most; in most

25. The one of the following criteria for planning of fire stations which is NOT mentioned in the above paragraph is
    A. comfort of firefighters
    B. proper location
    C. design for modern equipment
    D. efficiency of operation
    E. cost of construction

26. Of the following suggestions for improving the fire service, the one which would BEST deal with the problem discussed in the above paragraph would involve
    A. specialized training in the use of modern apparatus
    B. replacement of obsolete fire apparatus
    C. revision of zoning laws
    D. longer basic training for probationary firefighters
    E. reassignment of fire districts

26.____

Questions 27-29.

DIRECTIONS: The sentence listed below are part of a meaningful paragraph, but they are not given in their proper order. You are to decide what would be the BEST order in which to put the sentences so as to form a well-organized paragraph. Each sentence has a place in the paragraph; there are no extra sentences. You are then to answer Questions 27 through 29, inclusive, on the basis of your rearrangement of these scrambled sentences into a properly organized paragraph. It will help you in answering the questions to jot down the correct order of the sentences in the margins.

In 1887, some insurance companies organized an Inspection Department to advise their clients on all phases of fire prevention and protection. Probably this has been due to the smaller annual fire losses in Great Britain than in the United States. It tests various fire prevention devices and appliances and determines manufacturing hazards and their safeguards. Fire research began earlier in the United States and is more advanced than in Great Britain. Later, they established a laboratory specializing in electrical, mechanical, hydraulic, and chemical fields.

27. When the five sentences above are arranged in proper order, the paragraph starts with the sentence which begins
    A. In 1887   B. Probably this   C. It tests
    D. Fire research   E. Later they

27.____

28. In the last sentence listed above, *they* refers to
    A. insurance companies
    B. the United States and Great Britain
    C. the Inspection Department
    D. clients
    E. technicians

28.____

29. When the above paragraph is properly arranged, it ends with the words
    A. ...protection   B. ...the United States
    C. ...their safeguards   D. ...in Great Britain
    E. ...chemical fields

29.____

7 (#2)

Questions 30-32.

DIRECTIONS: Questions 30 through 32, inclusive, are to be answered with reference to the device shown below.

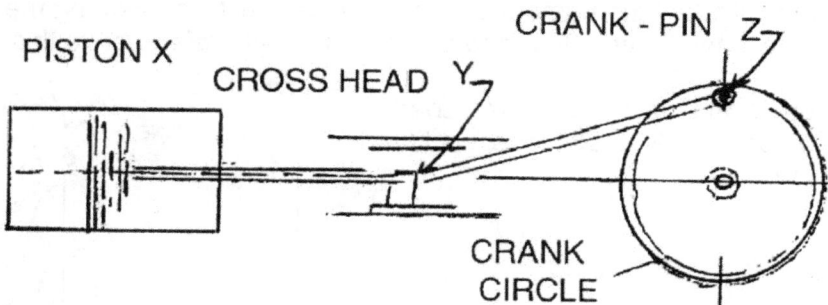

30. Assume that piston X is placed in its extreme left position so that X, Y, and Z are in a horizontal line.
If a horizontal force to the right is applied to the piston X, we may then expect that
   A. the crank-pin Z will revolve clockwise
   B. the crosshead Y will move in a direction opposite to that of X
   C. the crank-pin Z will revolve counterclockwise
   D. no movement will take place
   E. the crank-pin Z will oscillate back and forth

30.____

31. If we start from the position shown in the above diagram above and move piston X to the right, the result will be that
   A. the crank-pin Z will revolve counterclockwise and crosshead Y will move to the left
   B. the crank-pin Z will revolve clockwise and crosshead Y will move to the left
   C. the crank-pin Z will revolve counterclockwise and crosshead Y will move to the right
   D. the crank-pin Z will revolve clockwise and crosshead Y will move to the right
   E. cross Y will move to the left as piston X moves to the right

31.____

32. If crank-pin Z is moved closer to the center of the crank circle, then the length of the
   A. stroke of piston X is increased
   B. stroke of piston X is decreased
   C. stroke of piston X is unchanged
   D. rod between the piston X and crosshead Y is increased
   E. rod between the piston X and crosshead Y is decreased

32.____

Questions 33-34.

DIRECTIONS: The following figure represents schematically a block and fall tackle. The advantage derived from this machine is that the effect of the applied force is multiplied by the number of lines of rope directly supporting the load. Questions 33 and 34 are to be answered with reference to this figure.

33. Pull P is exerted on Line T to raise the Load L. The line in which the LARGEST strain is finally induced is line
    A. T
    B. U
    C. V
    D. X
    E. Y

34. If the largest pull P that two men can apply to Line T is 280 lbs., the MAXIMUM load L that they can raise without regard to frictional losses is MOST NEARLY _____ lbs.
    A. 1960
    B. 1680
    C. 1400
    D. 1260
    E. 1120

35. *Rules must be applied with discretion.*
    As used in this sentence, the word discretion means MOST NEARLY
    A. impartiality   B. judgment   C. severity
    D. patience   E. consistency

36. *The officer and his men ascended the stairs as rapidly as they could.*
    As used in this sentence, the word ascended means MOST NEARLY
    A. went up   B. washed down   C. chopped
    D. shored up   E. inspected

37. *The store's refusal to accept delivery of the merchandise was a violation of the express provisions of the contract.*
    As used in this sentence, the word express means MOST NEARLY
    A. clear   B. implied   C. penalty
    C. disputed   E. complicated

38. A fire engine carries 900 feet of 2½" hose, 500 feet of 2" hose, and 350 feet of 1½" hose.
    Of the total hose carried, the percentage of 1½" hose is MOST NEARLY
    A. 35   B. 30   C. 25   D. 20   E. 15

39. An engine company made 96 runs in the month of April which was a decrease of 20% from the number of runs made in March.
The number of runs made in March was MOST NEARLY
   A. 136   B. 128   C. 120   D. 110   E. 112

40. A water tank has a capacity of 6,000 gallons. Connected to the tank is a pump capable of supplying water at the rate of 25 gallons per minute which goes into operation automatically when the water in the tank falls to the one-half mark.
If we start with a full tank and drain the water from the tank at the rate of 50 gallons a minute, the tank can continue supplying water at the required rate for _____ hours.
   A. 2½   B. 3   C. 3½   D. 4   E. 4½

41. Three firefighters are assigned the task of cleaning fire apparatus which usually takes three men five hours to complete. After they have been working three hours, three additional firefighters are assigned to help them.
Assuming that they all work at the normal rate, the assignment of the additional men will reduce the time required to complete the task by _____ minutes.
   A. 20   B. 30   C. 40   D. 50   E. 60

42. Assume that at the beginning of the calendar year an employee was earning $48,000 per year. On July 1st, he received an increase of $2,400 per year. On November 1st, he was promoted to a position paying $60,000 per year.
The total earnings for the year were MOST NEARLY
   A. $51,000   B. $49,000   C. $50,000   D. $54,000   E. $53,000

43. Engine A leaves its firehouse at 1:48 P.M. and travels 3 miles to a fire at an average speed of 30 miles per hour. Engine B leaves its firehouse at 1:51 P.M. and travels 6 miles to the same fire at an average speed of 40 miles per hour.
From the above facts, we may conclude that Engine A arrives _____ Engine B.
   A. 3 minutes before   B. 6 minutes before
   C. 3 minutes after   D. 6 minutes after
   E. at the same time as

44. A widely used formula for calculating the quantity of water discharged from a hose is: $GPM = 29.7 d^2 \sqrt{P}$, where GPM = gallons per minute, d = diameter of the nozzle in inches, and P = pressure at the nozzle in pounds per square inch.
If it takes 1 minute to extinguish a fire using a 1½" nozzle at 100 pounds pressure per square inch, the number of gallons discharged is, according to the above formula, MOST NEARLY
   A. 730   B. 650   C. 710   D. 690   E. 670

45. The spring of a spring balance will stretch in proportion to the amount of weight placed on the balance.
If a 2-pound weight placed on a certain balance stretches the spring ¼", then a stretch in the spring of 1 ¾" will be caused by a weight of _____ pounds.
   A. 10   B. 12   C. 14   D. 16

KEY (CORRECT ANSWERS)

1.	D	11.	B	21.	E	31.	D	41.	E
2.	A	12.	E	22.	C	32.	B	42.	A
3.	A	13.	E	23.	C	33.	B	43.	B
4.	B	14.	C	24.	B	34.	B	44.	E
5.	D	15.	D	25.	E	35.	B	45.	C
6.	C	16.	D	26.	E	36.	A		
7.	B	17.	B	27.	D	37.	A		
8.	B	18.	A	28.	A	38.	D		
9.	E	19.	D	29.	C	39.	C		
10.	A	20.	B	30.	D	40.	B		

EXAMINATION SECTION
TEST 1

DIRECTIONS: Each question or incomplete statement is followed by several suggested answers or completions. Select the one that BEST answers the question or completes the statement. *PRINT THE LETTER OF THE CORRECT ANSWER IN THE SPACE AT THE RIGHT.*

Questions 1-5.

DIRECTIONS: Questions 1 through 5 are to be answered SOLELY on the basis of the following information and map.

A firefighter may be required to assist civilians who seek travel directions or referral to city agencies and facilities.

The following is a map of part of a city, where several public offices and other institutions are located. Each of the squares represents one city block. Street names are as shown. If there is an arrow next to the street name, it means the street is one way only in the direction of the arrow. If there is no arrow next to the street name, two-way traffic is allowed.

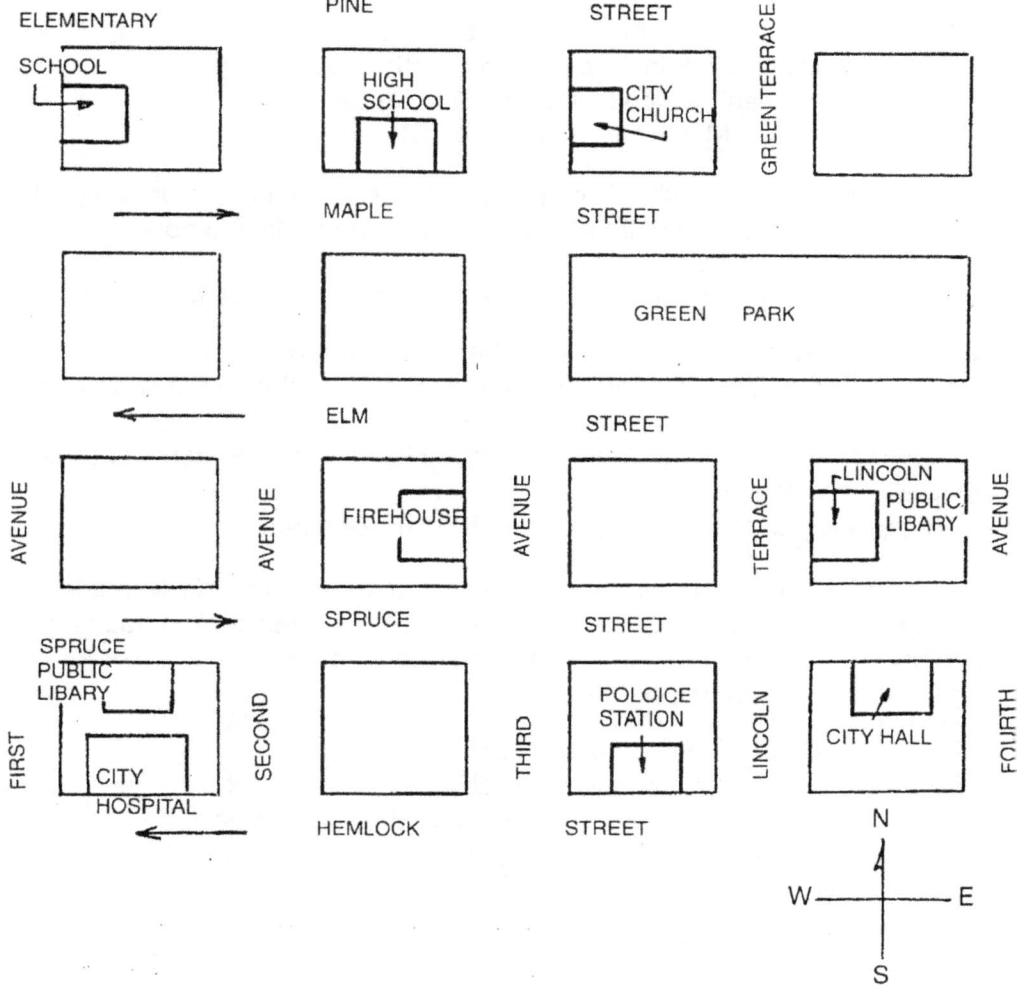

163

1. A woman whose handbag was stolen from her in Green Park asks a firefighter at the firehouse where to go to report the crime.
   The firefighter should tell the woman to go to the

   A. police station on Spruce St.
   B. police station on Hemlock St.
   C. city hall on Spruce St.
   D. city hall on Hemlock St.

2. A disabled senior citizen who lives on Green Terrace telephones the firehouse to ask which library is closest to her home.
   The firefighter should tell the senior citizen it is the

   A. Spruce Public Library on Lincoln Terrace
   B. Lincoln Public Library on Spruce Street
   C. Spruce Public Library on Spruce Street
   D. Lincoln Public Library on Lincoln Terrace

3. A woman calls the firehouse to ask for the exact location of City Hall.
   She should be told that it is on

   A. Hemlock Street, between Lincoln Terrace and Fourth Ave.
   B. Spruce Street, between Lincoln Terrace and Fourth Ave.
   C. Lincoln Terrace, between Spruce Street and Elm Street
   D. Green Terrace, between Maple Street and Pine Street

4. A delivery truck driver is having trouble finding the high school to make a delivery. The driver parks the truck across from the firehouse on Third Avenue facing north and goes into the firehouse to ask directions.
   In giving directions, the firefighter should tell the driver to go _____ to the school.

   A. north on Third Avenue to Pine Street and then make a right
   B. south on Third Avenue, make a left on Hemlock Street, and then make a right on Second Avenue
   C. north on Third Avenue, turn left on Elm Street, make a right on Second Avenue and go to Maple Street, then make another right
   D. north on Third Avenue to Maple Street, and then make a left

5. A man comes to the firehouse accompanied by his son and daughter. He wants to register his son in the high school and his daughter in the elementary school. He asks a firefighter which school is closest for him to walk to from the firehouse.
   The firefighter should tell the man that the

   A. high school is closer than the elementary school
   B. elementary school is closer than the high school
   C. elementary school and high school are the same distance away
   D. elementary school and the high school are in opposite directions

Questions 6-10.

DIRECTIONS: Questions 6 through 10 are to be answered SOLELY on the basis of the following passage.

Sometimes a fire engine leaving the scene of a fire must back out of a street because other fire engines have blocked the path in front of it. When the fire engine is backing up, each firefighter is given a duty to perform to help control automobile traffic and protect people walking nearby. Before the driver starts to slowly back up the fire engine, all the other firefighters are told the route he will take. They walk alongside and behind the slowly moving fire engine, guiding the driver, keeping traffic out of the street and warning people away from the path of the vehicle. As the fire engine, in reverse gear, approaches the intersection, the driver brings it to a full stop and waits for his supervisor to give the order to start moving again. If traffic is blocking the intersection, two firefighters enter the intersection to direct traffic. They clear the cars and people out of the intersection, making way for the fire engine to back into it. The driver then goes forward, turning into the intersection. Two other firefighters keep cars and people away from the front of the fire engine as it moves. Because of the extra care needed to control cars and protect people in the streets when a fire engine is backing up, it is better to drive a fire engine forward whenever possible.

6. A fire engine is leaving the scene of a fire. The street in front of it is blocked by people and other fire engines. Of the following, it would be BEST for the driver to

    A. put on the siren to clear a path
    B. back out of the street slowly
    C. drive on the sidewalk around the other fire engines
    D. move the other fire engines out of the way

7. Firefighters walk alongside and behind the fire engine when it is backing up in order to

    A. strengthen their legs and stay physically fit
    B. look around the neighborhood for fires
    C. insure that the engine moves slowly
    D. control traffic, protect people, and assist the driver

8. A fire engine going in reverse approaches an intersection blocked with cars and trucks. The driver should

    A. go forward and then try to back into the intersection at a different angle
    B. slowly enter the intersection as the firefighters guiding the driver give the signal to move
    C. back up through the intersection without stopping
    D. stop, then enter the intersection only when the supervisor gives the signal to move

9. The above passage states that the two firefighters who first enter the intersection

    A. clear the intersection of cars and people
    B. direct the cars past the fire engine when the engine is in forward gear
    C. see if the traffic signal is working properly
    D. set up barriers to block any traffic

10. The diagram to the right shows a fire engine backing slowly out of Jones Street. The letters indicate where firefighters are standing. Which firefighter is NOT in the correct position? Firefighter
    A. D
    B. E
    C. A
    D. C

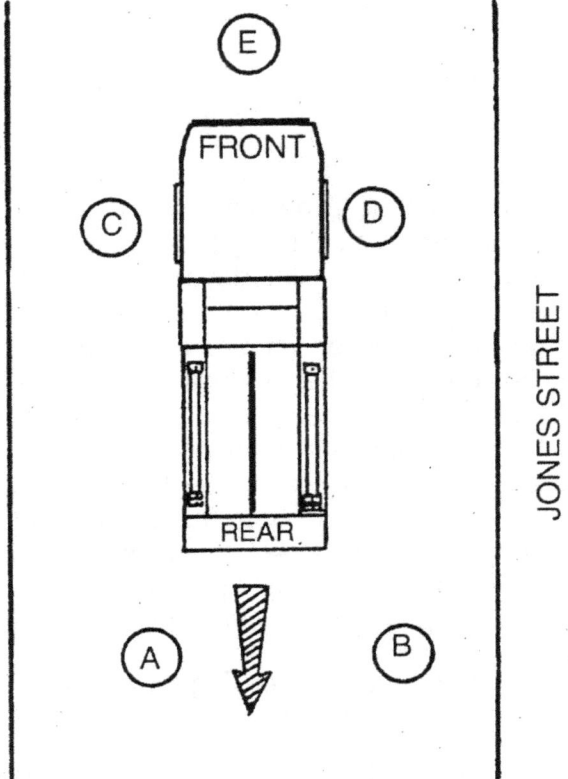

Questions 11-14.

DIRECTIONS: Questions 11 through 14 are to be answered SOLELY on the basis of the following passage.

About 48% of all reported fires are false alarms. False alarms add more risk of danger to firefighters, citizens, and property as well as waste the money and time of the fire department. When the first firefighters are called to a reported fire, they do not know if the alarm is for a real fire or is a false alarm. Until they have made sure that the alarm is false, they must not respond to a new alarm even if a real fire is burning and people's lives and property are in danger. If they do not find a fire or an emergency at the original location, then the firefighters radio the fire department that they have been called to a false alarm. The fire department radios back and tells the firefighters that they are in active service again and tells them where to respond for the next alarm. If that location is far from that of the false alarm, then the distance and the time it takes to get to the new location are increased. This means that firefighters will arrive later to help in fighting the real fire and the fire will have more time to burn. The fire will be bigger and more dangerous just because someone called the firefighters to a false alarm. In addition, each time the firefighters ride to the location of a false alarm, there is additional risk of unnecessary accidents and injuries to them and to citizens.

11. The MAIN point of the above passage is that false alarms

    A. seldom interrupt other activities in the firehouse
    B. occur more often during the winter

C. are rarely turned in by children
D. add more risk of danger to life and property

12. When firefighters are called to a false alarm, they must NOT respond to other alarms until they

    A. turn in a written report to the fire department
    B. take a vote and all agree to go
    C. are put back into active service by the fire department
    D. decide on the quickest route

13. Before firefighters get to the location of a reported fire, they

    A. finish eating their lunch at the firehouse
    B. do not know if the alarm is real or false
    C. search the neighborhood for the person who made the report
    D. do not know if the alarm is from an alarm box or telephone

14. The above passage states that false alarms

    A. shorten travel time to real fires
    B. give firefighters needed driving practice
    C. save money on fuel for the fire department
    D. account for about 48% of reported fires

Questions 15-18.

DIRECTIONS: Questions 15 through 18 are to be answered SOLELY on the basis of the following passage.

Fires in vacant buildings are a major problem for firefighters. People enter vacant buildings to remove building material or they damage stairs, floors, doors, and other parts of the building. The buildings are turned into dangerous structures with stairs missing, holes in the floors, weakened walls and loose bricks. Children and arsonists find large amounts of wood, paper, and other combustible materials in the buildings and start fires which damage and weaken the buildings even more. Firefighters have been injured putting out fires in these buildings due to these dangerous conditions. Most injuries caused while putting out fires in vacant buildings could be eliminated if all of these buildings were repaired. All such injuries could be eliminated if the buildings were demolished. Until then, firefighters should take extra care while putting out fires in vacant buildings.

15. The problem of fires in vacant buildings could be solved by

    A. repairing buildings
    B. closing up the cellar door and windows with bricks and cement
    C. arresting suspicious persons before they start the fires
    D. demolishing the buildings

16. Firefighters are injured putting out fires in vacant buildings because

    A. there are no tenants to help fight the fires
    B. conditions are dangerous in these buildings

C. they are not as careful when nobody lives in the buildings
D. the water in the buildings has been turned off

17. Vacant buildings often have

    A. occupied buildings on either side of them
    B. safe empty spaces where neighborhood children can play
    C. combustible materials inside them
    D. strong walls and floors that cannot burn

18. While firefighters are putting out fires in vacant buildings, they should

    A. be extra careful of missing stairs
    B. find the children who start the fires
    C. learn the reasons why the fires are set
    D. help to repair the buildings

Questions 19-20.

DIRECTIONS: Questions 19 and 20 are to be answered SOLELY on the basis of the following passage.

Firefighters inspect many different kinds of places to find fire hazards and have them reviewed. During these inspections, the firefighters try to learn as much as possible about the place. This knowledge is useful should the firefighters have to fight a fire at some later date at that location. When inspecting subways, firefighters are much concerned with the effects a fire might have on the passengers because, unless they have been trapped in a subway car during a fire, most subway riders do not think about the dangers involved in a fire in the subway. During a fire, the air in cars crowded with passengers may become intensely hot. The cars may fill with dense smoke. Lights may dim or go out altogether, leaving the passengers in darkness. Ventilation from fans and air conditioning may stop. The train may be stuck and unable to be moved through the tunnel to a station. Fear may send the trapped passengers into a panic. Firefighters must protect the passengers from the fire, heat, and smoke, calm them down, get them out quickly to a safe area, and put out the fire. To do this, firefighters may have to climb from street level down into the subway tunnel to reach a train stopped inside the tunnel. Before actually going on the tracks, they must be sure that the 600 volts of live electricity carried by the third rail is shut off. They may have to stretch fire hose a long distance down subway stairs, on platforms, and along the subway tracks to get the water to the fire and put it out. Subway fires are difficult to fight because of these special problems, but preparing for them in advance can help save the lives of both firefighters and passengers.

19. During a subway fire, a train is stuck in a tunnel. Firefighters have been ordered into the tunnel.
    Before firefighters actually step down on the tracks, they must be sure that

    A. all the passengers have been removed from the burning subway cars to a safe place
    B. they have stretched their fire hose a long distance to put water on the fire
    C. live electricity carried by the third rail is shut off
    D. the train is moved from the tunnel to the nearest station

20. According to the above passage, fire in the subway may leave passengers in subway cars in darkness.
    This occurs MAINLY because

    A. the lights may go out
    B. air in the cars may become very hot
    C. ventilation may stop
    D. people may panic

Questions 21-25.

DIRECTIONS: Questions 21 through 25 concern various forms, reports, or other documents that must be filed according to topic. Listed below are four topics numbered 1 through 4, under which forms, reports, and documents may be filed. In each question, choose the topic under which the form, report, or document concerned should be filed.
1. Equipment and supplies
2. Fire prevention
3. Personnel
4. Training

21. Under which topic would it be MOST appropriate to file a letter on a heroic act performed by a member of the fire company?

    A. 1   B. 2   C. 3   D. 4

22. Under which topic should a firefighter look for information about the fire company's new portable ladder?

    A. 1   B. 2   C. 3   D. 4

23. Under which topic should a firefighter locate a copy of the fire company's fire prevention building inspection schedule for the current year?

    A. 1   B. 2   C. 3   D. 4

24. Under which topic should a firefighter file a copy of a report on company property which has been damaged?

    A. 1   B. 2   C. 3   D. 4

25. Under which topic should a firefighter be able to locate a roster of firefighters assigned to the company?

    A. 1   B. 2   C. 3   D. 4

KEY (CORRECT ANSWERS)

1. B
2. D
3. B
4. C
5. A

6. B
7. D
8. D
9. A
10. B

11. D
12. C
13. B
14. D
15. D

16. B
17. C
18. A
19. C
20. A

21. C
22. A
23. B
24. A
25. C

TEST 2

DIRECTIONS: Each question or incomplete statement is followed by several suggested answers or completions. Select the one that BEST answers the question or completes the statement. *PRINT THE LETTER OF THE CORRECT ANSWER IN THE SPACE AT THE RIGHT.*

1. Firefighters must check gauges on fire engines so that defects are discovered and corrected. Some fire engines are equipped with gauges called. *Chargicators,* which indicate whether or not the electrical system is operating properly. When the fire engine's motor is running, the chargicator of a properly operating electrical system will show a reading of 13.5 to 14.2 volts on the scale. Which one of the following gauges shows a PROPERLY operating electrical system?

1.____

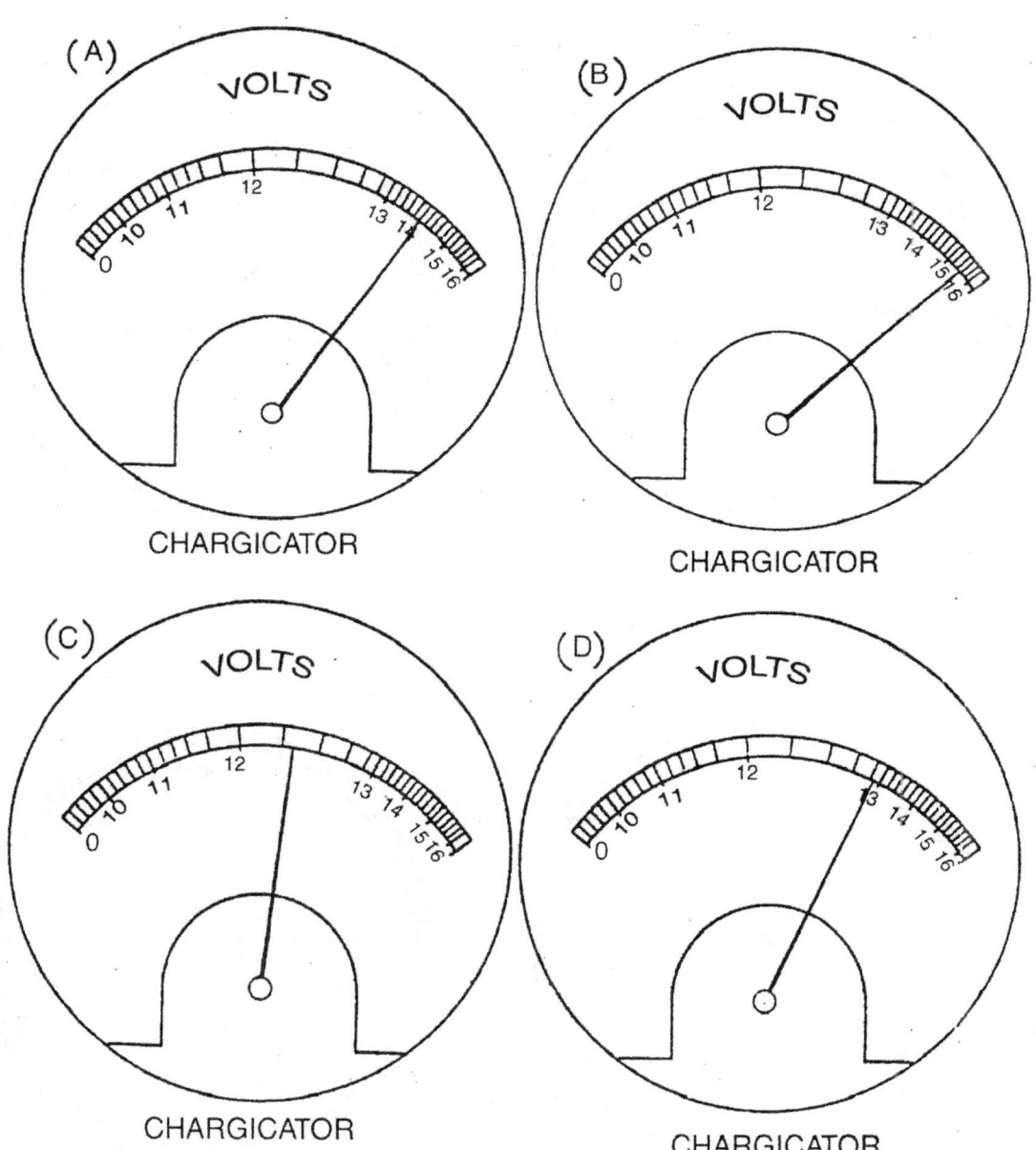

Questions 2-5.

DIRECTIONS: Questions 2 through 5 are to be answered SOLELY on the basis of the following facts and diagrams.

The gauges shown below in Diagrams I and II represent gauges on a fire engine's pump control panel at the scene of a fire. Diagram I gives the readings at 10 A.M., and Diagram II gives the readings at 10:15 A.M. Each diagram has one gauge labeled *Incoming* and one gauge marked *Outgoing*. The *Incoming* gauges show the pressure in pounds per square inch (psi) of the water coming into the pumps on the fire engine from a hydrant. The *Outgoing* gauges show the pressure in pounds per square inch (psi) of the water leaving the pumps on the fire engine. The pumps on the fire engine raise the pressure of the water coming from the hydrant to the higher pressures needed in the fire hoses.

DIAGRAM I

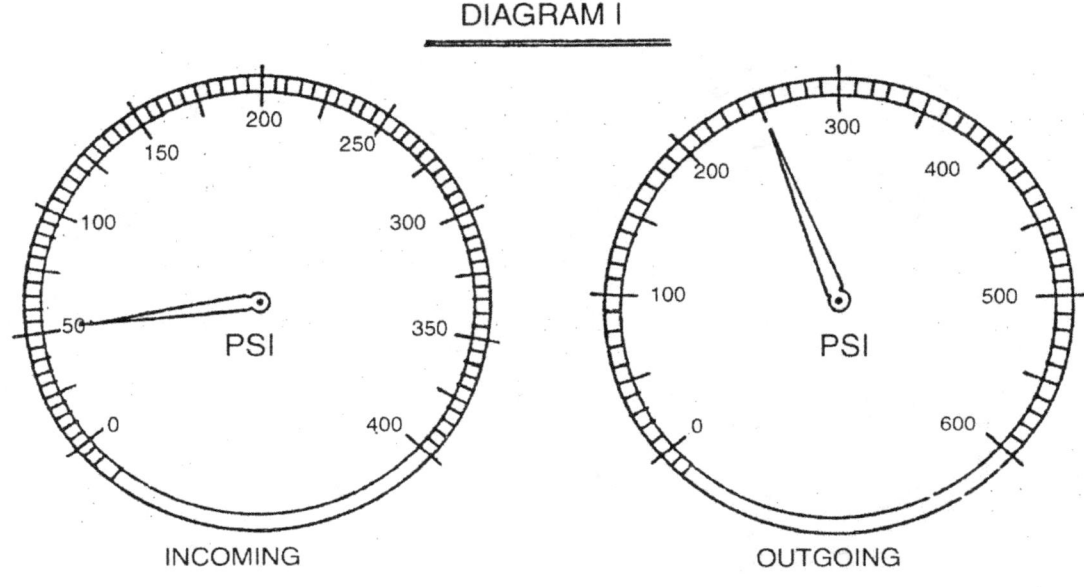

DIAGRAM II

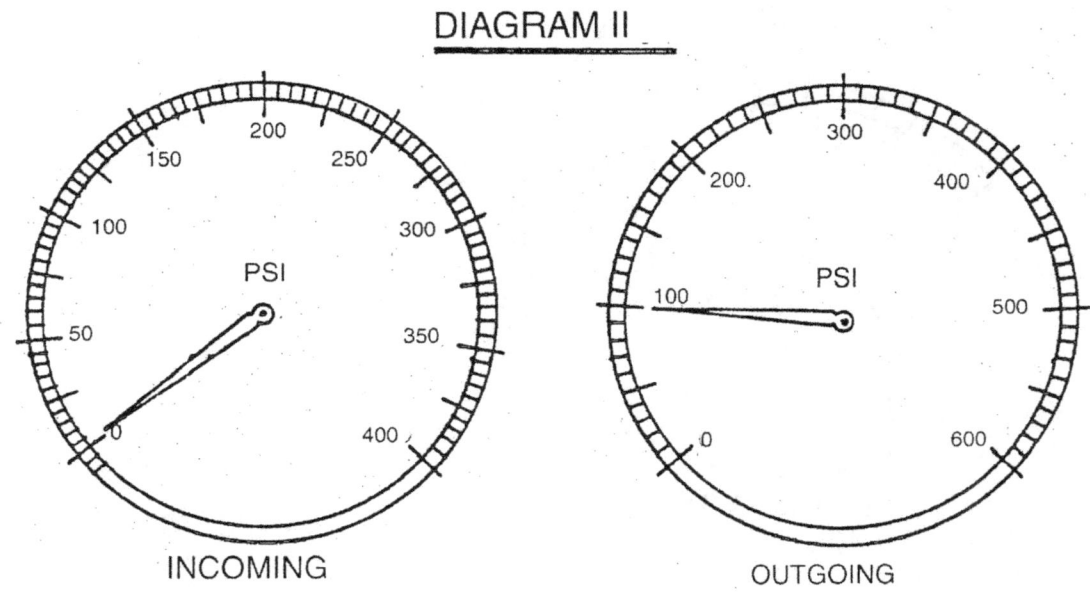

2. The firefighter looks at the gauges as shown in Diagram I and observes that the pressure, in pounds per square inch (psi), of the water coming into the pumps is MOST NEARLY

   A. 50   B. 250   C. 300   D. 500

3. The firefighter looks at the gauges shown in Diagram I and observes that the pressure, in pounds per square inch (psi), of the water going out of the pumps is MOST NEARLY

   A. 25   B. 50   C. 250   D. 500

4. Diagram II shows the incoming and outgoing water pressure fifteen minutes later. By looking at the gauges in Diagram II, the firefighter observes that the water _____ the pumps is _____ psi.

   A. going out of; at, 200
   B. going out of; at 5
   C. coming into; above 10
   D. coming into; below 10

5. The firefighter is able to determine that, between the time of Diagram I and the time of Diagram II, the pressure of the outgoing water from the pumps _____ by _____ psi.

   A. *increased;* 50
   B. *decreased;* 150
   C. *decreased;* 45
   D. *increased;* 145

Questions 6-11.

DIRECTIONS: Questions 6 through 11 are to be answered SOLELY on the basis of the following information.

In order to extinguish fires, firefighters must pull enough hose from the fire engine to reach the fire. Each length of hose is 50 feet long. The lengths of hose are attached together so that the water can go from the pump on the fire engine to a position where it will extinguish the fire.

6. If the total distance to reach the fire is 50 feet, what is the MINIMUM number of lengths of hose needed?

   A. 1   B. 2   C. 4   D. 4

7. If the total distance to reach the fire is 250 feet, what is the MINIMUM number of lengths of hose needed?

   A. 3   B. 4   C. 5   D. 6

8. If the total distance to reach the fire is 175 feet, what is the MINIMUM number of lengths of hose needed?

   A. 2   B. 3   C. 4   D. 5

9. If the total distance to reach the fire is 125 feet, what is the MINIMUM number of lengths of hose needed?

   A. 2   B. 3   C. 4   D. 5

10. If the total distance to reach the fire is 315 feet, what is the MINIMUM number of lengths of hose needed?

    A. 3   B. 5   C. 6   D. 7

11. If the total distance to reach the fire is 230 feet, what is the MINIMUM number of lengths of hose needed?

    A. 4   B. 5   C. 6   D. 7

Questions 12-13.

DIRECTIONS: Questions 12 and 13 are to be answered SOLELY on the basis of the following passage and diagrams.

Firefighters breathe through an air mask to protect their lungs from dangerous smoke when fighting fires. The air for the mask comes from a cylinder which the firefighter wears. A full cylinder contains 45 cubic feet of air when pressurized to 4500 pounds per square inch.

12. A gauge that firefighters read to tell how much air is left in the cylinder is pictured in the diagram at the right. The gauge indicates that the cylinder is
    A. full
    B. empty
    C. more than 3/4 full
    D. less than 1/2 full

13. A gauge which is part of the cylinder shows the pressure of the air in the cylinder in hundreds of pounds per square inch.
    Which of the following diagrams shows a cylinder which is more than half full?

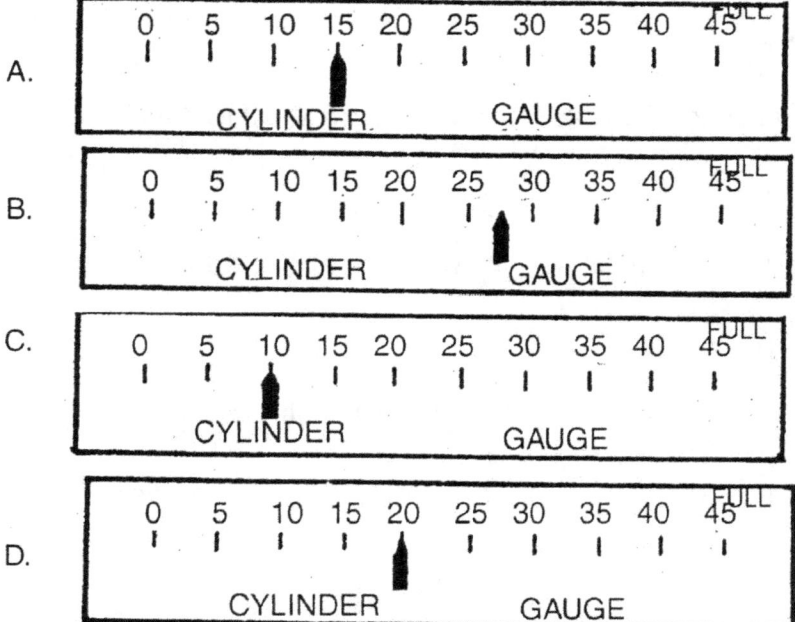

Questions 14-15.

DIRECTIONS: Questions 14 and 15 are to be answered SOLELY on the basis of the following passage.

The Fire Department uses a firehose nozzle with an automatically adjusting tip. The automatically adjusting nozzle tip keeps the water pressure at the tip constant even though the amount of water being pumped through the hose from the fire engine may vary. A partial loss of water in the hoseline does not result in the stream of water from the nozzle falling short of the target. A partial loss of water is caused by a kink in the hose somewhere between the fire engine pumping the water and the nozzle or by insufficient pressure being supplied by the fire engine pumping water into the hoseline.

The danger of this automatic nozzle is that as the nozzle tip adjusts to maintain constant water pressure, the number of gallons of water per minute flowing out of the nozzle is reduced. When the number of gallons of water per minute flowing from the nozzle is reduced, the nozzle is easier to handle and the stream of water coming from the nozzle appears to be adequate. However, since the number of gallons of flow is reduced, the cooling power of the hose stream will probably not be enough to fight the fire. If a firefighter can physically handle the hoseline alone, the nozzle is not discharging enough water, even though the stream coming out of the nozzle appears adequate. An adequate fire stream requires two firefighters to handle the hoseline.

14. An officer tells a firefighter to check why enough water is not coming out of a hoseline equipped with an automatic nozzle. The firefighter follows the hoseline from the nozzle back to the fire engine pumping the water into the hose but finds no kinks in the hose. The firefighter should inform the officer that the inadequate flow of water is PROBABLY due to

   A. a defective automatic nozzle
   B. the nozzle stream being aimed in the wrong direction
   C. insufficient pressure being supplied by the fire engine pumping water into the hoseline
   D. the fire engine not being connected to a hydrant

15. One firefighter alone is easily handling a hoseline equipped with an automatic nozzle. The hoseline's stream is reaching the fire.
According to the above passage, the firefighter should PROPERLY conclude that

   A. being able to handle the hoseline alone indicates extreme strength and excellent physical condition
   B. the stream of water coming from the nozzle is probably not an acceptable firefighting stream because not enough water is flowing
   C. the stream of water coming from the nozzle is adequate and is helping to save water
   D. the automatic nozzle has adjusted itself to provide the proper amount of water to fight the fire

Questions 16-17.

DIRECTIONS: Questions 16 and 17 are to be answered SOLELY on the basis of the following passage.

Firefighters at times are required to work in areas where the atmosphere contains contaminated smoke. To protect the firefighter from breathing the harmful smoke, a self-contained breathing mask is worn. The mask will supply the firefighter with a limited supply of pure breathing air. This will allow the firefighter to enter the smoke-filled area. The mask is lightweight and compact, which makes it less tiring and easier to move around with. The face mask is designed to give the firefighter the maximum visibility possible. The supply of breathing air is limited, and the rate of air used depends upon the exertion made by the firefighter. Although the mask will protect the firefighter from some types of contaminated smoke, it gives no protection from flame, heat, or heat exhaustion.

16. The rate at which the firefighter breathes the air from the mask will depend upon the

   A. amount of energy used by the firefighter
   B. amount of smoke the firefighter will breathe
   C. color of the flames that the firefighter will enter
   D. color of the heat that the firefighter will enter

17. According to the above passage, the mask will protect the firefighter from some types of

   A. flames   B. smoke
   C. heat   D. heat exhaustion

Questions 18-21.

DIRECTIONS: Questions 18 through 21 are to be answered SOLELY on the basis of the following passage.

In each firehouse, one firefighter is always on housewatch duty. Each 24-hour housewatch tour begins at 9 A.M. each day and is divided into eight 3-hour periods. The firefighter on housewatch is responsible for the correct receipt, acknowledgement, and report of every alarm signal from any source. Firefighters on housewatch are required to enter in the Company Journal the receipt of all alarms, as well as other matters required by Department regulations. All entries by the firefighter on housewatch should be written in blue or black ink. Any entries made by firefighters not on housewatch are made in red ink. Most entries, including receipt of alarms, are recorded in order, starting in the front of the Company Journal on Page 1.

Certain types of entries are recorded in special places in the Journal. When high level officers visit the company, those visits are recorded on Page 500. Company training drills and instruction periods are recorded on Page 497. The monthly meter readings of the utility companies which serve the firehouse are recorded on Page 493.

18. A firefighter is asked by the company officer to find out what alarms were received the previous day, August 25, between 1 A.M. and 2 A.M.
    Where in the Company Journal should the firefighter look to obtain this information?

   A. On Page 493
   B. Between Page 1 and Page 492, on the page for August 25
   C. On Page 500
   D. Between Page 497 and Page 500 on the page for August 25

19. A firefighter on housewatch is asked to find out how much electricity was used in the fire-   19._____
house between the last two meter readings taken by Con Edison.
On which one of the following pages of the Company Journal should the firefighter look
to find the last two electrical meter readings entered?

    A. 253   B. 493   C. 497   D. 500

20. A firefighter on housewatch duty is notified by a passing civilian of a rubbish fire around   20._____
the block. The company responds, extinguishes the rubbish fire, and returns to the firehouse.
The firefighter on housewatch should

    A. make no entry in the Company Journal of the receipt of the alarm because it was
       received orally from the civilian
    B. record the alarm in red ink in the Company Journal
    C. record the alarm in blue ink in the Company Journal
    D. ask the civilian to record the alarm in red ink in the Company Journal

21. The company officer asks the firefighter on housewatch to find out the last date on which   21._____
the company had a training drill on high-rise building fire operations.
On which one of the following pages of the Company Journal should the firefighter on
housewatch look to find the date of the training drill?

    A. 36   B. 493   C. 497   D. 500

Questions 22-23.

DIRECTIONS: Questions 22 and 23 are to be answered SOLELY on the basis of the following
              passage.

Fire Department regulations require that upon receiving an alarm while in the firehouse,
the officer of the fire company directs the firefighters to take positions in front of the firehouse.
The firefighters warn pedestrians and vehicles that the fire engine is leaving the firehouse.
The officer directs the driver of the fire engine to move the fire engine to the front of the firehouse and to stop to check for vehicles and pedestrian traffic. While the fire engine is
stopped, the firefighters will get on, and the officer will signal the driver to go to the alarm
location.

22. When do the firefighters who were sent to the front of the firehouse actually get on the   22._____
fire engine?

    A. As the fire engine turns into the street leaving the firehouse
    B. As the fire engine slows down while leaving the fire-house
    C. Inside the firehouse, before the fire engine is moved
    D. After the fire engine has been moved to the front of the firehouse and stopped

23. When responding to an alarm, why are the firefighters sent out of the firehouse before   23._____
the fire engine?
To

    A. make sure that the firehouse doors are fully opened
    B. go to the nearest corner to change the traffic signal

C. warn pedestrians and vehicles that the fire engine is coming out of the firehouse
D. give the firefighters time to put on their helmets and boots

24. When the engine oil drum in the firehouse is nearly empty, it must be replaced by a new drum full of oil. A firefighter gives the drum a kick. It sounds empty. The firefighter then checks the written log to see how many gallons of oil have been taken out of the drum so far. Checking the written log is

    A. *unnecessary,* since the oil drum sounded empty when the firefighter kicked it
    B. *necessary,* since the log should tell the firefighter exactly how much oil is left
    C. *unnecessary,* since the firefighter should avoid paperwork whenever possible
    D. *necessary,* since the firefighter should always try to keep busy with useful activity

25. The Fire Department provides each firehouse with such basic necessities as electric light bulbs. As the items are used up, new supplies are ordered before the old ones are all gone.
    Of the following, the BEST reason for ordering more electric light bulbs before the old ones are all gone is to

    A. decrease the amount of paperwork a firehouse company must complete
    B. be sure that there are always enough light bulbs on hand to replace those that burn out
    C. make sure that the firehouse has enough electric light bulbs to supply nearby firehouses
    D. decrease the cost of providing electricity to the firehouse

KEY (CORRECT ANSWERS)

1.	A	11.	B
2.	A	12.	D
3.	C	13.	B
4.	D	14.	C
5.	B	15.	B
6.	A	16.	A
7.	C	17.	B
8.	C	18.	B
9.	B	19.	B
10.	D	20.	C

21. C
22. D
23. C
24. B
25. B

EXAMINATION SECTION
TEST 1

DIRECTIONS: Each question or incomplete statement is followed by several suggested answers or completions. Select the one that BEST answers the question or completes the statement. *PRINT THE LETTER OF THE CORRECT ANSWER IN THE SPACE AT THE RIGHT.*

Questions 1-8.

DIRECTIONS: Questions 1 through 8 are to be answered SOLELY on the basis of the following Memory Scene 1. Study this scene carefully for five minutes. Then answer Questions 1 through 8. Do not refer back to this scene when answering the questions.

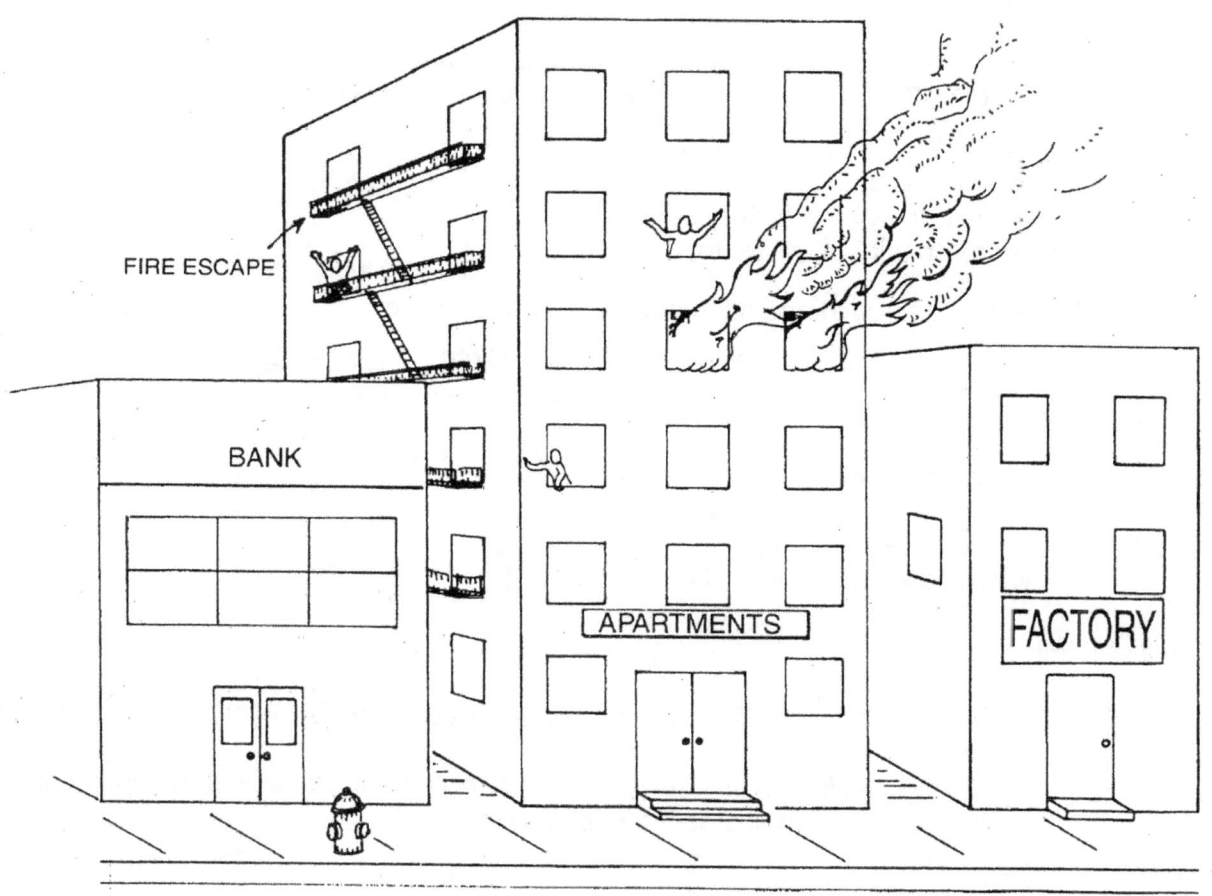

NOTE: THE GROUND FLOOR IS THE FIRST FLOOR

1. The fire is located on the _____ floor.   1._____
   A. first B. fourth C. fifth D. top

2. The smoke and flames are blowing _____ and to the _____.   2.___

   A. up; left   B. up; right
   C. down; left   D. down; right

3. There is a person on a fire escape on the _____ floor.   3.___

   A. second   B. third   C. fourth   D. fifth

4. Persons are visible in windows at the front of the building on fire on the _____ floors.   4.___

   A. second and third   B. third and fifth
   C. fourth and sixth   D. fifth and sixth

5. The person who is CLOSEST to the flames is in a _____ window on the _____ floor.   5.___

   A. front; third   B. front; fifth
   C. side; fifth   D. side; third

6. A firefighter is told to go to the roof of the building on fire.   6.___
   It would be CORRECT to state that the firefighter can cross directly to the roof from

   A. the roof of the bank
   B. the roof of the factory
   C. either the bank or the factory
   D. neither the bank nor the factory

7. On which side of the building on fire are fire escapes visible?   7.___

   A. Left   B. Front   C. Right   D. Rear

8. The hydrant on the sidewalk is   8.___

   A. in front of the bank
   B. between the bank and the apartments
   C. in front of the apartments
   D. between the apartments and the factory

Questions 9-16.

DIRECTIONS: Questions 9 through 16 are to be answered on the basis of the following floor plan.
Look at this floor plan of an apartment. It is on the 3rd floor of the building. The floor plan also indicates the public hallway.

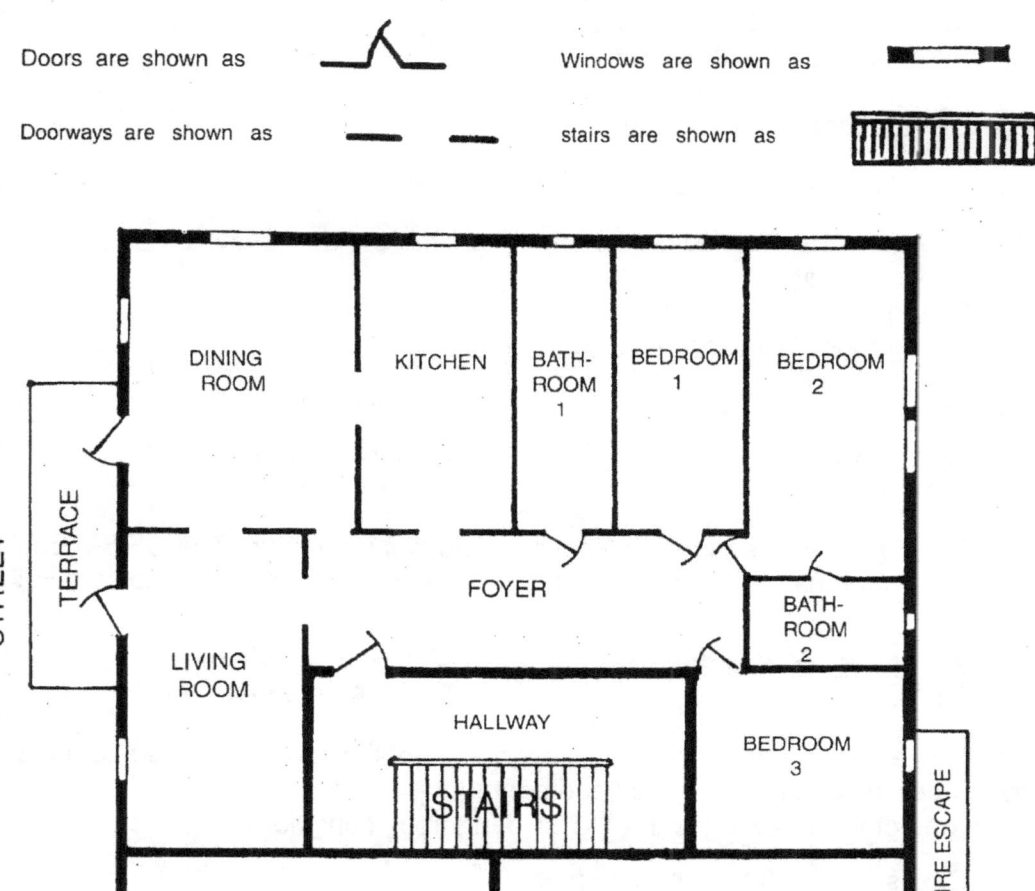

9. Which room is FARTHEST from the fire escape?

   A. Bedroom 2
   B. Bedroom 3
   C. Kitchen
   D. Dining room

10. Which one of the following rooms has ONLY one door or doorway?

    A. Living room
    B. Bedroom 1
    C. Kitchen
    D. Dining room

11. Which room can firefighters reach DIRECTLY from the fire escape?

    A. Dining room
    B. Living room
    C. Bedroom 1
    D. Bedroom 3

12. Which room does NOT have a door or doorway leading directly to the foyer?

    A. Bathroom 1
    B. Bathroom 2
    C. Bedroom 1
    D. Dining room

13. A firefighter leaving Bathroom 2 would be in

    A. bedroom 1
    B. bedroom 2
    C. bedroom 3
    D. the foyer

14. Firefighters on the terrace would be able to enter directly into which rooms?

    A. Bedroom 1 and bathroom 1
    B. Bedroom 2 and bathroom 2
    C. Dining room and kitchen
    D. Dining room and living room

15. Which rooms have AT LEAST one window on two sides of the building?

    A. Bedroom 2 and dining room
    B. Bedroom 2 and bedroom 3
    C. Dining room and living room
    D. Dining room, bedroom 2, and bedroom 3

16. Firefighters can enter the kitchen directly from the foyer and

    A. bedroom 1
    B. the living room
    C. bathroom 1
    D. the dining room

17. Firefighters are often required to rescue individuals from a fire. The GREATEST possibility of a firefighter having to rescue someone in a private home occurs between the hours of

    A. 7 A.M. and 11 A.M.
    B. 10 A.M. and 2 P.M.
    C. 2 P.M. and 6 P.M.
    D. 2 A.M. and 6 A.M.

18. At a fire in an apartment building, a firefighter is told to inform the lieutenant if she finds any dangerous conditions in the basement.
    Which one of the following is the MOST dangerous condition?

    A. Gas is leaking from a broken pipe.
    B. The sewer pipe is broken.
    C. Water is seeping into the basement.
    D. The electricity has been turned off.

19. Firefighters are required to use portable ladders to rescue people.
    When firefighters are positioning a portable ladder for a rescue, which one of the following would present the GREATEST threat to the firefighters' safety?

    A. A person to be rescued who is standing near an open window
    B. Tree branches which are close to the ladder
    C. A person to be rescued who is dressed in a long robe
    D. Overhead electrical wires which are close to the ladder

20. Firefighters are instructed to notify an officer whenever they attempt to rescue someone who is seriously endangered by fire or smoke. Firefighters respond to a fire in a 6-story apartment building. The fire is in a fourth floor apartment in the front of the building. Firefighters should notify an officer when they are attempting to rescue

    A. a person who disappears from a smoke-filled window on the fourth floor
    B. a person who is on the roof
    C. three persons on the third floor rear fire escape who appear to be very frightened
    D. two children who are locked in their apartment on the first floor

21. Firefighters who forcibly enter an apartment on fire may find conditions which indicate that they should immediately search for victims.
   Of the following conditions in an apartment on fire, which one would MOST clearly indicate to firefighters that they should immediately search for victims?

   A. There is a pot on the stove.
   B. The apartment door was chain-locked from the inside.
   C. Water is dripping into a pail.
   D. All the windows in the apartment are closed.

Questions 22-24.

DIRECTIONS: Questions 22 through 24 are to be answered SOLELY on the basis of the following passage.

When there is a fire in a subway train, it may be necessary for firefighters to evacuate people from the trains by way of the tunnels. In every tunnel, there are emergency exit areas which have stairways that can be used to evacuate people to the street from the track area. All emergency exits can be recognized by an exit sign near a group of five white lights.

There is a Blue Light Area which is located every 600 feet in the tunnel. These areas contain a power removal box, a telephone, and a fire extinguisher. Removal of power from the third rail is the first step firefighters must take when evacuating people through tunnels. When a firefighter uses the power removal box to turn off electrical power during evacuation procedures, the firefighter must immediately telephone the trainmaster and explain the reason for the power removal. Communication between the firefighter and the trainmaster is essential. If the trainmaster does not receive a phone call within four minutes after power removal, the power will be restored to the third rail.

22. When evacuating passengers through the subway tunnel, firefighters must FIRST

   A. telephone the trainmaster for assistance
   B. remove electrical power from the third rail
   C. locate the emergency exit in the tunnel
   D. go to the group of five white lights

23. Immediately after using the power removal box to turn off the electrical power, a firefighter should

   A. wait four minutes before calling the trainmaster
   B. begin evacuating passengers through the tunnel
   C. call the trainmaster and explain why the power was turned off
   D. touch the third rail to see if the electrical power has been turned off

24. A group of five white lights in a subway tunnel indicates that

   A. a telephone is available
   B. the electrical power is off in the third rail
   C. a fire extinguisher is available
   D. an emergency exit is located there

25. During a recent day tour with an engine company, Firefighter Sims was assigned to the control position on the hose. The company responded to the following alarms during this tour:

Alarm 1: At 9:30 A.M., the company responded to a fire on the first floor of an apartment building. At the fire scene, Firefighter Sims pulled the hose from the fire engine and assisted the driver in attaching the hose to the hydrant.

Alarm 2: At 11:00 A.M., the company responded to a fire on the third floor of a vacant building. Firefighter Sims pulled the hose from the fire engine and went to the building on fire.

Alarm 3: At 1:00 P.M., the company responded to a fire in a first-floor laundromat. Firefighter Sims pulled the hose from the fire engine and assisted the driver in attaching the hose to the hydrant.

Alarm 4: At 3:00 P.M., the company responded to a fire on the fourth floor of an apartment building. Firefighter Sims pulled the hose from the fire engine and went to the building on fire.

Alarm 5: At 5:45 P.M., the company responded to a fire on the second floor of a private house. Firefighter Sims pulled the hose from the fire engine and assisted the driver in attaching the hose to the hydrant.

The firefighter assigned to the control position assists the driver in attaching the hose to a hydrant when the fire is

- A. in an apartment building
- B. above the second floor
- C. in a vacant building
- D. below the third floor

KEY (CORRECT ANSWERS)

1.	B		11.	D
2.	B		12.	B
3.	D		13.	B
4.	B		14.	D
5.	B		15.	A
6.	D		16.	D
7.	A		17.	D
8.	A		18.	A
9.	D		19.	D
10.	B		20.	A

21. B
22. B
23. C
24. D
25. D

TEST 2

DIRECTIONS: Each question or incomplete statement is followed by several suggested answers or completions. Select the one that BEST answers the question or completes the statement. *PRINT THE LETTER OF THE CORRECT ANSWER IN THE SPACE AT THE RIGHT.*

Questions 1-3.

DIRECTIONS: Questions 1 through 3 are to be answered on the basis of the following floor plan and the paragraph which appears on the next page.

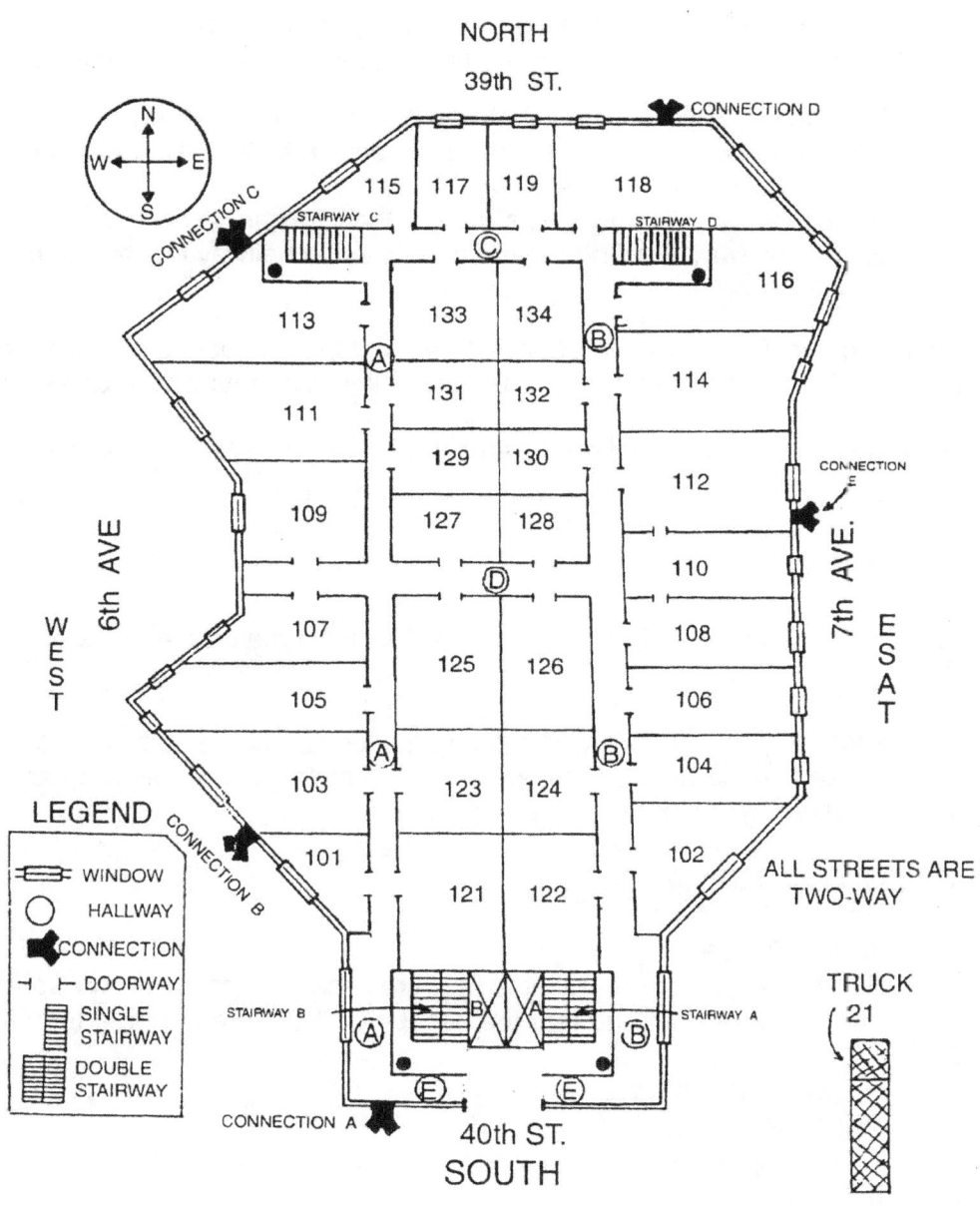

The floor plan represents a typical high-rise office building in midtown. Numbers shown indicate room numbers. The pipe connections for the water supply system are outside the building at street level. Firefighters attach hoses to those connections to send water into the pipes in the building.

185

2 (#2)

Questions 1 through 3 refer to a fire on the 1st floor in Room 111.

1. After fighting the fire in Room 111, firefighters are instructed to go immediately to the east-west hallway in the center of the building and search for victims in that hallway. Which one of the following lists ALL of the rooms that the firefighters should search?

    A. 115, 117, 118, 119, 133, and 134
    B. 125, 126, 127, 128, and 129
    C. 107, 109, 125, 126, 127, and 128
    D. 121, 122, 123, 124, 125, and 126

2. Firefighters are told to search Room 134. They enter the building from 40th Street. What is the SHORTEST route for the firefighters to take to reach this room?

    A. West in hallway E, north in hallway A, then east in hallway C
    B. West in hallway E, north in hallway A, east in hallway D, north in hallway B, then west in hallway C
    C. East in hallway E, north in hallway B, then west in hallway C
    D. East in hallway E, north in hallway B, west in hallway D, north in hallway A, then east in hallway C

3. Firefighters in Truck 21 have been ordered to attach a hose to a connection outside the building. The fire-fighters cannot use connection A because 40th Street is blocked by traffic.
What is the FIRST connection the firefighters can drive to? Connection

    A. B   B. C   C. D   D. E

Questions 4-6.

DIRECTIONS: Questions 4 through 6 are to be answered on the basis of the following passage.

Firefighters often know the appearance and construction features of apartments by recognizing the general features on the outside of the building. The following are some general features of different types of buildings in the city.

1. OLD LAW TENEMENTS:
   Height - 5 to 7 stories
   Width - 25 feet
   Fire Escapes - There will be a rear fire escape if there are two apartments per floor. There will be front and rear fire escapes if there are four apartments per floor.
2. ROW FRAMES:
   Height - 2 to 5 stories
   Width - 20 feet to 30 feet
   Fire Escapes - There will be a rear fire escape if the building is higher than 2 stories.
3. BROWNSTONES:
   Height - 3 to 5 stories
   Width - 20 feet to 25 feet
   Fire Escapes - If the brownstone has been changed from a private home to a multiple dwelling, there will be a rear fire escape. Unchanged brownstones have no fire escapes.

4. Upon arrival at a fire, a firefighter observes that the building is 3 stories high and 25 feet wide. There are fire escapes only in the rear of the building.
   The firefighter should conclude that the building is either a

   A. Row Frame or an unchanged Brownstone
   B. Row Frame or an Old Law Tenement with two apartments per floor
   C. changed Brownstone or an Old Law Tenement with four apartments per floor
   D. Row Frame or a changed Brownstone

5. At another fire, the building is 5 stories high and 25 feet wide. There is a front fire escape. The firefighters should conclude that this building has

   A. a rear fire escape because the building is a Row Frame higher than two stories
   B. a rear fire escape because the building is an Old Law Tenement with four apartments per floor
   C. no rear fire escape because the building is a Brown-stone that has been changed into a multiple dwelling
   D. no rear fire escape because the building has a front fire escape

6. At another fire, the building is 4 stories high and 30 feet wide. The building has no front fire escape.
   The firefighter should conclude that the building is a(n)

   A. Row Frame which has no rear fire escape
   B. Old Law Tenement which has four apartments per floor
   C. Row Frame which has a rear fire escape
   D. Brownstone which has been changed from a private home to a multiple dwelling

Questions 7-9.

DIRECTIONS: Questions 7 through 9 are to be answered on the basis of the following passage.

Firefighters use 2-way radios to alert other firefighters of dangerous conditions and of the need for help. Messages should begin with *MAY DAY* or *URGENT*. *MAY DAY* messages have priority over *URGENT* messages. Following is a list of specific emergencies and the messages which should be sent.

MAY DAY Messages:

1. When a collapse is probable in the area where the firefighters are working: *MAY DAY - MAY DAY, collapse probable, GET OUT.*
2. When a collapse has occurred in the area where the firefighters are working: *MAY DAY - MAY DAY, collapse occurred.* The firefighter should also give the location of the collapse. If there are trapped victims, the number and condition of the trapped victims is also given.
3. When a firefighter appears to be a heart attack victim: *MAY DAY - MAY DAY, CARDIAC.* The location of the victim is also given.
4. When anyone has a serious, life-threatening injury: *MAY DAY - MAY DAY.* The firefighter also describes the injury and gives the condition and the location of the victim.

Messages:

1. When anyone has a less serious injury which requires medical attention (for example, a broken arm): URGENT - URGENT. The firefighter also gives the type of injury and the location of the victim.
2. When the firefighters should leave the building and fight the fire from the outside: URGENT - URGENT, back out. The firefighter also indicates the area to be evacuated.
3. URGENT messages should also be sent when firefighters' lives are endangered due to a drastic loss of water pressure in the hose.

7. Firefighters are ordered to extinguish a fire on the third floor of an apartment building. As the firefighters are operating the hose on the third floor, the stairway collapses and cuts the hose.
What message should the firefighters send?

   A. URGENT - URGENT, back out
   B. URGENT - URGENT, we have a loss of water on the third floor
   C. MAY DAY - MAY DAY, collapse occurred on third floor stairway
   D. MAY DAY - MAY DAY, collapse probable, GET OUT

8. Two firefighters on the second floor of a vacant building are discussing the possibility of the floor's collapse. One of the firefighters clutches his chest and falls down. What message should the other firefighter send?

   A. MAY DAY - MAY DAY, firefighter collapse on the second floor
   B. MAY DAY - MAY DAY, CARDIAC on the second floor
   C. URGENT - URGENT, firefighter unconscious on the second floor
   D. URGENT - URGENT, collapse probable on the second floor

9. A firefighter has just decided that a collapse of the third floor is probable when he falls and breaks his wrist.
What is the FIRST message he should send?

   A. URGENT - URGENT, broken wrist on the third floor
   B. MAY DAY - MAY DAY, broken wrist on the third floor
   C. MAY DAY - MAY DAY, collapse probable, GET OUT
   D. URGENT - URGENT, back out, third floor

Questions 10-11.

DIRECTIONS: Questions 10 and 11 are to be answered on the basis of the following information and the diagram which appears on the next page.

An 8-story apartment building has scissor stairs beginning on the first floor and going to the roof. Scissor stairs are two separate stairways (Stairway A and Stairway B) that crisscross each other and lead to opposite sides of the building on each floor. Once a person has entered either stairway, the only way to cross over to the other stairway on any floor is by leaving the stairway and using the hallway on that floor. A person entering Stairway A, which starts on the east side of the building on the first floor, would end up on the west side of the building on the second floor, and back on the east side on the third floor. Similarly, a person entering Stairway B, which starts on the west side of the building on the first floor, would end up on the east side of the building on the second floor, and back on the west side on the third floor.

The apartment building has one water pipe for fighting fires. This pipe runs in a straight line near the stairway on the east side of the building from the first floor to the roof. There are water outlets for this pipe on each floor.

Both of the following questions involve a fire in an apartment on the west side of the 6th floor.

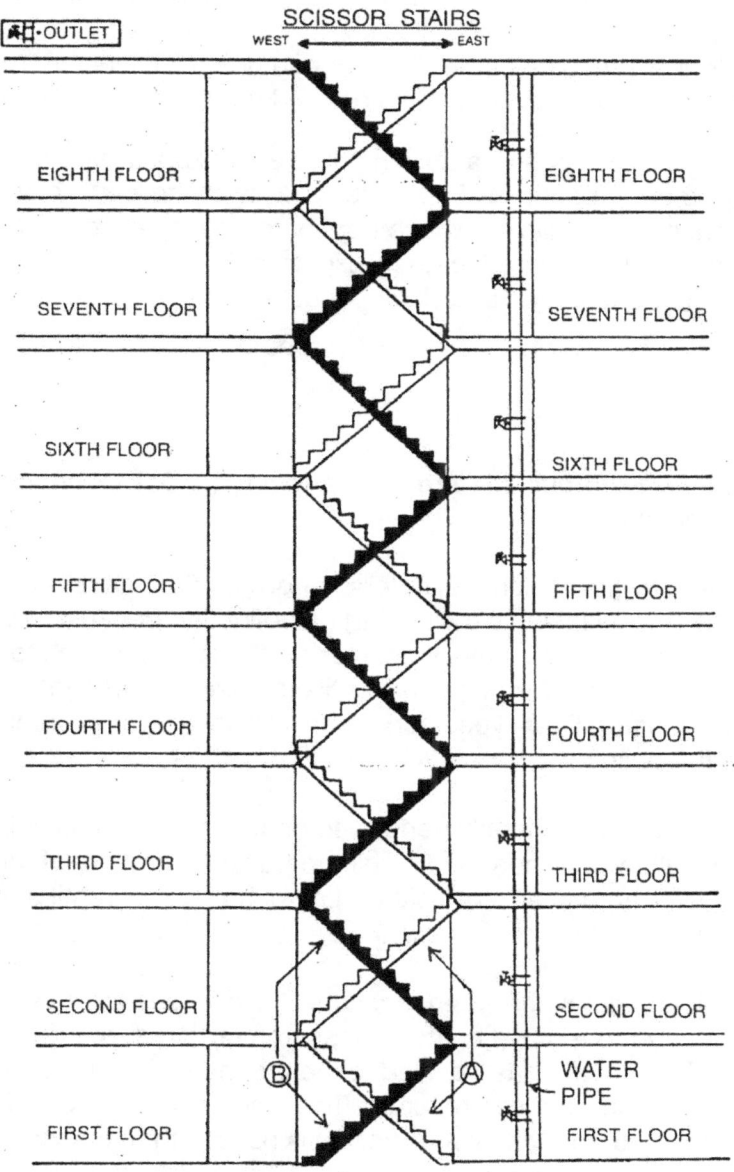

10. Firefighters are ordered to connect a hose to the nearest outlet below the fire. Upon reaching this outlet, they find that it is not usable.
Where is the next available outlet?
_____ floor near Stairway _____.

   A. 5th; B   B. 3rd; A   C. 4th; B   D. 4th; A

11. A firefighter working on the west side of the 7th floor is ordered to search for victims on the west side of the 8th floor. The door leading to the stairway on the west side of the 7th floor is jammed shut.
To reach the victims, the firefighter should take

   A. Stairway A to the 8th floor, and then go across the hallway to the west side of the floor
   B. Stairway B to the 8th floor, and then go across the hallway to the west side of the floor
   C. the hallway to the east side of the 7th floor and go up Stairway A
   D. the hallway to the east side of the 7th floor and go up Stairway B

12. Firefighters refer to the four sides of a building on fire as *exposures*. The front of the fire building is referred to as Exposure 1. Exposures 2, 3, and 4 follow in clock wise order. Firefighters are working at a building whose front entrance faces south. A firefighter who is in the center of the roof is ordered to go to Exposure 3.
To reach Exposure 3, the direction in which he must walk is

   A. east   B. west   C. south   D. north

Questions 13-17.

DIRECTIONS: Questions 13 through 17 are to be answered SOLELY on the basis of the following passage.

The most important activities which firefighters perform at fires are search, rescue, ventilation, and extinguishment. Ventilation is a vital part of firefighting because it prevents fire from spreading to other areas and because it enables firefighters to search for victims and to bring hoses closer to the fire area. Two types of ventilation used by firefighters are natural venting and mechanical venting. Both types permit the vertical and horizontal movement of smoke and gas from a fire building.

Natural vertical ventilation is generally performed on the roof of the building on fire by making an opening. This allows the heat and smoke to travel up and out of the fire building. Opening windows in the fire area is an example of natural horizontal ventilation. This allows the heat and smoke to travel out of the windows.

Mechanical ventilation takes place when mechanical devices, such as smoke ejectors or hoses with nozzles, are used to remove heated gases from an area. A smoke ejector might be used in a cellar fire when smoke has traveled to the far end of the cellar, creating a heavy smoke condition that cannot be removed naturally. The smoke ejector would be brought into the area to draw the smoke out of the cellar. A nozzle is used with a hose to create a fine spray of water. When directed towards an open window, the water spray pushes smoke and heated gases out of the window.

Extinguishment means bringing a hose to the fire and operating the nozzle to put water on the fire. The proper positioning of hoses is essential to firefighting tactics. Most lives are saved at fires by the proper positioning of hoses.

At each fire, firefighters must use the quickest and best method of extinguishment. There are times when an immediate and direct attack on the fire is required. This means that the hose is brought directly to the fire itself. A fire in a vacant lot, or a fire in the entrance of a building, calls for an immediate and direct attack on the fire.

It is generally the ladder company that is assigned the tasks of venting, search, and rescue while the engine company performs the task of extinguishment.

13. Ventilation performed at the roof is GENERALLY _____ ventilation.

    A. mechanical vertical
    B. natural vertical
    C. natural horizontal
    D. mechanical horizontal

14. When an immediate and direct attack on the fire is required, the hose is

    A. positioned between the building on fire and the building which the fire might spread to
    B. brought to a window in order to push smoke and gases out
    C. brought to the roof to push the smoke and gases out
    D. brought directly to the fire itself

15. Ladder companies are GENERALLY assigned the tasks of

    A. extinguishment, rescue, and search
    B. extinguishment, venting, and search
    C. venting, search, and rescue
    D. venting, rescue, and extinguishment

16. MOST lives are saved at fires by

    A. a systematic search
    B. the proper positioning of hoses
    C. the proper performance of ventilation
    D. the use of nozzles for ventilation and extinguishment

17. Ventilation enables firefighters to

    A. bring hoses to the fire and search for victims
    B. create a fine spray of water
    C. use a nozzle to remove smoke and gases
    D. use an ejector to draw smoke out of an area

Questions 18-19.

DIRECTIONS: Questions 18 and 19 are to be answered SOLELY on the basis of the following passage.

A new firefighter learns the following facts about his company's response area: All the factories are located between 9th Avenue and 12th Avenue, from 42nd Street to 51st Street; all the apartment buildings are located between 7th Avenue and 9th Avenue, from 47th Street to 51st Street; all the private houses are located between 5th Avenue and 9th Avenue, from 42nd. Street to 47th Street; and all the stores are located between 5th Avenue and 7th Avenue, from 47th Street to 51st Street.

The firefighter also learns that the apartment buildings are all between 4 and 6 stories; the private houses are all between 1 and 3 stories; the factories are all between 3 and 5 stories; and the stores are all either 1 or 2 stories.

18. An alarm is received for a fire located on 8th Avenue between 46th Street and 47th Street.
    A firefighter should assume that the fire is in a

    A. private house between 1 and 3 stories
    B. private house between 4 and 6 stories
    C. factory between 3 and 5 stories
    D. factory between 4 and 6 stories

18.___

19. The company responds to a fire on 47th Street between 6th Avenue and 7th Avenue. The firefighter should assume that he would be responding to a fire in a(n)

    A. store of either 1 or 2 stories
    B. factory between 3 and 5 stories
    C. apartment building between 4 and 6 stories
    D. private house between 4 and 6 stories

19.___

Questions 20-25.

DIRECTIONS: Questions 20 through 25 are to be answered on the basis of the following information and the diagram which appears on the next page.

At three o'clock in the morning, a fire alarm is received for the area shown in the diagram. A train loaded with highly flammable material is on fire. The entire area is surrounded by a ten-foot-high fence. At the time of the fire, Gate A is open and Gates B, C, and D are locked.

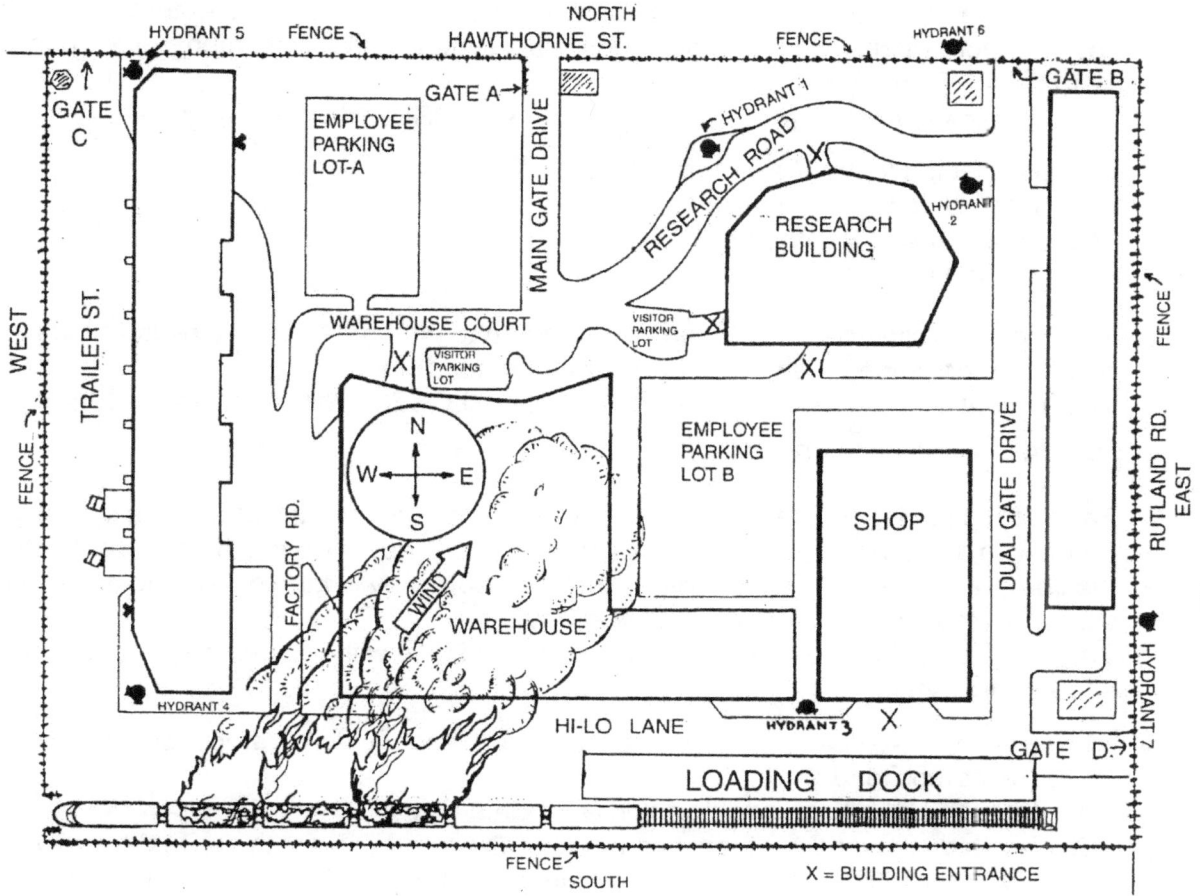

20. The first engine company arrives at the fire scene. The security guard at Gate A informs the firefighters of the location of the fire. Firefighter Jensen knows the area. He should inform the lieutenant that the way to drive to a hydrant that is as close to the fire as possible without passing through the smoke and flames is by going

    A. south on Main Gate Drive, east on Research Road, south on Dual Gate Drive, and west on Hi-Lo Lane to hydrant 3
    B. south on Main Gate Drive, west on Warehouse Court, south on Factory Road, and west on Hi-Lo Lane to hydrant 4
    C. south on Main Gate Drive and east on Research Road to hydrant 1
    D. east on Hawthorne Street and south on Rutland Road to hydrant 7

21. Firefighters at Employee Parking Lot A are ordered to drive their truck to the fence outside Gate D.
    Which of the following is the SHORTEST route the fire-fighters could take from Warehouse Court?

    A. South on Factory Road, then west on Hi-Lo Lane, and north on Trailer Street
    B. East on Research Road, and south on Dual Gate Drive
    C. North on Main Gate Drive, east on Hawthorne Street, and south on Rutland Road
    D. North on Main Gate Drive, west on Hawthorne Street, south on Trailer Street, and west on Hi-Lo Lane

22. The first ladder company arrives at the fire scene. As they are driving north on Rutland Road, firefighters see the fire through Gate D. They cut the locks and enter Gate D. The lieutenant orders a firefighter to go on foot from Gate D to the Research Building and to search it for occupants.
The entrance to the Research Building which is CLOSEST to this firefighter is

    A. connected to the Visitor Parking Lot
    B. located on Research Road
    C. connected to Parking Lot B
    D. located on Dual Gate Drive

23. The second engine company to arrive is ordered to attach a hose to a hydrant located outside of the fenced area and then to await further orders.
The hydrant outside of the fenced area which is CLOSEST to the flames is hydrant

    A. 6   B. 3   C. 4   D. 7

24. The second ladder company to arrive at the fire scene is met at Gate C by a security guard who gives them the keys to open all the gates. They drive south on Trailer Street to the corner of Hi-Lo Lane and Trailer Street. The company is then ordered to drive to the corner of Research Road and Dual Gate Drive.
Which is the SHORTEST route for the company to take with-out being exposed to the smoke and flames?

    A. East on Hi-Lo Lane, north on Factory Road, and east on Warehouse Court to Research Road
    B. East on Hi-Lo Lane and north on Dual Gate Drive
    C. North on Trailer Street, east on Hawthorne Street, and south on Dual Gate Drive
    D. North on Trailer Street, east on Hawthorne Street, south on Main Gate Drive, and east on Research Road

25. The heat from the fire in the railroad cars ignites the warehouse on the other side of Hi-Lo Lane. The officer of the first ladder company orders two firefighters who are on the west end of the loading dock to break the windows on the north side of the warehouse. Of the following, the SHORTEST way for the firefighters to reach the northwest corner of the warehouse without passing through the smoke and flames is to go

    A. east on Hi-Lo Lane, north on Dual Gate Drive, and then west on Research Road to the entrance on Warehouse Court
    B. west on Hi-Lo Lane, north on Factory Road, and then east on Warehouse Court to the Visitor Parking Lot on Warehouse Court
    C. east on Hi-Lo Lane, north on Rutland Road, west on Hawthorne Street, and then south on Main Gate Drive to the Visitor Parking Lot on Warehouse Court
    D. east on Hi-Lo Lane, north on Dual Gate Drive, west on Hawthorne Street, and then south on Main Gate Drive to the entrance on Warehouse Court

KEY (CORRECT ANSWERS)

1. C
2. C
3. D
4. D
5. B

6. C
7. C
8. B
9. C
10. C

11. C
12. D
13. B
14. D
15. C

16. B
17. A
18. A
19. A
20. A

21. C
22. C
23. D
24. C
25. A

READING COMPREHENSION
UNDERSTANDING WRITTEN MATERIALS
EXAMINATION SECTION

DIRECTIONS FOR THIS SECTION:

Each question or incomplete statement is followed by several suggested answers or completions. Select the one that *BEST* answers the question or completes the statement. *THEN, PRINT THE LETTER OF THE CORRECT ANSWER IN THE SPACE AT THE RIGHT.*

Your answers are to be based *ONLY* on the information that is given or that can be assumed from the reading passages.

TEST 1

Questions 1-5.

DIRECTIONS: Answer Questions 1 through 5 on the basis of the passage below.

Arsonists are people who set fires deliberately, They don't look like criminals, but they cost the nation millions of dollars in property loss, and sometimes loss of life. Arsonists set fires for many different reasons. Sometimes a shopkeeper sees no way out of losing his business, and sets fire to it so he can collect the insurance. Another type of arsonist wants revenge, and sets fire to the home or shop of someone he feels has treated him unfairly. Some arsonists just like the excitement of seeing the fire burn and watching the firefighters at work; arsonists of this type have even been known to help fight the fire.

1. The writer of the passage feels that arsonists
   A. usually return to the scene of the crime
   B. work at night   C. don't look like criminals
   D. never leave their fingerprints

2. An arsonist is a person who
   A. intentionally sets a fire   B. enjoys watching fires
   C. wants revenge   D. needs money

3. Arsonists have been known to help fight fires because they
   A. felt guilty   B. enjoyed the excitement
   C. wanted to earn money D. didn't want anyone hurt

4. Shopkeepers sometimes become arsonists in order to
   A. commit suicide   B. collect insurance money
   C. hide a crime   D. raise their prices

5. The *point* of this passage is that arsonists
   A. would make good firefighters   B. are not criminals
   C. are mentally ill   D. are not all alike

Questions 6-11.

DIRECTIONS: Answer Questions 6 through 11 on the basis of the passage below.

Water and ventilation are the keys to fire fighting. Firefighters put out most fires by hosing water on the burning material, and by letting the smoke and gases out. When burning material is soaked with cooling water it can no longer produce gases that burn. In a closed room, hot gases can raise the temperature enough for the room to burst into flame. This can happen even though the room is far away from the fire itself. Therefore, firefighters chop holes in roofs and smash windows in order to empty the house of gases quickly. This is called ventilation.

6. Burning material will stop giving off hot gases when it is
   A. allowed to burn freely   B. exposed to fresh air
   C. cooled with water   D. sprayed with chemicals

7. Hot gases cause a room to burn by
   A. creating a draft   B. exploding
   C. giving off sparks D. raising the room temperature

8. A room can burst into flames even though it is
   A. far from the fire   B. soaked with water
   C. well ventilated   D. cold and damp

9. Firefighters sometimes smash windows and chop holes in roofs in order to
   A. reach trapped victims   B. remove burning materials
   C. ventilate a building   D. escape from a fire

10. Ventilation is important in fire fighting because it
    A. releases trapped smoke and gases
    B. puts out flames by cooling them
    C. makes it easier for firefighters to breathe
    D. makes the flames easier to see and reach with a hose

11. Hot gases are *most* dangerous when they are in a room that is
    A. large   B. closed   C. damp   D. cool

Questions 12-15.

DIRECTIONS: Answer Questions 12 through 15 on the basis of the passage below.

When there is a large fire in an occupied apartment or tenement, the fire escapes often become overcrowded. To relieve this overcrowding, a portable ladder is often raised to the first level of the fire escape and put opposite to the drop ladder. For added help, an additional ladder can be raised from the ground to the second level. If the fire escape is located in the rear of the building, a "gooseneck" ladder that hooks over the roof can also be used. Then firefighters can help some occupants from the fire escape to the roof instead of to the ground.

Test 1

12. Portable ladders are raised to fire escapes so that
    A. firefighters can reach the roof from outside
    B. occupants can reach a higher level of the fire escape
    C. firefighters can enter windows more easily
    D. occupants can leave fire escapes more rapidly

    12._____

13. If all the ladders described in the passage are used, *how many* ways can the occupants reach the ground directly by ladder from the fire escape at the first level?
    A. 1   B. 2   C. 3   D. 4

    13._____

14. A "gooseneck" ladder is sometimes used
    A. opposite the drop ladder   B. from the top level
    C. from the first level   D. from the second level

    14._____

15. The *main* topic of the paragraph is:
    A. Relieving overcrowding on fire escapes
    B. Setting up and using portable ladders
    C. Rescuing occupants from apartments
    D. Using the roof to escape from fires

    15._____

Questions 16-20.

DIRECTIONS: Answer Questions 16 through 20 on the basis of the passage below.

Fire often travels inside the partitions of a burning building. Many partitions contain wooden studs that support the partitions. The studs leave a space for the fire to travel along. Flames may spread from the bottom to the upper floors through the partitions. Sparks from a fire in the upper part of a partition may fall and start a fire at the bottom. Some signs that a fire is spreading inside a partition are: (1) blistering paint, (2) discolored paint or wallpaper, or (3) partitions that feel hot to the touch. If any of these signs is present, the partition must be opened up to look for the fire. Finding cobwebs inside the partition is one sign that fire has not spread through the partition.

16. Fires can spread inside partitions because
    A. there are spaces between studs inside of partitions
    B. fires can burn anywhere
    C. partitions are made out of materials that burn easily
    D. partitions are usually painted or wallpapered

    16._____

17. Cobwebs inside a partition are a sign that the fire has not spread inside the partition because
    A. cobwebs are fire resistant
    B. fire destroys cobwebs easily
    C. spiders don't build cobwebs near fires
    D. cobwebs fill up the spaces between studs

    17._____

18. If a firefighter sees the paint on a partition beginning to blister, he should *first*
    A. wet down the partition
    B. check the partitions in other rooms
    C. chop a hole in the partition
    D. close windows and doors and leave the room

    18._____

19. *One* way to tell if fire is spreading within a partition is the
    A. temperature of the partition
    B. color of the smoke
    C. age of the plaster
    D. spacing of the studs

20. The *main* point of the passage is:
    A. How fire spreads inside partitions
    B. How cobwebs help firefighters
    C. How partitions are built
    D. How to keep fires from spreading

Questions 21-25.

DIRECTIONS: Answer Questions 21 through 25 on the basis of the passage below.

There is hardly a city in the country that is not short of fire protection in some areas within its boundaries. These municipalities have spread out and have re-shuffled their residential, business, and industrial districts without readjusting the existing protective fire forces, or creating new protection units. Fire stations are still situated according to the needs of earlier times and have not been altered or improved to house modern fire fighting equipment. They are neither efficient for carrying out their tasks nor livable for the men who must occupy them.

21. Of the following, the title which *BEST* describes the central idea of the above passage is:
    A. The Dynamic Nature of Contemporary Society
    B. The Cost of Fire Protection
    C. The Location and Design of Fire Stations
    D. The Design and Use of Fire Fighting Equipment
    E. The Growth of American Cities

22. According to the above passage, fire protection is inadequate in the United States in
    A. *most* areas of *some* cities
    B. *some* areas of *most* cities
    C. *some* areas in *all* cities
    D. *all* areas in *some* cities
    E. *most* areas in *most* cities

23. The *one* of the following criteria for planning of fire stations which is *NOT* mentioned in the above passage is:
    A. Comfort of firemen
    B. Proper location
    C. Design for modern equipment
    D. Efficiency of operation
    E. Cost of construction

24. Of the following suggestions for improving the fire service, the *one* which would *BEST* deal with the problem discussed in the passage above would involve
    A. specialized training in the use of modern fire apparatus
    B. replacement of obsolete fire apparatus
    C. revision of zoning laws
    D. longer basic training for probationary firemen
    E. reassignment of fire districts

25. The tone of the author of the passage above may BEST be characterized by which one of the following adjectives:
   A. Hopeful   B. Negative   C. Hopeless   D. Striving   E. Critical

TEST 2

Questions 1-6.

DIRECTIONS: Answer Questions 1 through 6 on the basis of the passage below.

During search operations the first step is usually to rescue victims who can be seen and heard, or those whose exact locations are known. Disorganized or careless search must be avoided since victims may be underneath rubble. Disorganized movement could cause injury or death. The best method is to start from the outer edge and work toward the center of an area. Sometimes a trapped or buried victim may be located by calling out or by tapping on pipes. Rescue workers should first call out, then have a period of silence to listen for sounds from a victim.

1. The *main* point of the paragraph is that
   A. firefighters should call and listen often
   B. trapped victims can usually be heard
   C. searching should be an organized procedure
   D. many victims are buried in fires

2. Normally, the *first* victims to be rescued during a search are those who are
   A. unconscious   B. trapped under rubble
   C. easy to see and hear   D. injured

3. When searching for buried victims, it is very important for firefighters to
   A. have periods of silence   B. keep moving constantly
   C. search rubble piles quickly
   D. stay away from rubble piles

4. The *best* way to search an area is
   A. around the edges   B. from center to edge
   C. from corner to corner   D. from edge to center

5. Disorganized movement by a rescue worker can cause
   A. panic and confusion   B. property destruction
   C. wasted time   D. death or injury

6. Tapping on pipes is a good way to locate victims because
   A. firefighters can use Morse code
   B. sound travels through a pipe
   C. firefighters can signal each other this way
   D. pipes usually aren't covered by rubble

Questions 7-10.

DIRECTIONS: Answer Questions 7 through 10 on the basis of the passage below.

When backing a fire truck into the firehouse, all firefighters should remain outside the building. Firefighters assigned to stop traffic should face traffic so they can alert the driver in case of an emergency. Additional firefighters should stand on the sidewalk in front of the firehouse to guide the driver. The truck should be slowly backed into the firehouse and immediately stopped upon orders of any firefighter. When the truck is completely in the firehouse, then and only then should the officer contact central headquarters for the placement of the company in service. Following this, the officer orders the entrance doors closed.

Use this diagram to help answer Questions 7 through 9. The letters indicate where firefighters are standing.

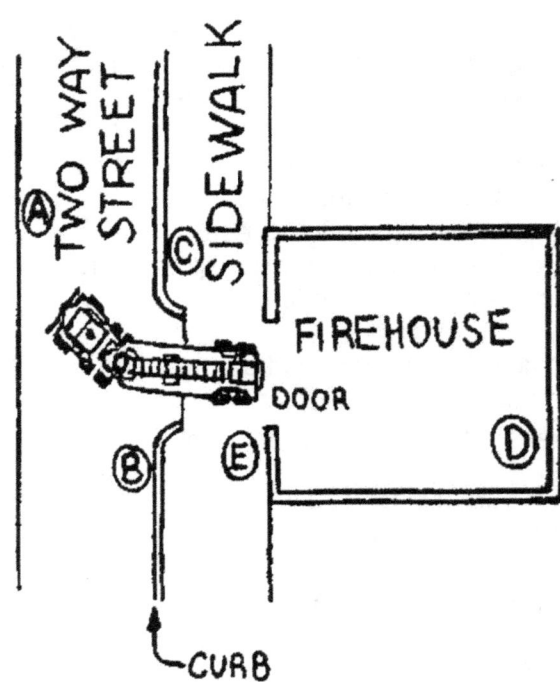

7. The truck is backing into the firehouse. *Which* firefighter is *NOT* needed according to the regulations?
   A. Firefighter A
   B. Firefighter B
   C. Firefighter C
   D. Firefighter D

8. *Which* firefighters are responsible for stopping cars? Firefighters
   A. A and C B. C and E C. A and B D. B and E

9. *Which* firefighters can order the truck to stop?
   A. Firefighters A and B only
   B. Firefighters C and E only
   C. Firefighter D only
   D. Any of them

10. When is central headquarters notified that the company is ready to be put in service? 10._____
    A. When the truck is returning from a fire
    B. After the truck is parked in the firehouse
    C. After the firehouse doors are closed
    D. When all of the firefighters have entered the firehouse

Questions 11-15.

DIRECTIONS: Answer Questions 11 through 15 on the basis of the passage below.

Unless they have had a fire, most people are not aware of the things firefighters do. Too often the public thinks of firefighters as lounging around a firehouse between fires. Firefighters can help change this image in small ways by their appearance, by greeting visitors who come to the firehouse, by their behavior on the street at a fire, and by treating the public in a courteous manner. For example, 90 percent of the rescues made by the average fire department take place at relatively small fires, not at spectacular extra alarm fires. The public rarely hears about them because the fire departments seldom let the press know about firefighters who have performed acts of bravery at routine fires.

11. What are firefighters doing when not fighting fires? 11._____
    A. Lounging around the firehouse
    B. Working on public relations projects
    C. Making repairs to the equipment
    D. The passage doesn't say

12. The passage places responsibility for improving the fire department's image on the 12._____
    A. fire department itself   B. press   C. public
    D. people rescued by firefighters

13. Most of the rescues made by firefighters take place at 13._____
    A. extra alarm fires
    B. special emergencies where no fire is involved
    C. relatively small fires   D. spectacularly large fires

14. The public rarely hears about rescues made by firefighters at routine fires because 14._____
    A. information about fires must be kept confidential
    B. fire departments seldom report these rescues to the press
    C. most of these rescues take place late at night
    D. reporters aren't interested in covering routine fires

15. What would be the BEST title for this passage? 15._____
    A. An Inside Look at the Fire Department
    B. Making the Most of Fire Prevention Week
    C. Improving the Fire Department's Public Image
    D. Brave Acts Performed by Firefighters

Questions 16-19.

DIRECTIONS: Answer Questions 16 through 19 on the basis of the passage below.

Ventilation, as used in fire-fighting operations, means opening up a building or structure in which a fire is burning to release the accumulated heat, smoke and gases. Lack of knowledge of the principles of ventilation on the part of firemen may result in unnecessary punishment due to ventilation being neglected or improperly handled. While ventilation itself extinguishes no fires, when used in an intelligent manner, it allows firemen to get at the fire more quickly, easily, and with less danger and hardship.

16. According to the above paragraph, the MOST important result of failure to apply the principles of ventilation at a fire may be
    A. loss of public confidence   B. disciplinary action
    C. waste of water   D. excessive use of equipment
    E. injury to firemen

16._____

17. It may be inferred from the above paragraph that the CHIEF advantage of ventilation is that it
    A. eliminates the need for gas masks
    B. reduces smoke damage
    C. permits firemen to work closer to the fire
    D. cools the fire
    E. enables firemen to use shorter hose lines

17._____

18. Knowledge of the principles of ventilation, as defined in the above paragraph, would be LEAST important in a fire in a
    A. tenement house   B. grocery store   C. ship's hold
    D. lumberyard   E. office building

18._____

19. We may conclude from the above paragraph that, for the well-trained and equipped fireman, ventilation is
    A. a simple matter   B. rarely necessary
    C. relatively unimportant   D. a basic tool
    E. sometimes a handicap

19._____

Questions 20-22.

DIRECTIONS: Answer Questions 20 through 22 on the basis of the passage below.

A fire of undetermined origin started in the warehouse shed of a flour mill. Although there was some delay in notifying the fire department, they practically succeeded in bringing the fire under control when a series of dust explosions occurred which caused the fire to spread and the main building was destroyed. The fire department's efforts were considerably handicapped because it was undermanned, and the water pressure in the vicinity was inadequate.

20. From the information contained in the above paragraph, it is MOST accurate to state that the cause of the fire was
    A. suspicious   B. unknown   C. accidental
    D. arson   E. spontaneous combustion

20._____

21. In the fire described above, the MOST important cause of the fire spreading to the main building was the
    A. series of dust explosions
    B. delay in notifying the fire department
    C. inadequate water pressure
    D. lack of manpower
    E. wooden construction of the building

21._____

22. In the fire described above, the fire department's efforts were handicapped CHIEFLY by
    A. poor leadership
    B. out-dated apparatus
    C. uncooperative company employees
    D. insufficient water pressure   E. poorly trained men

22._____

Questions 23-25.

DIRECTIONS: Answer Questions 23 through 25 on the basis of the passage below.

A flameproof fabric is defined as one which, when exposed to small sources of ignition such as sparks or smoldering cigarettes, does not burn beyond the vicinity of the source of the ignition. Cotton fabrics are the materials commonly used that are considered most hazardous. Other materials, such as acetate rayons and linens, are somewhat less hazardous, and woolens and some natural silk fabrics, even when untreated, are about the equal of the average treated cotton fabric insofar as flame-spread and ease of ignition are concerned. The method of application is to immerse the fabric in a flameproofing solution. The container used must be large enough so that all the fabric is thoroughly wet and there are no folds which the solution does not penetrate.

23. According to the above paragraph, a flameproof fabric is one which
    A. is unaffected by heat and smoke
    B. resists the spread of flames when ignited
    C. burns with a cold flame
    D. cannot be ignited by sparks or cigarettes
    E. may smolder but cannot burn

23._____

24. According to the above paragraph, woolen fabrics which have not been flameproofed are as likely to catch fire as
    A. treated silk fabrics
    B. treated acetate rayon fabrics
    C. untreated linen fabrics
    D. untreated synthetic fabrics
    E. treated cotton fabrics

24._____

25. In the method described above, the flameproofing solution is BEST applied to the fabric by
    A. sponging the fabric   B. spraying the fabric
    C. dipping the fabric   D. brushing the fabric
    E. sprinkling the fabric

25._____

KEYS (CORRECT ANSWER)

TEST 1

1. C	11. B		
2. A	12. D		
3. B	13. B		
4. B	14. B		
5. D	15. A		
6. C	16. A		
7. D	17. B		
8. A	18. C		
9. C	19. A		
10. A	20. A		

21. C
22. B
23. E
24. E
25. E

TEST 2

1. C	11. D
2. C	12. A
3. A	13. C
4. D	14. B
5. D	15. C
6. B	16. E
7. D	17. C
8. C	18. D
9. D	19. D
10. B	20. B

21. A
22. D
23. B
24. E
25. C

READING COMPREHENSION
UNDERSTANDING AND INTERPRETING WRITTEN MATERIAL

EXAMINATION SECTION
TEST 1

DIRECTIONS: Each question or incomplete statement is followed by several suggested answers or completions. Select the one that BEST answers the question or completes the statement. *PRINT THE LETTER OF THE COREECT ANSWER IN THE SPACE AT THE RIGHT.*

Questions 1-3.

DIRECTIONS: Questions 1 through 3 are to be answered SOLELY on the basis of the following paragraph.

When wood products are heated sufficiently under fire conditions, they undergo thermal decomposition and evolve various combustible gases or vapors which burn as the familiar flames. After these volatile decomposition products of the wood are driven off, the combustible residue is essentially carbon which on further heating undergoes surface combustion reactions with the oxygen of the air, producing considerable heat (glowing), but usually very little flame.

1. The one of the following explanations of thermal decomposition that is MOST accurate is that it is a process by which

    A. heat is transferred from solid substances to gaseous substances
    B. a substance is consumed during the course of a fire
    C. a substance is broken down into component parts when subjected to heat
    D. heat is generated until the ignition point of the substance is reached

    1.____

2. The one of the following statements that is MOST accurate is that pure carbon has an ignition temperature which, compared to the combustible vapors of wood, is

    A. lower
    B. approximately the same
    C. higher
    D. higher or lower, depending upon the variety of wood involved

    2.____

3. A substance which burns with a large amount of flames is one that

    A. contains a large amount of inorganic material
    B. produces during the burning process a large amount of pure carbon
    C. contains a large amount of calories per unit of combustibles
    D. produces during the burning process a large amount of combustible gases or vapors

    3.____

Questions 4-7.

DIRECTIONS: Questions 4 through 7 are to be answered SOLELY on the basis of the following paragraph.

For the five year period 1996-2000, inclusive, the average annual fire loss in the United States amounted to approximately $2,709,760,000. Included in this estimate is $2,045,332,000 damage to buildings and contents, and $564,328,000 average annual loss in aircraft, motor vehicles, forest and other miscellaneous fires not involving buildings. Preliminary estimates indicate that the total United States fire loss in 1981 was $3,230,000,000. These are property damage fire losses only and do not include indirect losses resulting from fires which are just as real and sometimes far more serious than property damage losses. But because evaluation of indirect monetary losses is usually very difficult, their importance in the national fire waste picture is often overlooked.

4. According to the data in the above paragraph, the BEST of the following estimates of the total direct fire loss in the United States for the six year period 1996-2001, inclusive, is

    A. $2,800,000,000   B. $5,400,000,000
    C. $14,000,000,000   D. $16,800,000,000

5. The BEST example of an indirect fire loss, as that term is used in the above paragraph, is monetary loss due to

    A. smoke or water damage to exposures
    B. condemnation of foodstuffs following a fire
    C. interruption of business following a fire
    D. forcible entry by firemen operating at a fire

6. Suppose that during the period 2001-2005 the average annual fire loss to buildings and contents increases 10 percent and the average annual loss due to fires not involving buildings decreases 10 percent.
The MOST valid of the following conclusions is that the average annual fire loss for the 2001-2005 period, compared to the losses for the 1996-2000 period,

    A. will increase
    B. will decrease
    C. will be unchanged
    D. cannot be calculated from the information given

7. If a comparison is made between total annual direct and indirect fire losses on the basis of the information given in the above paragraph, the MOST valid of the following conclusions is that

    A. generally direct losses are higher
    B. generally indirect losses are higher
    C. generally direct and indirect losses are approximately equal
    D. there is not sufficient information to determine which is higher or if they are approximately equal

Questions 8-10.

DIRECTIONS: Questions 8 through 10 are to be answered SOLELY on the basis of the following paragraph.

The soda-acid fire extinguisher is the commonest type of water solution extinguisher in which pressure is used to expel the water. The chemicals used are sodium bicarbonate (baking soda) and sulfuric acid. The sodium bicarbonate is dissolved in water, and this solution is the extinguishing agent. The extinguishing value of the stream is that of an equal quantity of water.

8. According to the above paragraph, the soda-acid extinguisher, compared to others of the same type, is the

   A. most widely used
   B. most effective in putting out fire
   C. cheapest to operate
   D. easiest to operate

9. In the soda-acid extinguisher, the fire is put out by a solution of sodium bicarbonate and

   A. sulfuric acid   B. baking soda
   C. soda-acid   D. water

10. According to the above paragraph, the sodium bicarbonate solution, compared to water, is

    A. *more* effective in putting out fires
    B. *less* effective in putting out fires
    C. *equally* effective in putting out fires
    D. *more* or *less* effective, depending upon the type of fire

Questions 11-13.

DIRECTIONS: Questions 11 through 13 are to be answered SOLELY on the basis of the following paragraph.

The average daily flow of water through public water systems in American cities ranges generally between 40 and 250 gallons per capita, depending upon the underground leakage in the system, the amount of waste in domestic premises, and the quantity used for industrial purposes. The problem of supplying this water has become serious in many cities. Supplies, once adequate, in many cases have become seriously deficient, due to greater demands with increased population and growing industrial use of water. Water works, operating on fixed schedules of water charges, have in many cases not been able to afford the heavy capital expenditures necessary to provide adequate supply, storage, and distribution facilities. Thus, the adequacy of a public water supply for fire protection in any given location cannot properly be taken for granted.

11. The four programs listed below are possible ways by which American communities might try to reduce the seriousness of the water shortage problem.
    The one of the four programs which does NOT directly follow from the paragraph above is the program of

    A. regular replacement of old street water mains by new ones
    B. inspection and repair of leaky plumbing fixtures
    C. fire prevention inspection and education to reduce the amount of water used to extinguish fires
    D. research into industrial processes to reduce the amount of water used in those processes

12. The MAIN conclusion reached by the author of the above paragraph is

    A. there is a waste of precious natural resources in America
    B. communities have failed to control the industrial use of water
    C. a need exists for increasing the revenue of water works to build up adequate supplies of water
    D. fire departments cannot assume that they will always have the necessary supply of water available to fight fires

13. Per capita consumption of water of a community is determined by the formula

    A. $\dfrac{\text{Population}}{\text{Total consumption in gallons}} = $ per capita consumption in gallons

    B. $\dfrac{\text{Total consumption in gallons}}{\text{Population}} = $ per capita consumption in gallons

    C. Total consumption in gallons x population = per capita consumption in gallons
    D. Total consumption in gallons - population = Per capita consumption in gallons

Questions 14-17.

DIRECTIONS: Questions 14 through 17 are to be answered SOLELY on the basis of the following paragraph.

Language performs an essentially social function; it helps us to get along together, to communicate and achieve a great measure of concerted action. Words are signs which have significance by convention, and those people who do not adopt the conventions simply fail to communicate. They do not *get along* and a social force arises which encourages them to achieve the correct associations. *Correct* means as used by other members of the social group. Some of the vital points about language are brought home to an Englishman when visiting America, and vice versa, because our vocabularies are nearly the same—but not quite.

14. *Communicate*, as that word is used in the above paragraph, means to

    A. make ourselves understood
    B. send written messages
    C. move other persons to concerted action
    D. use language in its traditional or conventional sense

15. Usage of a word is *correct*, as that term is defined in the above paragraph, when the word is used as it is

    A. defined in standard dictionaries
    B. used by the majority of persons throughout the world who speak the same language
    C. used by the majority of educated persons who speak the same language
    D. used by other persons with whom we are associating

16. In the above paragraph, the author is concerned PRIMARILY with the 16.____
    A. meaning of words
    B. pronunciation of words
    C. structure of sentences
    D. origin and development of language

17. According to the above paragraph, the MAIN language problem of an Englishman, while 17.____
    visiting America, stems from the fact that an Englishman
    A. uses some words that have different meanings for Americans
    B. has different social values than the Americans
    C. has had more exposure to non-English speaking persons than Americans have had
    D. pronounces words differently than Americans do

Questions 18-21.

DIRECTIONS: Questions 18 through 21 are to be answered SOLELY on the basis of the following paragraph.

Whenever a social group has become so efficiently organized that it has gained access to an adequate supply of food and has learned to distribute it among its members so well that wealth considerably exceeds immediate demands, it can be depended upon to utilize its surplus energy in an attempt to enlarge the sphere in which it is active. The structure of ant colonies renders them particularly prone to this sort of expansionist policy. With very few exceptions, ants of any given colony are hostile to those of any other community, even of the same species, and this condition is bound to produce preliminary bickering among colonies which are closely associated.

18. According to the above paragraph, a social group is wealthy when it 18.____
    A. is efficiently organized
    B. controls large territories
    C. contains energetic members
    D. produces and distributes food reserves

19. According to the above paragraph, the structure of an ant colony is its 19.____
    A. social organization   B. nest arrangement
    C. territorial extent   D. food-gathering activities

20. It follows from the above paragraph that the LEAST expansionist society would be one 20.____
    that has
    A. great poverty generally
    B. more than sufficient wealth to meet its immediate demands
    C. great wealth generally
    D. wide inequality between its richest and poorest members

21. According to the above paragraph, an ant generally is hostile EXCEPT to other 21.____

   A. insects
   B. ants
   C. ants of the same species
   D. ants of the same colony

Questions 22-25.

DIRECTIONS: Questions 22 through 25 are to be answered SOLELY on the basis of the following paragraph.

Steel used in boiler construction must be of a higher quality than steel used in general construction. The boiler steel must be capable of sustaining loads at elevated temperatures. Temperature has a more serious effect upon the boiler fabrication than has the pressure. The material for bolts and studs is conditioned by tempering. The tempering temperature is at least 100F higher than the service operating temperature. All materials used in boiler construction must be creep resistant to minimize the relaxation in service. Fire box quality plate is used for any part of a boiler exposed to the fire or products of combustion. For parts of the boiler subject to pressure and not exposed to fire or products of combustion, flange quality plate is used. A small percentage of molybdenum is added to steel in the manufacture of superheater tubes, piping, and valves to increase the ability of these parts to withstand high temperature.

22. Material for bolts and studs used on boilers is conditioned for service by 22.____

   A. tempering   B. re-tightening
   C. forging   D. anodizing

23. The part of a boiler that is exposed to products of combustion is made of 23.____

   A. alloy materials   B. firebox quality plate
   C. flange quality plate   D. carbon steel

24. Temperature has a MORE serious effect upon boiler fabrication than has the 24.____

   A. vibration   B. steam   C. relaxation   D. pressure

25. When comparing steel used in boiler construction to steel used in general construction, it can be said that steel used in boiler construction must be of a 25.____

   A. high-weld strength   B. low-carbon content
   C. lower quality   D. higher quality

KEY (CORRECT ANSWERS)

1. C
2. C
3. D
4. D
5. C

6. A
7. D
8. A
9. D
10. C

11. C
12. D
13. B
14. A
15. D

16. A
17. A
18. D
19. A
20. A

21. D
22. A
23. B
24. D
25. D

TEST 2

Questions 1-3.

DIRECTIONS: Questions 1 through 3 are to be answered SOLELY on the basis of the following paragraph.

A fire of undetermined origin started in the warehouse shed of a flour mill. Although there was some delay in notifying the fire department, they practically succeeded in bringing the fire under control when a series of dust explosions occurred which caused the fire to spread and the main building was destroyed. The fire department's efforts were considerably handicapped because it was undermanned, and the water pressure in the vicinity was inadequate.

1. From the information contained in the above paragraph, it is MOST accurate to state that the cause of the fire was

    A. suspicious
    B. unknown
    C. accidental
    D. spontaneous combustion

2. In the fire described above, the MOST important cause of the fire spreading to the main building was the

    A. series of dust explosions
    B. delay in notifying the fire department
    C. inadequate water pressure
    D. wooden construction of the building

3. In the fire described above, the fire department's efforts were handicapped CHIEFLY by

    A. poor leadership
    B. outdated apparatus
    C. uncooperative company employees
    D. insufficient water pressure

Questions 4-6.

DIRECTIONS: Questions 4 through 6 are to be answered SOLELY on the basis of the following paragraph.

A flameproof fabric is defined as one which, when exposed to small sources of ignition such as sparks or smoldering cigarettes, does not burn beyond the vicinity of the source of the ignition. Cotton fabrics are the materials commonly used that are considered most hazardous. Other materials, such as acetate rayons and linens, are somewhat less hazardous, and woolens and some natural silk fabrics, even when untreated, are about the equal of the average treated cotton fabric insofar as flame spread and ease of ignition are concerned. The method of application is to immerse the fabric in a flameproofing solution. The container used must be large enough so that all the fabric is thoroughly wet and there are no folds which the solution does not penetrate.

4. According to the above paragraph, a flameproof fabric is one which
   A. is unaffected by heat and smoke
   B. resists the spread of flames when ignited
   C. cannot be ignited by sparks or cigarettes
   D. may smolder but cannot burn

5. According to the above paragraph, woolen fabrics which have not been flameproofed are as likely to catch fire as
   A. treated silk fabrics
   B. untreated linen fabrics
   C. untreated synthetic fabrics
   D. treated cotton fabrics

6. In the method described above, the flameproofing solution is BEST applied to the fabric by _____ the fabric.
   A. sponging   B. spraying   C. dipping   D. brushing

Questions 7-10.

DIRECTIONS: Questions 7 through 10 are to be answered SOLELY on the basis of the following paragraph.

There is hardly a city in the country that is not short of fire protection in some areas within its boundaries. These municipalities have spread out and have re-shuffled their residential, business, and industrial districts without readjusting the existing protective fire forces or creating new protection units. Fire stations are still situated according to the needs of earlier times and have not been altered or improved to house modern fire fighting equipment. They are neither efficient for carrying out their tasks nor livable for the men who must occupy them.

7. Of the following, the title which BEST describes the central idea of the above paragraph is
   A. THE DYNAMIC NATURE OF CONTEMPORARY SOCIETY
   B. THE COST OF FIRE PROTECTION
   C. THE LOCATION AND DESIGN OF FIRE STATIONS
   D. THE DESIGN AND USE OF FIRE FIGHTING EQUIPMENT

8. According to the above paragraph, fire protection is inadequate in the United States in _____ areas _____ cities.
   A. most; of some
   B. some; of most
   C. some; in all
   D. most; in most

9. The one of the following criteria for planning of fire stations which is NOT mentioned in the above paragraph is

   A. proper location
   B. design for modern equipment
   C. efficiency of operation
   D. cost of construction

10. Of the following suggestions for improving the fire service, the one which would BEST deal with the problems discussed in the above paragraph would involve

    A. specialized training in the use of modern fire apparatus
    B. replacement of obsolete fire apparatus
    C. longer basic training for probationary firemen
    D. reassignment of fire districts

Questions 11-14.

DIRECTIONS: Questions 11 through 14 are to be answered SOLELY on the basis of the following paragraph.

Gravity tanks for sprinkler systems shall contain an available quantity of water sufficient to supply 25 percent of the number of sprinkler heads in the average protected fire area for twenty minutes, and in any case at least 5,000 gallons. Where there are more than 200 and not more than 400 sprinklers in such average protected fire area, the available quantity of water in excess of 20,000 gallons need not be greater than an amount sufficient to supply 12 1/2 percent of the sprinklers in excess of 200 in such average protected fire area for a period of twenty minutes. If the number of sprinklers in such average fire area exceeds 400, the available quantity of water in excess of 30,000 gallons need not be greater than an amount sufficient to supply six and one-fourth percent of the sprinklers in excess of four hundred in such average protected fire area for a period of twenty minutes.

11. In establishing the required capacity of the gravity tanks for sprinkler systems, the assumption contained in the above paragraph is that the average discharge per minute from sprinkler heads will be _____ gallons.

    A. 20   B. 22   C. 25   D. 28

12. A sprinkler system containing 500 sprinkler heads requires gravity tanks with a minimum capacity of approximately _____ gallons.

    A. 32,500   B. 35,000   C. 37,500   D. 40,000

13. A sprinkler system contains 600 sprinkler heads in the protected fire area. If the minimum requirements of the above paragraph have been met, the gravity tanks should be able to supply for twenty minutes approximately _____ heads.

    A. 88   B. 94   C. 100   D. 106

14. The one of the following graphs which MOST accurately represents the gravity tanks' capacity requirements for sprinkler systems built in accordance with the requirements of the above paragraph is

14._____

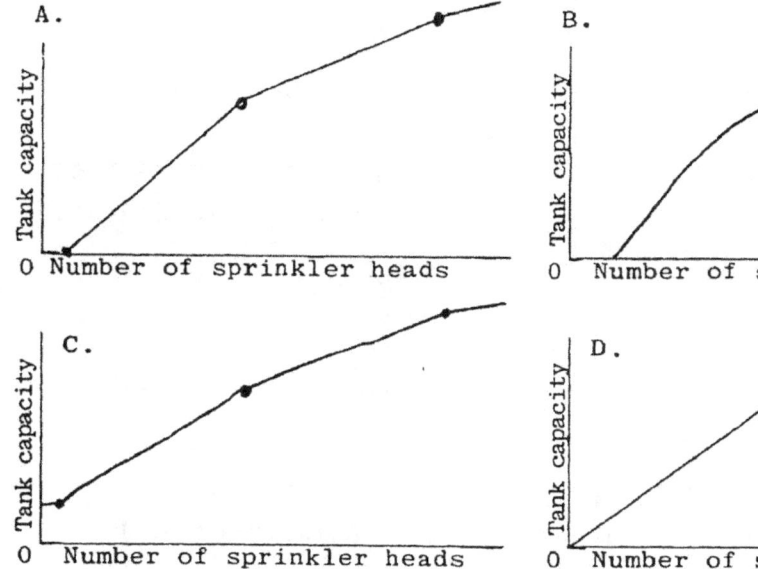

Questions 15-18.

DIRECTIONS: Questions 15 through 18 are to be answered SOLELY on the basis of the following paragraph.

A mixture of a combustible vapor and air will burn only when the proportion of fuel to air lies within a certain range, i.e., between the upper and lower limits of flammability. If a third, non-combustible gas is now added to the mixture, the limits will be narrowed. As increasing amounts of diluent are added, the limits come closer until, at a certain critical concentration, they will converge. This is the peak concentration. It is the minimum amount of diluent that will inhibit the combustion of any fuel-air mixture.

15. If additional diluent is added beyond the peak concentration, the flammable limits of the mixture will

15._____

    A. converge rapidly
    B. diverge slowly
    C. diverge rapidly
    D. not be affected

16. If the four numbers listed below were peak concentration values obtained in a test of four diluents, then the MOST efficient diluent would have the value of

16._____

    A. 7.5   B. 10   C. 12.5   D. 15

17. The word *inhibit,* as used in the last sentence of the above paragraph, means MOST NEARLY

17._____

    A. slow the rate of
    B. prevent entirely the occurrence of
    C. reduce the intensity of
    D. retard to an appreciable extent the manifestation of

18. The one of the graphs below which BEST represents the process described in the above paragraph is

A.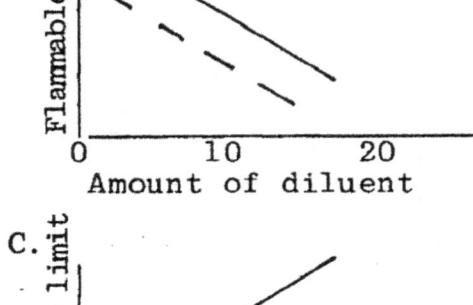
B.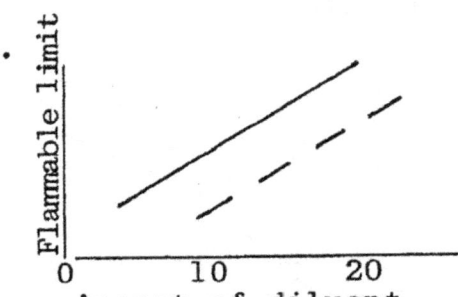
C.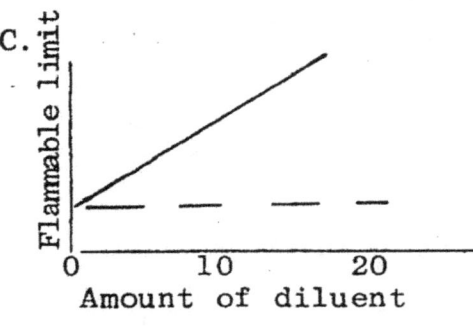
D.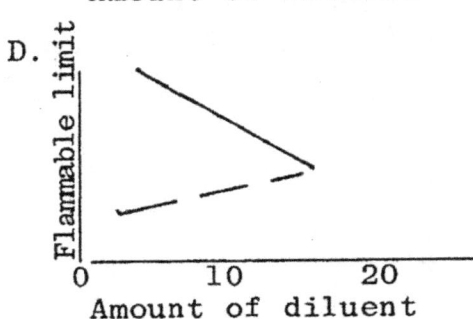

———————— Upper flammable limits
— — — — — — Lower flammable limits

Questions 19-22.

DIRECTIONS: Questions 19 through 22 are to be answered SOLELY on the basis of the following paragraph.

The unadjusted loss per $1000 valuation has only a very limited usefulness in evaluating the efficiency of a fire department, for it depends upon the assumption that other factors will remain constant from time to time and city to city. It might be expected that high fire department operation expenditures would tend to be associated with a low fire loss. A statistical study of the loss and cost data in more than 100 cities failed to reveal any such correlation. The lack of relationship, although to some extent due to failure to make the most efficacious expenditure of fire protection funds, must be attributed in part at least to the obscuring effect of variations in the natural, physical, and moral factors which affect fire risk.

19. One reason for the failure to obtain the expected relationship between fire department expenditures and fire loss data which is stated in the above paragraph is the

    A. changing dollar valuation of property
    B. unsettling effects of rapid technological innovations
    C. inefficiency of some fire department activities
    D. statistical errors made by the investigators

20. We may conclude that *the unadjusted loss per $1000* figure is useful in comparing the fire departments of two cities   20._____

    A. only if the cities are of comparable size
    B. only if adjustments are made for other factors which affect fire loss
    C. under no circumstances
    D. only if properly controlled experimental conditions can be obtained

21. The one of the following factors which affect fire risk that is MOST adequately reflected in the *unadjusted loss per $1000 valuation* index is   21._____

    A. fire department operation expenditures
    B. physical characteristics of the city
    C. type of structures most prevalent in the city
    D. total worth of property in the city

22. According to the above paragraph, cities which spend larger sums on their fire departments   22._____

    A. tend to have lower fire losses than cities which spend smaller sums on their fire departments
    B. do not tend to have lower fire losses than cities which spend smaller sums on their fire departments
    C. tend to have higher fire losses than cities which spend smaller sums on their fire departments
    D. do not tend to have the same total property valuation as cities which spend smaller sums on their fire departments

Questions 23-25.

DIRECTIONS: Questions 23 through 25 are to be answered SOLELY on the basis of the following paragraph.

    Shafts extending into the top story, except those stair shafts where the stairs do not continue to the roof, shall be carried through and at least two feet above the roof. Every shaft extending above the roof, except open shafts and elevator shafts, shall be enclosed at the top with a roof of materials having a fire resistive rating of one hour and a metal skylight covering at least three-quarters of the area of the shaft in the top story, except that skylights over stair shafts shall have an area not less than one-tenth the area of the shaft in the top story, but shall be not less than fifteen square feet in area. Any shaft terminating below the top story of a structure and those stair shafts not required to extend through the roof shall have the top enclosed with materials having the same fire resistive rating as required for the shaft enclosure.

23. The above paragraph states that the elevator shafts which extend into the top story are   23._____

    A. not required to have a skylight but are required to extend at least two feet above the roof
    B. neither required to have a skylight nor to extend above the roof
    C. required to have a skylight covering at least three-quarters of the area of the shaft in the top story and to extend at least two feet above the roof
    D. required to have a skylight covering at least three-quarters of the area of the shaft in the top story but are not required to extend above the roof

24. The one of the following skylights which meets the requirements of the above paragraph is a skylight measuring

   A. 4' x 4' over a stair shaft which, on the top story, measures 20' x 9'
   B. 4 1/2' x 3 1/2' over a pipe shaft which, on the top story, measures 5' x 4'
   C. 2 1/2' x 1 1/2' over a dumbwaiter shaft which, on the top story, measures 2 1/2' x 2 1/2'
   D. 4' x 3' over a stair shaft which, on the top story, measures 15' x 6'

25. Suppose that in a Class I building a shaft which does not go to the roof is required to have a three-hour fire resistive rating.
   In regard to the material enclosing the top of this shaft, the above paragraph

   A. states that a one-hour fire resistive rating is required
   B. states that a three-hour fire resistive rating is required
   C. implies that no fire resistive rating is required
   D. neither states nor implies anything about the fire resistive rating

KEY (CORRECT ANSWERS)

1. B		11. A	
2. A		12. A	
3. D		13. A	
4. B		14. C	
5. D		15. D	
6. C		16. A	
7. C		17. B	
8. B		18. D	
9. D		19. C	
10. D		20. B	

21. D
22. B
23. A
24. B
25. B

www.ingramcontent.com/pod-product-compliance
Lightning Source LLC
Chambersburg PA
CBHW081807300426
44116CB00014B/2266